TEACHING FOR BETTER USE
OF LIBRARIES

CONTRIBUTIONS TO LIBRARY LITERATURE
John David Marshall, Editor

BOOKS, LIBRARIES, LIBRARIANS, Selected by
John David Marshall (with Wayne Shirley and Louis
Shores), 1955. #1

OF, BY, AND FOR LIBRARIANS, Selected by John
David Marshall, 1960. #2

AN AMERICAN LIBRARY HISTORY READER,
Selected by John David Marshall, 1961. #3

BETTER LIBRARIES MAKE BETTER SCHOOLS,
Selected by Charles L. Trinkner, 1962. #4

REFERENCE SERVICES, Selected by Arthur Ray
Rowland, 1964. #5

READINGS IN LIBRARY CATALOGUING, Edited
by R. K. Olding, 1966. #6

THE LIBRARY IN THE UNIVERSITY: UNIVERSITY
OF TENNESSEE LIBRARY LECTURES, 1849–1966,
1967. #7

THE CATALOG AND CATALOGING, Selected by
Arthur Ray Rowland, 1968. #8

TEACHING FOR THE BETTER USE OF LIBRARIES,
Selected by Charles L. Trinkner, with an Introduction
by Florrinell Morton, 1969. #9

TEACHING FOR BETTER USE OF LIBRARIES

Contributions to Library Literature #9

Selected by

CHARLES L. TRINKNER

Introduction by
FLORRINELL F. MORTON

THE SHOE STRING PRESS, INC.

HAMDEN, CONNECTICUT

1970

SBN 208 00975 2
Library of Congress Catalog Card Number: 73-99445
Printed in the United States of America

Dedicated to
Marian, the Librarian

CONTENTS

CONTENTS

CONTENTS

Part III: THE INSTRUCTIONAL APPROACH

CONTENTS

CONTENTS

ACKNOWLEDGMENTS

The editor thanks the authors and publishers with whose permission the articles in this book have been reprinted. Bibliographic data about each of these articles is given below, in the order in which the articles appear in the text.

1. Chase Dane. "Library Instruction in a Vacuum," Education, 74:121–124, October, 1953. Reprinted by permission of author and publisher.

2. Helen M. Carpenter. "Study Skills: Treasure Hunt for Information," Instructor, 74:27–28, January, 1965. Reprinted by permission of author and publisher.

3. Vernon S. Gerlach and Irene Farnbach. "How to Teach Library Skills Without Really Being There," Library Journal, 89:921–922, February 15, 1964. Reprinted by permission of authors and publisher.

4. Valentine Jones. "Teaching Library Skills to Elementary Students," Texas Outlook, 50:16–17, April, 1966. Reprinted by permission of authors and publisher.

5. Martha Dallmann. "The Development of Locational Skills," Grade Teacher, 75:56–57, January, 1958. Reprinted by permission of author and publisher.

6. Gertrude Stacy. "The Fourth Grade and the Card Catalog," Wilson Library Bulletin, 29:643–644, April, 1955. Reprinted by permission of author and publisher.

7. Barbara A. Monroe. "They Compete to Learn to Catalog," Library Journal, 81:990–991; Junior Libraries, 2:62–63, April 15, 1956. Reprinted by permission of publisher.

ACKNOWLEDGMENTS

8. Bessie L. Pugh. "Teaching Children to Use the Dictionary," Volta Review, 63:178–185, April, 1961. Reprinted by permission of author and publisher.

9. Grace M. Shakin. "Teaching Children to Use Reference Books," Instructor, 71:92–93, November, 1961. Reprinted by permission of author and publisher.

10. Marilyn Robbins. "Teaching Library Skills to Junior High Honor Students," Science Teacher, 32:48, February, 1965. Reprinted by permission of author and publisher.

11. Albert Nissman. "Re-Searching in the Library," Clearing House, 35:37–39, September, 1960. Reprinted by permission of author and publisher.

12. Bernice K. Donehue. "Sliding Toward Progress," School Libraries, 11:25–27, March, 1962. Reprinted by permission of author and publisher.

13. Helen Reed and Maryline Conrey. "A High School Course in Library Skills," School Library Association of California Bulletin, 33:7–8, January, 1962. Reprinted by permission of authors and publisher.

14. Ralph W. McComb. "Orientation and Library Instruction," Drexel Library Quarterly, 2:248–249, July, 1966. Reprinted by permission of author and publisher.

15. Robert L. Foose. "The Library: A Writing Laboratory," National Education Association Journal, 49:28–29, December, 1960. Reprinted by permission of author and publisher.

16. B. Agard Evans. "Training the Library User," Aslib Proceedings, 3:239–244, November, 1951. Reprinted by permission of author and publisher.

17. Robert U. Jameson. "Who Should Use the School Library—How," Wilson Library Bulletin, 29:230–232, November, 1954. Reprinted by permission of author and publisher.

ACKNOWLEDGMENTS

18. Leah M. Serck. "We Learn about the Library," Grade Teacher, 78:102–104, November, 1960. Reprinted by permission of author and publisher.

19. Beatrice Herrmann and Ann Shaffner. "Effective Library Instruction in the Creative Elementary School Library," Wilson Library Bulletin, 37:65–67, September, 1962. Reprinted by permission of authors and publisher.

20. Leona B. Ayres. "Learning the Library in Grades K–6," Library Journal, 87:276–277, January 15, 1962; School Library Journal, 8:28–29, January, 1962. Reprinted by permission of author and publisher.

21. Esther Pinch. "Wauwatosa Elementary Schools Teach Good Library Habits," Library Journal, 75:253–254, February 15, 1950. Reprinted by permission of author and publisher.

22. Alene Taylor. "First Graders in the Library," North Carolina Libraries, 20:73–74, Spring, 1962. Reprinted by permission of author and publisher.

23. Elaine Lapidus. "Library Lesson Period in the Elementary School," Wilson Library Bulletin, 35:712–713, May, 1961. Reprinted by permission of author and publisher.

24. D. I. Colley. "Teaching Children to Use Books," Library Association Record, 53:114–119, April, 1951. Reprinted by permission of publisher.

25. A. H. Watkins. "The Library and School Leavers," Librarian and Book World, 38:193–194, August, 1949. Reprinted by permission of author and publisher.

26. Elisabeth Hurd. "Now I Use the Library Even More: Musings by a Sixth-Grader," Instructor, 74:69, November, 1964. Reprinted by permission of author and publisher.

27. Bernice L. Dunten. "How to Make the Library Function: Teaching the Use of the Library," Medical Library Association Bulletin, 41:410–413, October, 1953. Reprinted by permission of author and publisher.

ACKNOWLEDGMENTS

28. William H. Osterle. "The High School Library as a Preparation for College," Catholic Library World, 22:111–114, January, 1951. Reprinted by permission of author and publisher.

29. Mildred Eyres. "Orientation of the Use of the College Library," South Dakota Library Bulletin, 47:142–144, October, 1961. Reprinted by permission of author and publisher.

30. Donald D. Ranstead and Sherman H. Spencer. "Freshman Library Orientation Program," Library Journal, 86:152–154, January 15, 1959. Reprinted by permission of authors and publisher.

31. Eleanor Devlin. "Thoughts on Freshman Orientation," Catholic Library World, 29:23–27, October, 1957. Reprinted by permission of author and publisher.

32. Byrd Fanita Sawyer. "We Can Use Our Library!" Wilson Library Bulletin, 32:432–434, February, 1958. Reprinted by permission of author and publisher.

33. Mary Ann Blatt. "Library Instruction in the Limelight—and Other Assorted Colors," Maryland Libraries, 30:18–20, Winter, 1964. Reprinted by permission of author and publisher.

34. Carolyn Leopold. "Beyond the DDC: The Teaching of Library Skills Can Be an Intellectual Adventure," Library Journal, 93:3930–3931, October 15, 1968. Reprinted by permission of author and publisher.

35. Edna S. Macon. "School Librarians and Teachers," Kentucky Library Association Bulletin, 25:14–16, July, 1961. Reprinted by permission of author and publisher.

36. Dorothy Ligda. "Do-It-Yourself Tape Recording for Library Instruction," Library Journal, 86:4009–4010, November 15, 1961; School Library Journal, 8:23–24, November, 1961. Reprinted by permission of author and publisher.

ACKNOWLEDGMENTS

37. Hilda P. Shufro. "A Workshop Project on Using the Elementary School Library," Instructor, 74:98, February, 1965. Reprinted by permission of author and publisher.

38. Griff L. Jones. "Teaching Library Practice to the Low I.Q.'s," Wilson Library Bulletin, 31:621, April, 1957. Reprinted by permission of publisher.

39. Frederic R. Hartz. "Library Instruction in the Secondary School," Journal of Secondary Education, 41:201–205, May, 1966. Reprinted by permission of author and publisher.

40. Lillian L. Shapiro. "Teaching Correlated Lessons in the Vocational High School Library," Wilson Library Bulletin, 29:632–633, April, 1955. Reprinted by permission of author and publisher.

41. Dorothy Roche. "The School Library: Each Teacher's Responsibility," Wilson Library Bulletin, 31:630–631, April, 1957. Reprinted by permission of author and publisher.

42. Gladys Barreto Spencer. "High School Library Instruction," Wilson Library Bulletin, 24:371–372, January, 1950. Reprinted by permission of author and publisher.

43. Martin Rossoff. "Blueprint for Library Teaching," Wilson Library Bulletin, 27:70–72, September, 1952. Reprinted by permission of author and publisher.

44. Loraine J. Kelleher. "We Used Our Camera," Wilson Library Bulletin, 31:527–528, March, 1957. Reprinted by permission of author and publisher.

45. Alice E. Johnson. "Library Instruction 'En Masse,'" School Libraries, 11:21–23, January, 1962. Reprinted by permission of author and publisher.

ACKNOWLEDGMENTS

46. Muriel Bennett. "The Role of the Resource Unit in Library Instruction," Illinois Libraries, 35:150–153, April, 1953. Reprinted by permission of author and publisher.

47. Kermit Dehl. "The Place of the Library in a High School Developmental Reading Room," Illinois Libraries, 31:49–52, January, 1949. Reprinted by permission of author and publisher.

48. Mary Young Hale. "Instruction in the Use of the Library," Tennessee Librarian, 5:47–52, April, 1953. Reprinted by permission of author and publisher.

49. Virginia Clark. "Teaching Students to Use the Library: Whose Responsibility?" College and Research Libraries, 21:369–372, September, 1960. Reprinted by permission of publisher.

50. E. J. Josey. "The Role of the College Library Staff in Instruction in the Use of the Library," College and Research Libraries, 23:492–498, November, 1962. Reprinted by permission of author and publisher.

51. Helen M. Brown. "The Librarian as Teacher in the College Library," College and Research Libraries, 10:119–123, April, 1949. Reprinted by permission of author and publisher.

52. Edward G. Holley and Robert W. Oram. "University Library Orientation by Television," College and Research Libraries, 23:485–491, November, 1962. Reprinted by permission of authors and publisher.

53. Sidney E. Matthews. "A Military College Initiates a Library Instructional Program," College and Research Libraries, 23:482–484, November, 1962. Reprinted by permission of author and publisher.

54. Annie May Alston. "The Happy Medium in Library Instruction at the College Level," College and Research

ACKNOWLEDGMENTS

Libraries, 21:469–470, November, 1960. Reprinted by
permission of publisher.

55. LeMoyne W. Anderson. "Library Instruction at the University of Illinois in Chicago," Illinois Libraries, 39:118–
121, April, 1957. Reprinted by permission of author and
publisher.

56. William S. Budington. "Teaching the Use of Engineering
Libraries," College and Research Libraries, 12:268–272,
July, 1951. Reprinted by permission of author and pub-
lisher.

57. Hugh Pritchard, Edmund G. Miller, Alice H. Savidge, and
Ezra C. Fitch. "Library Exercise for Freshmen," Library Journal, 84:2576–2578, September 15, 1959. Reprinted by permission of authors and publisher.

58. Annie May Alston. "Library Instruction on the General
Education Level," Arkansas Libraries, 10:7–9, July,
1953. Reprinted by permission of author and publisher.

INTRODUCTION

Possibly there has never been a better time for librarians to take a serious look at their programs of instruction in library use, and this volume of collected articles on the subject can serve as a starting point for such a study. The many changes in education that are now taking place — changes in content emphases, changes in teaching methods, changes in placement levels of subject matter—are affecting the nature of libraries, their collections, their services, their interrelations with the academic institution of which they are a part, their extra-relations with libraries from which their users have come, will go, or are using concurrently, and, consequently, the instruction in their use.

The articles selected for inclusion in Teaching for Better Use of Libraries span a period of nineteen years, from 1949 through 1968; reflect many points of view; and represent every level of instruction from kindergarten through college to graduate and professional education. For each level of instruction, the articles vary in their treatment as to their emphasis on fundamental objectives and basic considerations, course or program content, skills and competencies to be developed, or teaching methods and techniques to be used in the presentation of the subject.

Three of the fifty-eight articles were published in 1949, and the others are divided almost equally between those published in the fifties and in the sixties. While more than half of the articles come from College and Research Libraries, Library Journal and Wilson Library Bulletin, twenty other library science journals are represented, of which four are foreign and nine are state library association publications. Six in the field of education bring the total number of journals to twenty-nine.

INTRODUCTION

While not organized for the purpose, the collection
provides a quick way to take a retrospective look at the
literature of library instruction and to see what, insofar
as these selections can be considered representative, was
engaging the attention of librarians at any one time in
respect to this subject. The years 1949–1959 are represented by twenty-eight articles, half of which are concerned with introducing the high school student to his library and developing in him the skills he will need to
make effective use of it. Five are directed at teaching
library use to elementary school pupils, and seven to college and university students. Three of the articles are
devoted to special needs of students in medicine, pharmacy,
and engineering. The thirty selections appearing in print
from 1960 through 1968 show an almost even division between elementary and high school libraries, with only a
few articles devoted to college and university libraries
and none to special subject areas.

What, if anything, is the significance that can be attached to these figures? One might be that instruction in
the use of libraries still must go on at every level, despite
the growth in the number of schools, elementary and secondary, served by libraries, and the improvement in quality of collection and services provided by these libraries.
In other words, the high school will continue to find that
its students will need instruction in the use of the library
even when each will have experienced centralized libraries
in elementary as well as in junior high schools. And, in
turn, the colleges and universities will find their students
requiring assistance in the further development of library
skills, though the high schools from which they come have
vastly improved libraries, and programs of instruction in
their use. And so it goes, from kindergarten through graduate and professional education.

Another significance of this breakdown by level of instruction and, in fact, a corollary of the first, is the necessity it suggests for the coordination of effort at the various

INTRODUCTION

levels. While we can be quite certain that the varying library
backgrounds of our students which is cited as a major problem in library instruction in one of the earliest articles in
the collection, and in a number of the later articles, will continue to plague us, this does not absolve us from the necessity for coordination. More and more, if library instruction
is to be both effective and palatable, we must deal with it at
each level as a segment of a cumulative body of knowledge
and skills which builds upon that segment which precedes it,
and into that segment which will follow. This requires perspective on that part of the instruction for which each has
primary responsibility, and an interest in and knowledge of
the totality of the library instruction which students are to
experience throughout the entire period of their formal education.

As would be expected, the articles published during the
past several years reflect an increased concern for effective use of libraries in the elementary grades and for the
needs of special kinds of students—the superior student, the
student with a low IQ, the college-bound student, the high
school drop-out. Also, the reader will see in these more
recent articles the influence of the newer techniques, devices, and teaching methods on library instruction. Team
teaching, and the appropriate use of small and large group
instruction are making their contributions to this, as to
other areas of instruction. Television, tape recordings for
self and group instruction, slides, transparencies, and 8MM
cartridges are effective devices for use in library instruction as elsewhere in the curriculum, and the librarian of the
sixties appears to be exploiting these to an increasing extent.

The reader may look in this volume in vain for articles
that will indicate an effect on library instruction of the growing use by the student of libraries in addition to that of the
institution at which he is in attendance. In teaching for better use of libraries, surely this increase in the use of multiple libraries must be, and is no doubt being, taken into
consideration despite the absence of articles reporting it.

INTRODUCTION

Another gap in the literature which the reader will regret, but in this instance will expect, is that of articles which describe the library instruction given in the various Knapp Foundation Project schools. We have much to learn from the librarians and teachers in these schools, where the important role of the library is recognized and where collection and staff sufficient to achieve it are provided.

The reference librarian on one side of the reference desk and the inquiring library user on the other—the library's counterpart to Mark Hopkins and his student on the log—is still viewed by many with nostalgia as the best method of teaching the use of the library. Integration of library instruction into all subject fields remains every librarian's ideal. These ideas continue to be expressed throughout the literature of instruction in library use. But continuing increase in enrollments, greater emphasis in teaching on the use of library materials, expanding knowledge in various fields and all that is concomitant to it, continue to make more or less formalized instruction necessary. As Maryline Conrey and Helen Reed expressed it for high school libraries in 1962, and the same holds true today, and at every level: "If each high school had two or more librarians, if all teachers were library minded and well acquainted with resources, and if pressure to cover textbook material—and classroom pressures in general—were less, there would probably be little need for a special course in library skills."*

A course as such may not be the answer in every situation, but planned instruction spread throughout the years of his formal education and directed toward the stu-

---

* "A High School Course in Library Skills," School Library Association of California Bulletin, Vol. 33, no. 2, p. 8, January, 1962.

INTRODUCTION

dent's needs at any given time is essential to any educational program that would develop him into an effective, independent user of libraries. The library profession is indebted to the editor for bringing together in one convenient volume the thinking of many librarians on this subject, and their experience in many different kinds of situations. The sharing of these ideas and experiences can lead to teaching for better use of libraries—a shared responsibility of school, college, and public librarians.

Florrinell F. Morton
Director, Library School
Louisiana State University

PREFACE

Most librarians will agree that instruction in library usage is most acutely needed. The purpose of Teaching for Better Use of Libraries is to provide librarians, in both academic and non-academic libraries, with guidelines for improving the use of their resources through effective library instruction. This text will help librarians, teachers, and administrators to answer such questions as —How and when should library skills be introduced and taught? Whose responsibility should it be? Should it be an on-going process through all levels of education? What skills need to be taught in our schools and colleges? Are teachers thoroughly familiar with the library and its services? How many teachers are familiar with a broad range of resources to which they can direct their students?

As library instruction spreads throughout all levels of education, the foundations for skill in research must be laid long before the student reaches the university. It is necessary to develop a competency in searching for information early in the learning process in order to keep pace with not only academic progress but with rapid societal-technical changes and knowledge explosion. More and more, the student will live with self-instruction techniques and independent study because of rapidly increasing student enrollments and population explosion. The ability to use the library on his own will be the deciding factor in academic success and eventual occupational success.

A survey of the literature on the subject of teaching the use of the library definitely places the responsibility for this vital task on the librarian. The first order of business in acknowledging this responsibility is to care-

PREFACE

plan, schedule, cooperate, and guide the teacher in establishing a framework of means for improving the student's library skills. All educators should understand the need for guiding and helping youngsters to make effective use of library resources. It is a cooperative assignment for the teacher and librarian to decide when library experience is most beneficial to the student.

There are three basic aspects of program content for teaching the use of the library: (1) Use of the library, its card catalog, classification system, organization of materials, reference tools, audio-visual equipment, etc.; (2) Use of the book, its author, title, index, etc. and (3) Use of the individual reference tool, the encyclopedia, the dictionary, the periodical index, fact book, atlases, etc. All three should be approached in terms of the problem at hand rather than prescribing busy work assignments. The separate library course, the orientation lecture and individual instruction are various approaches used to help students to understand the library.

Library learning, like the ideal counseling situation, is most effective when placed on a person-to-person basis. However, it is not possible to reach everyone with personal attention and it is necessary to use group instruction. Librarians are constantly faced with the problem of building better attitudes toward their libraries along with establishing the library as a prime resource for lifelong learning.

Grateful acknowledgment is made to the individual authors and the publishers for permission to use their material in Teaching for Better Use of Libraries.

Charles L. Trinkner

Librarian
Pensacola, Florida

PART I: TEACHING LIBRARY SKILLS

1. LIBRARY INSTRUCTION IN A VACUUM

Chase Dane

School librarians and teachers all agree that students must be taught how to use the library. The problem, however, is to decide which method of instruction should be used: group or individual? Both methods have been tried, and both have been successful and both have been unsuccessful. Some librarians, indeed, have sought to evade a decision by employing a combination of the two. Perhaps neither method will ever prove satisfactory in all situations. And yet, recognizing the need for instruction in the use of the library, the subject must be taught somehow. It may be well, therefore, before adopting one method or the other, or both, to consider them carefully. But no matter which method is finally used the most important thing is to remember that library instruction must never be given in a vacuum. It must never be taught in itself and for itself. The library is a tool, and lessons in library usage must teach the student how to use that tool.

Group instruction has many things to recommend it. It can be given much more rapidly, and to many more students, than individual instruction. By this method the librarian can insure that every student will have had at least some instruction in the use of the library. This method also lends itself well to the use of visual aids: films, posters, charts, over-sized catalog cards. And in a large school it is probably the only method by which the librarian can reach all students.

But group instruction also has many things which do not recommend it. It is often difficult to give group instruction and still make it meaningful. To do this the librarian and the teacher must work together very closely. And in a large school, where group instruction has its greatest value, this

3

is usually a difficult problem in itself. Such cooperation frequently has to be imposed by the administration, and requires very careful planning. Much of the effectiveness of group instruction is lost if even only a few teachers fail to follow up with more detailed instruction or application in the classroom. And group instruction makes it difficult to repeat material. One student, if properly motivated, will gladly listen to a second lesson on the same subject if he did not learn the first one thoroughly. But many students, no matter how carefully motivated, will not willingly listen to two lessons on the same topic.

Too often, too, group instruction is not related to a project. A lesson in the use of the card catalog will not be remembered if students do not feel that they need to know how to use it. But if a lesson in the use of the card catalog is given in connection with a term paper in a history class, then the students will understand why they have to learn that lesson. And the lesson will, of course, be remembered much longer. When, however, students learn how to use the Readers' Guide but have no need to use it for several months, they will have to be taught that lesson all over again.

One further weakness of this method lies in the fact that it cannot be easily carried to completion by one person. As has already been pointed out, group instruction, if it is to be effective, must be followed up by application in the classroom. For if it is not so followed up it simply becomes instruction in a vacuum. But this means that the librarian who gives the instruction cannot also see that it is applied correctly. Thus the librarian has very little opportunity to judge the effectiveness of her lessons in how to use the library. Such a method also makes it difficult for the librarian to see how her lessons can be improved if they are unsatisfactory.

But individual instruction likewise has its advantages and disadvantages. Perhaps the greatest value of this method is that instruction in the use of the library is given when the student needs it most. The student who must compile a bibliography comes to the library for help and receives the

instruction which will aid him most. This kind of learning
is thoroughly motivated. And lessons taught in this way will
usually be remembered for a long time. By this method
also the librarian does not waste time imparting knowledge
which will never be used. When a large group of students
is taught how to use the library the problem always arises
of how much these students should be taught. The needs of
all students are not the same and this multiplicity of needs
cannot be solved by group instruction. Individual needs, however, can be met by individual instruction. By this method,
therefore, the librarian does not teach too little to some students and too much to others. Each student receives only
the instruction which he needs at the time.

Another important benefit of individual instruction is
that it allows students to proceed at their own pace. The
fast learner is not held back by the slow learner. Also,
this method makes it possible to repeat lessons for some
students without boring, and without taking the time of other
students who have already learned the lesson. And finally,
but not necessarily individual instruction is apt to be more
thorough than group instruction. Lessons so taught can be
made more concentrated; more information can be imparted
in less time.

Individual instruction, however, also has its drawbacks.
This method makes it very difficult to cover all students; indeed, all students will not receive instruction unless they ask
for it or unless some kind of a program is established to see
that they receive it. Perhaps a more important drawback is
the fact that not all students will be ready at the same time
to begin work on a project. Thus when a bibliography of magazine articles is required for a science class not all students
in the class will be trained to carry out the assignment. If
only a few have not been trained they can, of course, be
trained at the last minute by the librarian. But if, on the
other hand, a great many students lack such training, this
will obviously not be possible. In such a case the librarian
will have to resort to group instruction or the science teacher

will have to postpone the assignment until all students have received the necessary training.

Neither method, therefore, is completely satisfactory. A combination of the two does, however, have certain advantages. Group instruction makes it possible for the librarian to give all students a certain basic training — a training which will benefit all students whether they are preparing for college, for business, for trade, or for agriculture. And individual instruction can then be given only to students who did not learn the basic lesson thoroughly, or who need more advanced and specialized training. In this way the librarian can take advantage of the chief values of each method. In this way, too, she can avoid most of the weaknesses of each method.

But regardless of which method is finally adopted the librarian must not neglect the use of repetition. For to be effective, lessons in the use of the library must be repeated frequently. This repetition must, of course, be varied as much as possible to avoid monotony. For if the lessons become monotonous they will lose their effectiveness no matter how often they are repeated. Also, if the lessons become monotonous they may lead to a growing dislike of the library — and thus work against the very thing the librarian is trying to achieve. To avoid this error it may be wise for the librarian to grade the lessons in such a way that while material is repeated it is always presented on a more advanced level.

Furthermore, to achieve the greatest good, the program of library instruction must not overlook the necessity for cooperation between teacher and librarian. All work must be planned in advance so that when students come to the library for instruction they will have a need for that which is then presented to them. This means that a project should first be set up in the classroom which will involve problems in the use of the library. Moreover, this project, whether it is a term paper or a bibliography, must be important because of its relation to subject matter as well as because it provides a reason for learning how to use the library. A project must not be adopted simply because it requires the use of library materials. When a project results from this kind of cooperation between teacher and librarian it will be mutually beneficial to both. The teacher and the librarian will have an equal desire to complete the project successfully; and the student cannot but benefit as a result of this.

But in addition to cooperation between teacher and librarian there must also be cooperation between the librarians of the several schools within a system. The junior high school librarian must know what instruction in the use of the library has been given by the elementary school librarian. She must know this in order to avoid useless repetition; and in order to build on the knowledge which the students have already received. In a like manner the high school librarian must know what has been done by the junior high school librarian, and for the same reasons. For only in this way can library instruction be truly helpful to the student.

If possible, this cooperation between librarians should include the public librarian. The public library has many resources not available in the school library; and the public librarian is, of course, best fitted to give instruction in the use of these materials. The overall program of library instruction should, indeed, include visits to the public library. And during these visits simple group instruction can be given in the use of the special materials in the library. Individual instruction can be given at any time when students go to the public library for help on special projects. And finally, the public library can continue, informally, the lessons in the use of books which were begun in the school library. There is really no good reason why library instruction should stop when students leave school. Perhaps one reason for the great difference in the quantitative use of the library between people in school and people out of school is that there is no program for continued library instruction.

Greater cooperation among all librarians, school and public, may do something to contribute to the improvement of this unfortunate situation.

In conclusion it should be pointed out again that different situations will require different methods of library instruction. In one school group instruction may be the only possible solution to this difficult problem; in another school the best method may be a combination of the two. But before deciding on the adoption of a method all the factors involved must be considered carefully. And the most important of these factors is the meaningfulness of the instruction given. Library instruction must be properly motivated; and it must be put to use as soon as it is given. Library instruction must be taken out of the vacuum in which it is now too often taught.

2. STUDY SKILLS: TREASURE HUNT FOR INFORMATION

Helen M. Carpenter

Treasure hunts provide captivating entertainment at parties; they also suggest a stimulating approach to skill development in locating data at school. The search for information can be as exciting and beneficial as the hunt for contrived rewards hidden by a resourceful hostess.

Why Bother? The nature of our times and the requirements of responsible citizenship make facility in locating information an imperative for every citizen. Knowledge in all fields has become so vast and complex that no single source, not even an encyclopedia, can be a complete compendium. Multiple sources need to be consulted.

In addition, multiplicity and rapidity of changes in living make knowledge obsolescent at a faster rate than ever

8

before. Educators are coming to realize that "learning how to learn" is perhaps the most valuable contribution the school can make to individuals whose mature years will occur in the twenty-first century. At the very core of independent learning is the ability to locate information.

Finally, the most important reason of all is the need for responsible citizens to be aware of varying points of view on problems confronting the nation and humanity. Only if its citizens use a balanced, intelligent approach to issues can a democracy survive the appeals of demagogues and dictators. Once again the ability to gather information is central — this time to discharging the obligations of democratic citizenship.

What to Remember. All the study skills that we have discussed this year deal with gaining information — reading pictures, looking and listening on study trips, asking questions, interpreting graphic materials. The focus this month is on developing facility with more comprehensive sources: 1) using a library, be it in the classroom, school, or community; 2) knowing the kind of source to consult—atlas, dictionary, encyclopedia—for different sorts of information; and 3) learning the arrangement of material within a specific reference, as a textbook, a periodical index, or an almanac.

From the earliest primary years, the school program should provide for systematic development of skills in each of these three categories. Standards of competency are usually indicated, but it is important for teachers to remember that some children in a class may be able to move beyond the achievement level set for a grade. For example, some third- and fourth-graders whose reading vocabularies are developed will be able to use the front-page table of contents of a newspaper to find the kind of information desired—a competency usually associated with higher grades.

Two basic skills underlie all others in the gathering of information. One, facility with alphabetical order, is relatively easy, and most children reach a functional level during the primary years. The other, analysis to determine

9

key words as guides in the search, is subtle and elusive. It needs continual emphasis and should begin in the early primary grades with the examining of the titles of books for clues to contents.

   How to Do It. Many practice activities are necessary to develop skills involved in locating information. Educational literature abounds in suggestions. A few recommendations are included here as indicative of the direction such activities should take. It is important to keep in mind that all activities should be functional. The process of locating necessary or vital information should be taught with reference to a specific report, a class question, or such—not in isolation.

Activities which develop a favorable attitude toward research:

   1. Wide reading and an enthusiastic approach by the teacher to discovery of information
   2. Treating location of data as a treasure hunt, with child competing against his own growth record
   3. Constant sharing of facts and ideas found in search
   4. Using "Let's look it up" in every plausible application
   5. Surrounding children in classroom with much material for reading and reference, permitting them enough time and enough freedom of movement for frequent use

To develop facility in using the library:

Primary grades:

   1. Locate pertinent shelves and check out books with guidance
   2. Look at magazines
   3. Listen to stories

STUDY SKILLS

Intermediate grades:

1. Make slides, for classroom use, of catalog cards showing item listed by subject, author, and title
2. List things to remember in interpreting data on catalog cards
3. Make a chart of Dewey Classification System for classroom
4. Draw chart of library showing location of various materials

To develop facility in using various kinds of materials:

1. Examine textbooks or reading books to learn parts of a book—title, title page, table of contents, and so on, through meaningful exercises begun in the first grade
2. Make charts listing available kinds of reference books and other reference sources, as dictionaries, encyclopedias, atlases, guides, almanacs, newspapers, magazines
3. Follow with separate lists of all the items of each category available, as encyclopedias: Compton's Pictured Encyclopedia and World Book Encyclopedia
4. Prepare rules to keep in mind in using each category, based on arrangement of material in a specific source
5. Dramatize through charades or "What Am I" game a miscellany of terms facilitating data collection, such as guide words, key words, cross reference, index
6. Summarize learnings and procedures by making posters or slides of steps in the process of locating information from many sources

Developing skills in gathering data is not a comfortable pursuit for either the lazy student or the teacher; but for those who bestir themselves, life becomes more zestful both inside and outside school.

3. HOW TO TEACH LIBRARY SKILLS
WITHOUT REALLY BEING THERE

Vernon S. Gerlach and Irene Farnbach

Have you ever wished during one of your library class periods that you could be at the card catalog, the reference shelves and several other places, all at the same time, to give individual help to a host of neophyte library-users? A new instructional medium, just being introduced to education, enables you to be at every learning center in your library—by proxy.

This new ubiquitous slave is an 8MM cartridge projector. It is inexpensive, and maintenance-free except for the usual periodic lamp replacement. When used with a small desktop side-projection screen, the projector becomes a device for self-instruction or for small-group work. (Some models are equipped with a zoom lens which allows the teacher to project a screen-size picture for teaching an entire class if he wishes.)

Light in weight and portable, the projector can be used at any learning center in the library. When used as a self-teaching device, the film in its cartridge can be inserted into the projector by even a first-grader; he merely turns on a switch and focuses. He may then view the film, which is stored as a continuous loop in the plastic cartridge, as many times as necessary.

Films used with this projector are called single-concept films. Based upon a rigorous task analysis, they require responses from the learner. This gives the medium the flavor of programed learning, though it is not a teaching machine or program in the popular sense of these terms.

Sealed into cartridges, the continuous-loop films are never touched. There is no threading, no film maintenance.

The small cartridges are easily titled, cataloged and stored. Since the films are sealed in the cartridges, you never find yourself showing a film about the facts of life which was delivered to you in a can marked "Know Your Library." The pictures are never projected upside down and backwards as sometimes happens with conventional educational films.

At present the size of the cartridge limits the length of a single-concept film to four minutes. Consequently, there can be no meandering from the single idea and no distracting cinematographical techniques just for effect. They are matter-of-fact, no-nonsense, let's-get-down-to-business teaching tools.

When library science is taught with this new device, complex behavior is analyzed step by step and each identifiable skill is portrayed in a separate film. A series of films used to teach the use of the card catalog to elementary school children would be titled as follows:

1) Using the Outside Guides, 2) Using the Inside Guides, 3) Finding a Book by Using the Subject Card, 4) Finding a Book by Using the Title Card, 5) Finding a Book by Using the Author Card, 6) Using the Cross Reference Cards. Depending upon the age and achievement level of the children, more films on filing rules for the card catalog could be added.

A very important advantage in the use of cartridge films over other educational films is that responsive actions are required of the student at various points in the presentation. At appropriate intervals, the word STOP is flashed on the screen. The learner then stops the projector and performs the action he has just seen. The projector can be stopped at any frame, either by depressing a button on the top of the machine, which permits the viewing of a single frame, or by turning the projector switch off, which at the same time turns off the projection lamp. After the learner has completed the action to be learned, he releases the stop button or turns on the projector, and the lesson continues until he reaches the next "stop" frame.

13

In group presentation of any of these films, the stop intervals can be used for discussion or questions about the action just presented. In this way misconceptions can be prevented and faulty practices corrected before they become habitual.

Another way to elicit the learner's response is by using a film manual to accompany each film. The stop interval in this case directs the learner to the manual for specific verbal instruction to supplement the pictured action, which he then performs before starting the film again. These responses, action required of the student, are a vital part of learning which has been neglected or impossible with the educational films now in general use in teaching library skills.

Although some single-concept 8MM films in cartridges are being produced, they are not readily available as yet. Though this is apparently a disadvantage, it can very easily become a blessing in disguise to the ambitious teacher, since, in order to take advantage of all the opportunities for good teaching with this new medium, you become the producer. Knowing the needs of your own students, you can tailor-make the films to meet their needs.

Not only is this not a difficult job, but it can become a most exciting activity. The films can be made with no more elaborate equipment than is used in making 8MM home movies. If you do not have an 8MM camera, perhaps you could interest a fellow teacher or friend who has one to do the photography for you. Or, if there is a photography club in your school, perhaps some of its members could be your camera crew.

That teachers who have little or no training in cinematography can produce effective films of the kind described in this article is amply attested to by the experience of 12 graduate students in a workshop at Arizona State University during the summer of 1963. Applying the principles of programed instruction to motion picture production, these students produced over 20 films of sufficiently high quality to

merit the plaudits of some of the nation's leaders in the
field of audio-visual education.

To give you help in planning, shooting and editing your
films, there are many good books about making home
movies which set forth principles of moviemaking that apply
to producing single-concept films. They can help you with
techniques of lighting, cinematography, continuity and editing.

The exciting advantages of this medium for the teaching of library skills and the satisfaction of doing a good job
better will make the effort well worthwhile.

4. TEACHING LIBRARY SKILLS
TO ELEMENTARY STUDENTS

Valentine Jones

Any child over the age of six knows it takes three things
to make a seesaw work: a child on each end and a board in
between.

In a sense, the library program in any school is like the
children and the board. It takes cooperation between the
classroom teacher and the librarian, plus the support of the
administration.

At Velasco Elementary in the Brazosport ISD, the principal cooperates to the fullest by making the library available and attractive to our students, whether they are searching for factual information or recreational reading.

We begin teaching library skills in the first grade. Students come to the library each week from the beginning of
school and the teacher selects books for her class and checks
them out in her name.

To stimulate the child's interest in reading, even before he can choose his own books, the librarian reads from books which will be within his reading capacity before the end of the first grade. Instruction is given by demonstrating the proper way to handle books, and an explanation is given in detail regarding the behavior expected in the library.

About mid-term we begin to play an alphabet game, in which a letter is given and the students are to answer with the next letter of the alphabet. Correlated with this game is an explanation of the arrangement of shelves by author (a new word at this time). These exercises are used preceding the time students are permitted to choose their own books.

We review library shelving, courtesy, rules, and fines at the beginning of the second grade. The alphabet game is continued, this time extending it to include asking for the preceding letter. This is still presented as an enjoyable and challenging game.

Our easy books are on the shelves in alphabetical order by author. Students are taught to return a book to its proper place on the shelf if they decide not to check it out. By the end of the year the students are very proud of their ability to locate their favorite book or author.

About once a month we devote part of the period to listening to oral reports from students who have particularly enjoyed their book. This experience gives the child practice in expressing himself without previous preparation. It also gives the teacher and librarian the opportunity of being sure that he is attempting to read on his level of comprehension.

About half of each 30-minute library period is devoted to teaching library skills during the first part of the school year. The third grade covers the alphabetizing of names as well as letters.

By mid-term most of the third-grade students are prepared to read books which are more difficult than those which are classified as easy. As their reading skills progress, they are allowed to go to the more difficult shelves.

TEACHING LIBRARY SKILLS

The librarian must depend on the cooperation of the teacher in order to determine this step. We must wait for the students' natural curiosity to guide us to the next step.

When they notice and question books having numbers, we know it is time to begin an explanation of the Dewey decimal classification system. We tell them only of the classifications in hundreds and give them a list of these in terminology which is more easily understood by the student, i.e. 400—Language Man Speaks, and 500—General Science What God Gave Man.

It is really rewarding to see these children who were reading easy books at the beginning of the year searching for a book on an animal, an airplane, a person, or a country with the aid of their list. The look of triumph on their faces when they are successful in their search, and the imperative necessity to tell their librarian or teacher, makes all the time and effort worthwhile.

We discuss the Dewey decimal classification in greater detail in the fourth grade. Students are given the same list to make notes for themselves. We practice finding where various titles of books are located in our library and why. It is surprising how many of these titles are circulated.

The students are introduced to the card catalog and are taught to recognize author, title, and subject heading cards. Again we teach alphabetizing, but this time by author name, title, and subject heading. Card catalog alphabetizing seems to be more difficult for the fourth-grade students as they want to alphabetize by letters alone and not word by word.

In the fifth and sixth grades we review all that has been taught in the fourth grade. This is important, as we have a great number of students transfer into our school from districts where library skills are not taught or from districts where a library is not available to elementary students.

Fifth-graders are introduced to the use of reference books and materials after the classroom teacher assigns research papers. This coordination can come only through cooperation between the teacher and the librarian.

In our district we are stressing the use of reference books and materials in addition to encyclopedias. The children really appreciate subject books with an index in the back of the book as this makes locating of materials so much easier.

In the sixth grade we put into practical use the library skills which have been taught.

Different hard-to-find topics are given to groups of students. Each group is made up of four or five students and they work as a team to find all they can about their topic. These topics may range from a certain subject, period of time, or location. They are to find not only the factual material, but also fiction if any is available.

In their reports they need to tell only the classification number, title, author, and why they had used the book. Each group has several weeks to work up the report.

We try to have all organized library skills classes completed by Thanksgiving of each year. Naturally, library skills will continue to be taught with each library session to individual students whenever they need or ask for assistance.

About once a month, during the rest of the year, we have students report on the books they have read. One word of caution probably needs to be added here.

It is invaluable to the librarian to have read the books on which the children make oral book reports. It is extremely easy for an average child to give a description which would ruin a book for the rest of his class.

At this point the librarian must attempt to "sell" the book. If not, it could be an injustice to all of the students because not every child will like Alice in Wonderland or Hurry Home, Candy, both of which are excellent books.

The teaching of library skills in the elementary grades is not only beneficial to students but is a time-saver for teachers and librarians as well.

Several fifth- and sixth-grade teachers send students to the library to select books pertaining to the topic they are studying in the classroom. Very few students who have had library skills instruction need any help from the librarian. This saves time and gives those students a feeling of importance and accomplishment by helping the teacher and fellow-students.

We also use students from the fourth, fifth, and sixth grades as library helpers. They begin their training by pasting pockets and date-due slips in the new books and checking books in and out for their class.

By the time they are fifth- and sixth-grade students, they file the new cards in the card catalog and are able to shelve any of the books. Needless to say, this saves a lot of time for the librarian. Without library skills instruction beginning in the first grade, few, if any, of these students would be able to help.

The third-, fourth-, fifth-, and sixth-grade students are given written tests before Thanksgiving each year to evaluate their knowledge of library skills which have been presented. These tests are prepared, administered, and graded by the librarian.

These tests are then made available to the teachers and <u>may be</u> considered as a part of the students' language arts grade. Many teachers have found this method helpful in locating individual weaknesses in other basic skills.

It is this seesaw idea that enables the students to learn basic skills, not only in the library but also in the classroom. This cooperation between librarian and classroom teacher with the support of the administration is an essential ingredient for an effective library program.

5. THE DEVELOPMENT OF LOCATIONAL SKILLS

Martha Dallmann

In this article, suggestions for teaching three types of locational skills are given: (1) developing efficiency in locating information in a nonreference book (2) acquiring skill in using encyclopedias and (3) learning to find materials in a library.

BASIC CONSIDERATIONS

The teacher should take inventory of what skills her pupils already possess. Even in the beginning of the fourth grade, the teacher will find that many of the pupils have some ability to locate information in print. It is upon this foundation of what the children already know that the teacher needs to build, rather than upon some theoretical conceptions of what skills boys and girls should have when they enter her grade.

Develop skills in terms of the resources available. When you are teaching boys and girls to use the index of a book, use the indexes of books that the children already have. Similarly, when teaching encyclopedia usage, use those encyclopedias that are provided in the school or that the boys and girls have in their homes. And again, when teaching how to find materials in the library, let the children learn in terms of the library facilities which are available, either in the room, or the school or the public library.

The boys and girls should be given a thorough foundation in the techniques and skills needed in locating information. These skills include finding words arranged in alphabetical order, using entry words, locating a page rapidly and knowing for what type of information to look in a given kind

20

of book. Unless, for example, a pupil is efficient in finding words in alphabetical order, he will have trouble when using the dictionary, an index, an encyclopedia and the card catalogue of a library.

LOCATING INFORMATION IN A NONREFERENCE BOOK

Essential knowledge and skills. Some time before the pupil leaves the elementary school he should have learned the purpose and location of the parts of a book that serve as aids to finding information in the book: the introduction or preface, the table of contents, the appendix and the index. He should know how to use these divisions of a book to locate information in the book. Furthermore, he should be able to use chapter headings, center heads and side heads as aids in locating information. He should also know that not all books have these various means for facilitating the location of information, and he should realize in what types of books each is likely to be found—for example, he should not look for an index in a book of fiction.

Since the introduction to a book often gives some clue as to what to expect in it, boys and girls should learn what type of aid they may be able to find in the introduction and how to make use of the information there. They also need to realize that the sole purpose of most introductions is not, however, to help the reader learn to locate information within the book.

The pupils should realize that the table of contents can be very valuable in finding information. They need to know that it contains chapter headings, at times divided into subheadings; that the chapters are listed in the contents in order of appearance in the book; and that the page on which each chapter begins is given. They should acquire efficiency in using the contents to decide, in the case of some books, where to look for information on a given topic.

Important points for children to learn about the index are:

1. If there is an index, it is almost invariably located in the back part of the book.

2. The topics are given in alphabetical order.

3. The main entries in an index are usually subdivided.

4. References indicate on what pages information on main entries and subdivisions can be found.

The following skills in using the index are some of the most significant ones: (1) ability to decide under what key words to look for information on a specific topic or question (2) speed in finding an entry in an index (3) skill in interpreting the various types of information given in an index and (4) ability to make effective use of a reference in an index after it has been located.

The boys and girls should also learn what type of information is likely to be given in appendices to books and how to make use of this information. At times this involves learning how to interpret tables. They should also learn how to use chapter headings, center headings and side headings in such a way that they do not spend time looking for information in parts of the book where it is not likely to be given.

Methods. In teaching this topic of how to find information in a book, the teacher should utilize meaningful classroom situations as much as seems profitable. Most of the work should not be in the form of exercises; a large part of the needed practice should be obtained as the boys and girls need to find information on some problem or question of significance that confronts them. Frequently, however, some of the pupils will need supplementary practice exercises.

The following are a few of the ways to develop skill in finding information in a nonreference book:

1. Ask the boys and girls to find as quickly as they can, but without haste or tension, the title of a story in one of their basal reading books.

2. Provide incentive for making a table of contents or an index for a notebook that is being made either as a class, a committee or an individual project.

3. Have some of the children report on the type of information given in the introductions to various books they

are using. Ask them to note in particular that which serves as an aid to finding information within the books.

4. Have the boys and girls decide which one of several specified words would probably be the entry word to use when trying to locate information on a specified question.

USING ENCYCLOPEDIAS

Essential knowledge and skills. The boys and girls should learn what types of information can be found in an encyclopedia, how the information is arranged, what aids to the speedy finding of material are given in each set of encyclopedias and what method each has for giving references to material in addition to that included in the encyclopedia. The pupil should also be helped to develop skill in finding and utilizing material found in the encyclopedia.

Methods. The following are some procedures to help boys and girls use encyclopedias effectively:

1. When introducing the use of the encyclopedia, ask each child to browse through some volume until he can report one fact that he finds particularly interesting or significant.

2. After you have written on the chalkboard a diagram showing the volume guides of an encyclopedia, have the pupils tell the number of the volume in which they would look for information on a topic that you mention, such as George Washington Carver, the Battle of New Orleans, or state flowers.

3. Show the pupils the filmstrip, "How to Use an Encyclopedia," published by the Popular Science Publishing Company (distributed by McGraw-Hill Book Co., 330 W. 42nd St., New York 36, N.Y.).

4. Help the boys and girls make arrangements for a "quiz program" in which questions will be asked that are answered in one or more related articles in the encyclopedia. Let a committee of boys and girls, under your guidance, prepare the list of questions. They should inform the rest

of the class of the articles on which they will base the questions, but they should not tell their classmates beforehand what the questions will be.

FINDING MATERIALS IN THE LIBRARY

Pupils should learn the meaning and use of the following: the card catalogue, its arrangement and value; the three most common types of library cards—the title card, the author card and the subject card; the arrangement of the books on the shelves; the placement of magazines in the library.

The teacher can do the following to help the boys and girls learn more about the library and how to use it:

1. Help the boys and girls make a card catalogue of books in their room library. Have them include title cards, author cards, subject cards, guide cards and See also cards.

2. Suggest that a committee make a large diagram showing the placement of books in their room or school library.

3. Take the boys and girls to the public library so that the librarian can explain to them the arrangement in their local library of books and magazines.

4. Have the pupils put on a skit showing how to behave when in a library.

6. THE FOURTH GRADE AND THE CARD CATALOG

Gertrude Stacy

Too many adults appear to be afraid of the card catalog. It has no terrors for our fourth graders. Our library is only a classroom in an old building, soon to be abandoned, but it is a lively room full of activity and very popular with the fourth grades.

Since space is limited, free access to the library is not permitted below the fourth grade. Regular instruction in library procedures begins soon after school opens in the fall, with lessons on the use of the card catalog given early. Before these lessons are taught, the little newcomers watch the older children using the card catalog and many ask timidly if they may look in the "little boxes." Permission is given and if possible, a personal lesson takes place at once. There is no better time to teach anything than in response to need or when interest is high.

Before the card catalog can be meaningful to these young children, a lesson devoted to the placing of books on the shelves is needed. The librarian becomes a "postman" with a "package" (book) to deliver. She walks through the "200 block," the "300 block," etc., until the right section is reached:

"How does the postman know which is the right house?" "Each house has a number."

"How does he know which package or letter to deliver?" "By the name on the package or letter."

"Suppose he does not know your name, or you have a visitor who is receiving mail?" "He looks at the number on the letter!" "Right. Our books are placed on the shelves by number, just as mail is put into your boxes by number. This

25

book belongs here because the number on the book is the same as the number on this shelf."

Some practice in putting books on the shelves takes place at this time, beginning with the more alert pupils and using only nonfiction, to tie it in with the postman-and-numbers theme. The children usually continue this on their own at intermissions, and the mistakes they make are corrected without comment later. (They soon catch each others' mistakes!)

GIANT CARDS

The first formal lesson on the card catalog is given with large 15"x 25" cards in a Visograph, a primary reading device of plastic and cardboard, made by the John C. Winston Company. Since most people ask for a book by title, the first card shown is a title card for a book about Mexico, a fourth grade unit:

"You remember, last week we put books on the shelves by number? We found that each book has its own special place on the shelf. Sometimes we want to know if the library has a certain book and where it can be found. We can always find this out by looking in the card catalog. How many of you know what that is? Point to it."

"Now, everyone raise his left hand. Point to this number in the upper left-hand corner of this card I am holding. This card is just like a card in one of the drawers in the card catalog. This number in the upper left-hand corner is the 'address' of the book. It tells us where the book is kept on the shelves. If it is in the library today, it will be on the shelf marked 917.2. Every book in our library has at least one card for it; most of them have at least three."

The class is told that the number in the upper left-hand corner of the card is the same as the number on the spine of the book. The term call number is given, and if there is time, an explanation of the meaning of the term. The title is ascertained, and the librarian asks the class what "block" the book will be found in, and elicits the answer "900 block." Some child sitting near the correct shelf is asked to locate the book. He is assured of success, since the librarian has placed a copy there just before the lesson is begun. He brings it to her proudly. This is a big moment in his young life! He is then asked to see how many pages the book has.

"That's right. 273 pages. Is there anything on this card that might tell us that?"

The children usually find the information at once. (The number of pages is used as a starting point because pages have more meaning to young children than author, publisher, etc.)

"I wonder if anyone can see what else this card tells us about the book?"

Since the title has already been established, someone is sure to mention it. The word author is explained, preferably by a child, and the author line is indicated. Now comes the participation in the lesson by pupils. The Visograph permits underlining and circling of different parts of the card with a special crayon easily erased with tissue. The "address" of the book is circled, the title underlined, the number of pages, the author, and finally the date indicated. No attempt is made to teach publisher unless the pupils ask about it. The terms "call number" and "address" are used interchangeably, over and over. The number of pages is stressed chiefly to give emphasis to the fact that the number that tells where the book is kept is in the upper left-hand corner of the card. (Occasionally pupils ask where "273 p." is unless this point is clarified in the beginning.)

The title card is then set aside in plain sight and the author card is shown. The likenesses and difference are elicited from the pupils and the terms author card and title card are used frequently by the librarian. Review takes place with this second card as the various parts are underlined or circled, again and again, with constant participation by the pupils at the Visograph. This is continued with a subject card and that term is added to their vocabularies.

ALPHABETICAL ARRANGEMENT

At this point, the alphabetical arrangement of the card catalog is explained and first letters are discussed, underlined, or circled. Volunteers go to the card catalog to find copies of each of the cards being displayed.

In review, the various uses of the card catalog are given and a placard showing these uses in childlike language is placed above the catalog. At a later date, title analytics and see references are taught, but this is enough for one lesson. It is reviewed briefly the following week, and participation of a different sort then takes place.

Orange practice cards exactly like the cards in the card catalog for books on the shelves in the right places on the day of the lesson are passed to one half the class. Each child is asked to go to the right shelf and to take the book indicated on his card to his table. When all of the books have been located, the children with books give them to neighbors who have no books. They watch to see their neighbors return the books to the proper shelves.

A third lesson involves another set of orange cards. These are to be matched to cards in the card catalog. Since we have only fifteen drawers, not all of the class can take part in this activity at once. The others get library books to take home while they are waiting. Then the process is reversed. Most children are eager to match several cards and this is encouraged while interest is high, and continued at intermissions. Once in a while, the title card is found when it should be the main entry or a subject card. Since this causes conflict in the use of a drawer, the error is discovered almost before it happens.

For young children it is not enough to be told about the card catalog. There must be both formal instruction and incidental learning, followed by much <u>practice</u>. For that reason, if a child asks whether we have a book or where it can be found, the answer is never "yes" or "no" or "back in 595." It is <u>always</u> looked up in the card catalog. The librarian <u>never</u> knows the name of the author of a book to be renewed. The child is directed to look it up under title and ascertain the author's name. If he cannot pronounce it, he brings the drawer to the librarian and is always surprised (the first time) that she has his card ready to be stamped again.

It is gratifying to watch a nine year old playing a game alone—looking up a book in the card catalog and locating it on the shelves. It is a source of satisfaction to the librarian to know that even if her patrons are so short their noses barely miss the top drawers, they are growing in the knowledge that the card catalog is a useful tool in any library.

7. THEY COMPETE TO LEARN THE CATALOG

Barbara A. Monroe

Twenty-six sixth-graders are learning how to make effective use of the library; and what's more, they are enjoying themselves. We're having library instruction. If we named the class "Library Instruction," the youngsters would undoubtedly be puzzled or even incredulous. Library instruction connotes listening to explanations, taking tests, doing homework. But this is fun!

The teacher and the librarian were concerned because the sixth grade did not know how to use the library efficiently. A weekly 45 minute period was set aside for instruction, and the teacher and librarian, working together, developed

the following procedure. The first day that the children
came into the library, they were asked to sit in four heterogeneous groups which were also used for various classroom activities. Each group chose a leader. At a signal
from the bell, the leader from each group came to the desk
and chose a slip of paper, on which was written the title or
the author of a book. Each group conferred for one minute,
the members advising the leader as to the best and quickest
way of locating the book. Then the search was on! The four
leaders set forth with subdued (in deference to the nature of
the room in which they were working), but enthusiastic,
cheering in the background. If, at the end of two minutes,
the leader was unable to locate his book, he passed on the
slip of paper and the information which he had accumulated
concerning it to the person at his right. If three people in
the group were unsuccessful, activity was suspended until
the next round.

Four points were awarded the group which found the
correct book first, three points to the second, two to the
third, and one to the fourth. If the group made three attempts without results, it received no points. A follow-up
session occupied the last portion of the period. Children
asked questions concerning the books which they had had
difficulty locating. The librarian helped with the solutions
and also brought up other questions which needed group discussion and clarification. The children left the library reluctantly at the end of the period, begging to repeat the
"game" soon.

It was repeated the next week, but with a new twist. Instead of authors and titles of fact books on the slips of paper,
we listed subjects and asked the children to locate informational books about these subjects. The third week, the slips
contained reference questions. The children brought the answers to the librarian in the form of reference books opened
to the pages where the requested information could be found.
The fourth week children were anxious to search on the fiction shelves for particular books, books written by certain

authors, and books about definite subjects. And in the grand finale in the last week all the techniques of the past weeks were employed in a final review.

But the end has not yet come. We intend, from time to time, to repeat some of the ideas, as well as introduce new ones into this same structure. Five aspects of the activity are of value. We are pleased with the soundness of the procedure; we are delighted with the diagnostic opportunities; the follow-up sessions at the end of each period provide the right information at the right time; the organization and the content make evaluation possible; the children are enjoying the experience.

EDUCATIONAL VALUE

Let's examine the technique for its educational value. What are its merits? The most important is that all children have an opportunity to participate. In less than 30 minutes, each child has at least one turn at the actual search. This aspect is accentuated by the passing of the slip to another person after two minutes have passed. Moreover, all members of each group have an opportunity to suggest and advise every time a new slip of paper is chosen. Secondly, all children are able to attain success in the activity. Jane, who has very little knowledge of the card catalog or the books about rocks, can profit from Jim and Bill's suggestions and find the requested book. Thirdly, the timing is good. Because of the "three times and the group is out" stipulation, one group is not active for a long period of time while other groups are waiting for something to happen. Also, the two minute time limit for each searcher eliminates the impatience which other members of the group might feel toward one embarrassed member who is left on the spot for too long a time. Lastly, the plan lends itself to the presentation of varied skills, ideas, and information.

Diagnostically, the scheme works beautifully. It points out individual and group strengths and weaknesses very clearly,

at a time when the children are completely oblivious to being observed. The teacher and librarian, sitting on the side-
lines, quickly notice that many children thumb through an
enormous number of catalog cards one by one. We notice
Sarah heading for the encyclopedia to find the pronunciation
of a proper noun. We realize instantly that she is not aware
that proper nouns are included in the dictionary. And then
there is Elizabeth. She has been right in the vicinity of Hugh
Lofting's books for a long time now. Why doesn't she pull
out one and bring it over? Maybe the author's name isn't
evident on the outside of the book. Doesn't she know where
to look for it inside? Most of the children are forgetting
their call numbers enroute from the catalog to the shelves.
The librarian takes notes of all these observations. Now
she knows what the children need to learn and what areas
need the most concentration.

FOLLOW-UP SESSION

The din is over, and we're ready for the follow-up session. Hands are waving. We're glad, because we hope that
most of the incentive for learning will come from the children. Mary wonders why she couldn't find a book about the
Civil War by looking through cards in the "C" drawer of the
catalog. Children in other groups are also puzzled. Aha!
thinks the librarian, they didn't realize that the cards for
each period of our country's development are arranged
chronologically in the "U" drawer as a part of United States
history. Now is the time to straighten this out.

When the children have exhausted their questions, the
librarian glances quickly over her notes. This is the time
to consider the everlasting thumbing through individual
cards in the catalog. How can we locate the cards we need
more quickly? Elizabeth had difficulty finding the author's
name in the books she was looking at. Where can we find
author's names in the books? What kind of reference do we
head for when we are asked for definitions, synonyms, and

pronunciations? Yes, the dictionary, even if we are dealing
with a proper noun. And next time let's all write down on
the slip of paper the call numbers and other information
from the card catalog which will help us find our book. This
will help us in our search and also be of assistance to the
next person in case we need to pass on the job.

Evaluation is a continuous process. Each week questions are included which directly and indirectly involve learnings from previous weeks. In this way we can constantly
build upon sound bases, making sure that one concept is mastered before we attempt to teach another one which is dependent upon it.

It is impossible to overestimate the last value of the activity. When children thoroughly enjoy a learning experience,
all things are possible. And it came about because a teacher
and a librarian joined forces.

8. TEACHING CHILDREN TO USE THE DICTIONARY

Bessie L. Pugh

If education is to be a continuous process throughout
life, it is imperative that children be taught as many self-
help techniques as possible while they are in school; and
since scientific studies show a high positive relationship
between success and the size of one's vocabulary, systemat-
atic training in the efficient use of the dictionary should be
emphasized.

With the excellent picture dictionaries now available,
preschool children should develop the dictionary habit.
After looking at the pictures in these books repeatedly,
some children automatically turn to the front if you ask

them to show you an apple or a ball and toward the back if you ask to see a turkey. Other children need guidance in discovering the fact that all dictionaries follow the same pattern in arranging the sequence of words.

Even before children know the names of the letters, they should have the alphabet displayed on the classroom wall and be shown that words having a beginning letter that matches a letter on the left in the alphabet will be toward the front of the dictionary; those having an initial letter which matches a letter toward the right will be near the back of the book; and those beginning with a letter in the middle of the alphabet will be near the middle of the book. The fact that we do not have an equal number of words beginning with each letter will, of course, skew the dictionary arrangement somewhat.

As soon as a child has two or three basic sight words in his vocabulary which begin with the same letter, these words should be grouped and attention called to the fact that pictures of these words are found close together in the dictionary. Their relative place in the dictionary can also be associated with the relative position of the initial letter in the alphabet. All children will not be able to make this association, but those who are capable of doing so should have the opportunity to see the application of this self-help technique.

To test children's understanding of this arrangement, they should be asked to locate rapidly certain pictured words in their dictionaries so the teacher can observe whether or not they make use of the explanation.

The next step in developing locational skills in the use of the dictionary is to have the children themselves arrange lists of words alphabetically according to the initial letter, as follows:

a	cat	e	egg
b	horse	f	goose
c	fish	g	apple
d	book	h	dog

34

TEACHING CHILDREN TO USE THE DICTIONARY

When children's vocabularies have grown to the point
where they need to alphabetize according to the first two
letters in a word, charts should be used as visual reminders
to look at the second letter as well as the first; as illustrated below:

a	corn	b	aby	c	at
a	irplane	b	ee	c	ent
a	pple	b	ook	c	hair
a	rm	b	us	c	omb

The same procedure should be continued when they have
need for alphabetizing according to the first three letters:

bo	at	do	ctor	pi	ano
bo	ne	do	g	pi	cture
bo	ok	do	ll	pi	g
bo	w	do	or	pi	llow
bo	x	do	ve	pi	pe

After children pass beyond the picture dictionary stage
and are required to get the meaning of words from definitions
alone, great care must be taken to make this a successful experience from the beginning. To do this, the following principle should be observed in beginning dictionary practice:
Never ask a child to look up the meaning of a word unless
you know what he will find as a definition. Oftentimes there
is no familiar synonym given for the particular word on which
the child is seeking help. Finding an unfamiliar definition to
an unfamiliar word discourages a child from further attempts
to use the dictionary. Conversely, when a child's first efforts
are highly successful, he is eager to try the same technique
again.

In the initial states of developing dictionary skills, it is
usually easier and more satisfactory for the teacher to prepare her own sentences containing unfamiliar words to be
looked up. In this way she can control the difficulty of sentence structure and guard against having more than one unfamiliar word to a sentence. Furthermore, by controlling

the tense of the verbs, the degree of adjectives and adverbs, and the singular and plural forms of nouns, she can eliminate the necessity of making structural changes in words before they can be substituted in context.

The dictionary defines nouns only in the singular, verbs only in the infinitive forms, and adjectives and adverbs only in the positive degree. Consequently, if a child encounters the word "elves" in his reading and looks that word up, he will merely discover that elves is the "plural of elf;" and if he does not know what elves are he probably does not know what an elf is either. Having made one unsuccessful attempt to find out, the child may not even turn to the word "elf" to see what it means. Likewise, if a child looks up the meaning of "slew" and finds "pt. slay" or "See slay," he may become frustrated in his efforts to utilize the aid of a dictionary.

Even if a child turns to the word "slay" and finds it means "kill" he will still have to change "kill" to "killed" before he can substitute it correctly in context. If the definition given is, "kill with violence," the definition must also be split and the direct object inserted after the verb "kill," as the following sentence illustrates:

> David slew Goliath.
> David killed Goliath with violence.

Children will never become efficient users of the dictionary if they are permitted to stop short of making all structural changes in word forms required to make grammatically correct sentences.

By constructing her own sentences initially, a teacher can eliminate the necessity for any structural changes in words and concentrate solely upon finding the correct synonym to clarify the context, as in the following sentences:

> I heard a peculiar noise.
> I heard a strange noise.
> A whale is an enormous animal.
> A whale is a huge animal.

TEACHING CHILDREN TO USE THE DICTIONARY

(Children at this stage should know that we use "an" before words beginning with a, e, i, o or the short u sound and "a" before all other words.)

John will <u>purchase</u> a birthday gift for his mother.
John will <u>buy</u> a birthday gift for his mother.
The man's <u>annual</u> earnings are $6,000.
The man's <u>yearly</u> earnings are $6,000.
We use sprays to get rid of <u>vermin</u>.
We use sprays to get rid of <u>small troublesome animals, such as fleas, bedbugs, mice, and rats.</u>

After children can successfully substitute definitions that require no structural changes in words, they should be taught to define words requiring minimal changes, such as changing singular nouns to the plural form and substituting the past tense of verbs for the present tense. Gradually sentences involving additional changes can be introduced. The following sentences illustrate such changes:

The soldiers used <u>grenades</u>.
   A grenade means <u>a hand</u> bomb.
   <u>Grenades</u> mean <u>hand bombs</u>.
The soldiers used <u>hand bombs</u>.

Trouble never <u>ceases</u>.
   <u>Cease</u> means <u>stop</u>.
   <u>Ceases</u> means <u>stops</u>.
Trouble never <u>stops</u>.

Columbus liked to watch the ships at the <u>wharves</u>.
   A <u>wharf</u> means <u>a platform built out from shore</u> beside which ships load and unload.
   <u>Wharves</u> mean <u>platforms built out from shore</u> beside which ships load and unload.
Columbus liked to watch the ships at the <u>platforms built out from shore by which ships load and unload.</u>

The soldiers spied an enemy plane.
  Spy means see.
  Spied means saw.
The soldiers saw an enemy plane.

Sam shone on his arithmetic test.
  Shine means do very well.
  Shone means did very well.
Sam did very well on his arithmetic test.

The men were scaling the mountain with difficulty.
  Scale means climb.
  Scaling means climbing.
The men were climbing the mountain with difficulty.

The farmers were tilling the ground.
  Till means plow.
  Tilling means plowing.
The farmers were plowing the ground.

The farmers had dwelt on their land for many years.
  Dwell means live.
  Dwelt means lived.
The farmers had lived on their land for many years.

Multiple meanings of words also need to be stressed and children should be trained to use contextual clues in deciding which of the several meanings of a word to select for a particular sentence. In the following sentence the word "dwelt" has an entirely different meaning from the one in the previous sentence:

The teacher had dwelt on ways to use the dictionary.
  Dwell means put stress on.
  Dwelt means put stress on. (In this case there is a structural difference between "dwell" and "dwelt" but no structural change is required in the definition as all verb forms of "put" are "put.")
The teacher had put stress on ways to use the dictionary.
  Another definition for "dwell on" is "speak about for a long time" and if this definition is used, it will necessitate

38

a change in the word order of the sentence in addition to the structural changes in the verb form.

The sentence will then read as follows:

The teacher had <u>spoken about</u> ways to use the dictionary <u>for a long time.</u>

Sentences requiring both structural changes and the splitting of definitions by the insertion of direct objects in order to permit correct rephrasing with the substituted definition require a great deal of practice before proficiency is attained. However, the improvement in reading and the increased understanding of language more than justify the effort expended.

Sometimes it requires more understanding of a situation than that contained in a definition to select the correct meaning for a word. For example the word <u>scan</u> has two quite different meanings: (a) look at closely; examine with care; and (b) glance at; look over hastily. If a sentence states that Mr. Jones <u>scans</u> the newspaper every morning before he goes to work, either definition substituted for <u>scans</u> would produce a grammatically correct sentence. However, the sentence will not be semantically correct unless one knows which meaning correctly applies to the situation.

Sometimes deaf children make correct application of all the dictionary skills they have been taught and yet formulate odd-sounding sentences which fail to convey a word's true meaning.

To check the comprehension of the word "penetrated," I once asked a child to use it in a sentence. He wrote, "Mrs. Moore <u>penetrated</u> our room this morning."

<u>Penetrate</u> means <u>enter and pass through.</u>

<u>Penetrated</u> means <u>entered and passed through.</u>

"Mrs. Moore <u>entered and passed through</u> our room this morning."

Although the child correctly applied his dictionary skills, the lack of semantic understanding was obvious. Therefore, a teacher must develop semantic understanding in conjunction with dictionary skills at all levels.

Before children can correctly substitute dictionary definitions of adjectives and adverbs in context, they must know not only the positive degree of these words but also the comparative and superlative forms in order to make the proper structural changes. The following sentences illustrate this necessity:

The whale is the largest animal in the world.
Large means big.
Largest means biggest.
(The pupil must know that the "g" has to be doubled in forming the superlative degree of "big.")
The whale is the biggest animal in the world.

A city was built near the broadest part of the river.
Broad means wide.
Broadest means widest.
(The pupil needs to know that widest has only one "e.")
A city was built near the widest part of the river.

My dog's hair looks the sleekest after I brush it well.
Sleek means shiny.
Sleekest means shiniest.
(The "y" must be changed to "i" before adding "est.")
My dog's hair looks the shiniest after I brush it well.

Sometimes adjectives and adverbs that form their comparative and superlative degrees by adding "er" and "est" are defined by synonyms that form the comparative and superlative degree by using more and most before the positive degree and vice versa, as in the following examples:
Spot is the friskiest dog I ever saw.
Frisky means playful.
Friskiest means most playful.
Spot is the most playful dog I ever saw.

Jane is the <u>most fortunate girl</u> I know.
   <u>Fortunate</u> means <u>lucky</u>.
   <u>Most fortunate</u> means <u>luckiest</u>.
Jane is the <u>luckiest</u> girl I know.

In the following sentence, an understanding of facts not to be found in the definition is essential to the correct rephrasing of the sentence semantically:

John is the <u>stoutest</u> boy in our class.

Stoutest can mean either fattest or strongest, and either synonym would make a grammatically correct statement; so without knowing whether John's strength or obesity is referred to, one cannot determine the correct synonym for stoutest.

Effective use of the dictionary requires even more than the ability to determine which of the multiple meanings for a particular part of speech applies to a given context; it necessitates, first, the ability to recognize what part of speech a word is from its usage in a sentence. For example, the word <u>still</u> can be used as an adjective, an adverb, a noun, and a verb. Within these classifications, there are also multiple meanings according to contextual usage. The teacher, therefore, should construct sentences illustrating the various usages of a particular word not only as different parts of speech but also with multiple meanings for each part of speech. Then by requiring the pupils to match definitions and context according to both multiple meanings and parts of speech, she can evaluate a child's progress in this skill in the following way:

still—adj. (1) without noise
         (2) soft; low
         (3) without waves
    v. (1) make quiet
    n. (1) silence
         (2) apparatus for making alcohol
  adv. (1) up to this or that time
         (2) even; yet

41

(Adv. 2) You must work still harder if you hope to succeed.
(Adj. 3) The ocean was still during our trip.
(N. 2) The officers found the still and arrested two men.
(Adv. 1) Mary was late to school because she was still in bed at 8:30.
(Adj. 2) Joan of Arc heard a still small voice speak to her.
(V. 1) Sometimes a mother can still a crying child by singing to it.
(Adj. 1) We can work better when the room is still.

Oftentimes an understanding of prefixes and suffixes is an aid in recognition of parts of speech despite the fact that there are exceptions to most rules. Furthermore, it is difficult at times for a pupil to recognize the difference between a group of letters used as a prefix or suffix and the same group of letters when they constitute part of the root word, such as preview and present; contentment and ferment; pious and dangerous; pretty and loyalty.

Nevertheless, children should learn to associate the prefixes ness, ment, etc., with nouns; the suffixes less, ous, able, etc., with adjectives; and the suffix ly with adjectives and adverbs.

Although the prefix un is most often used with adjectives, it is frequently used with verbs, such as untie, uncover, unfasten, etc., and it may be used with nouns, such as unbeliever. Dis is another prefix which can be used with either nouns, adjectives, or verbs, and practice in determining which part of speech applies to a given context is necessary.

Sometimes the prefixes dis and un can be added to the same word resulting in entirely different meanings, as the following sentences demonstrate:

John is unlike his father.
John dislikes his father.

The dictionary does not list all words according to prefixes; so in cases where this is not done, a child must be able to omit the prefix and find the root word. Then he will have to attach the meaning of the prefix to the definition of the root word.

42

TEACHING CHILDREN TO USE THE DICTIONARY

It is difficult for a person not familiar with the problems involved in teaching language to the deaf to realize the difficulty caused by the small words—especially the prepositions. A single preposition may have fifteen to twenty different meanings according to its usage in a sentence. One of the most troublesome situations arises when a preposition is used in connection with a verb to give new meaning to the verb. This can be illustrated by adding various prepositions to the verb take and defining them as they are used in context:

Billy did not take to his new sister at first.
Billy did not like his new sister at first.
The baby takes after her father.
The baby resembles her father.
I was taken in by a clever salesman.
I was deceived by a clever salesman.
Ruth takes up with the wrong type of girls.
Ruth associates with the wrong type of girls.
John thought so well of himself the other boys tried to take him down at times.
John thought so well of himself the other boys tried to humble him at times.
Mr. Smith took up a new kind of business recently.
Mr. Smith started a new kind of business recently.
The students couldn't take in all the professor said.
The students couldn't understand all the professor said.
Sally can take off a number of movie stars.
Sally can mimic a number of movie stars.
The teachers take off copies of materials on the ditto machine.
The teachers reproduce copies of materials on the ditto machine.
Some people take on a lot when they are sick.
Some people show their feelings a lot when they are sick.
The factory will take on more men.
The factory will employ more men.

Additional meanings for the verb <u>take</u> also occur when
it is followed by certain nouns or phrases:
After one victory the soldiers <u>took heart</u>.
After one victory the soldiers <u>gained courage</u>.
Where did the accident <u>take place</u>?
Where did the accident <u>happen</u>?
The speaker <u>took the floor</u>.
The speaker <u>arose to speak</u>.
The child <u>took</u> her father's death <u>to heart</u>.
The child <u>was</u> <u>saddened</u> by her father's death.
The teacher <u>took</u> the boys <u>to task</u> for fighting.
The teacher <u>scolded</u> the boys for fighting.

As soon as dictionary practice is begun, explanations
of the mechanics involved in using a dictionary efficiently
should keep pace with the selection of correct definitions.
Pupils should be told that the numbers 1, 2, 3, etc., are used
to indicate different meanings for a word while the semicolon is used to separate synonymous terms. They should
also be informed that italicized words are not definitions but
illustrations of correct usage in a phrase or sentence. For
example, a child who is looking up the meaning of the word
<u>rich</u> in the sentence—Mrs. Jones likes rich food—may find
definitions such as the following:

Rich, adj. (1) wealthy; well-to-do; having much money
           (2) having plenty of butter, eggs, flavoring,
               etc.
           (3) producing or yielding abundantly; fertile;
               <u>rich soil</u>, <u>rich mine</u>.
           (4) costly; elegant; <u>rich dress</u>.

If the child understands that all three definitions listed
under "1" are synonyms and can interpret the words "having much money," he will eliminate all the terms under "1"
as suitable for the context even though he is not familiar
with the words wealthy and well-to-do. When he tries substituting the second definition in context and sees that it
clarifies the sentence, he should also see that the position

TEACHING CHILDREN TO USE THE DICTIONARY

of the modifier must be changed when this definition is substituted for rich. The sentence will then read: Mrs. Jones likes food having plenty of butter, eggs, or flavoring.

Although the italicized words in the third and fourth definitions are used merely to help clarify the words which precede them, deaf children often seize upon some familiar word in the italicized group (such as dress in this instance) and substitute it for the word to be defined (rich) even though the two words are not used as the same part of speech.

Frequently deaf children try to pick a single word out of a phrase used as a definition and substitute it alone as a definition, such as using the word eggs instead of the complete phrase having plenty of butter, eggs, flavoring, etc.

In teaching children how to use the dictionary, the meaning of all abbreviations should be carefully explained and illustrated, such as n., v., adj., adv., prep., conj., interj., pl., pt., pp., Colloq., Syn. and Ant.

Without knowing that Ant. refers to a word of opposite meaning, children attempt to use antonyms as synonyms. Even when a child understands the meaning of the word antonym, he becomes confused, at times, by circuitous definitions which lead to wrong assumptions, such as hard—not soft; soft—not hard; and hard—not easy; easy—not hard. Since both easy and hard are defined as not soft, it is logical to conclude that easy and soft are synonymous. Apparently this was the line of reasoning followed by one of my pupils who rated her book as "a little soft" when asked if it was hard for her.

In the fall of 1960 Scholastic Magazine began publication of classroom weeklies designed to meet the needs of children on each grade level. To illustrate the suitability of News Pilot for the first grade, a picture of Goldilocks and the Three Bears was used, supplemented by the caption ". . . not too hard . . . not too 'soft'. . . JUST RIGHT!"

I was impressed by the fact that the misuse of the word soft by a deaf child, with no attempt at humor, and the consciously contrived misuse of the same word by one who

45

knows better constitutes the difference between a language error and a form of humor. It also presents a challenge to the teacher to develop the deaf child's language understanding to the point where he, too, can recognize and appreciate this difference.

Of all the self-help techniques a deaf child will need after leaving school none is more important than the ability to use the dictionary as an aid to correct pronunciation of new words encountered in reading. This entails an understanding of diacritical marks and the ability to use all kinds of pronunciation keys—not just the diacritical marks used by a single dictionary. Many texts contain glossaries with diacritical marks which are unlike those in the classroom dictionary if a single dictionary is used.

It has always been my policy to have at least three different kinds of dictionaries in the room. This not only gives the children the opportunity to learn how to use more than one type of pronunciation key, but it also increases their chance of finding a meaningful definition to an unfamiliar word. As children advance in their dictionary skills, I make it a practice never to assist a child until he has consulted at least three dictionaries and applied all his known skills to finding out a word's meaning by himself.

To get the correct pronunciation of a new word from the dictionary, one must be able to make correct use of the accent mark as well as the diacritical marks.

In selecting the correct definition for a heteronym, the task is simplified if one knows which pronunciation to use and this is sometimes solely a matter of accent. For example, the word <u>invalid</u> means one thing if it is accented on the first syllable and something quite different if the accent falls on the second syllable.

Deaf children need to be made aware of the fact that there are a number of other heteronyms which are identical in spelling although quite different in meaning and pronunciation, as the following sentences illustrate:

TEACHING CHILDREN TO USE THE DICTIONARY

Jane asked me to wait a <u>minute</u>.
There are <u>minute</u> dust particles in the air.
The farmer sold a <u>sow</u> and six pigs.
Farmers do not <u>sow</u> seed by hand.
Have you <u>wound</u> your watch today?
The soldier's <u>wound</u> was not serious.
The <u>wind</u> blows a lot in Kansas.
It is easy to drive on a road that does not <u>wind</u>.
What <u>does</u> a snake eat?
I saw a fawn and two <u>does</u>.
Which <u>row</u> do you sit in?
The boys got into a <u>row</u> over a girl.

Deaf children who have had systematic instruction in the use of the dictionary from the time they enter school should have a fair degree of proficiency in all these skills when they reach the sixth grade. However, a constantly expanding vocabulary will bring to light many additional understandings necessary for natural and fluent use of the English language.

In summarizing, the following skills are essential to the effective use of the dictionary as a self-help technique:

I. The ability to alphabetize correctly by the use of one or more letters.
II. The ability to find, select, and substitute in context synonyms for words requiring no structural changes.
III. The ability to make the following structural changes:
   A. Pluralizing nouns
   B. Adding "s" for the third person, singular number, present tense verb form.
   C. Changing irregular verbs to the past tense forms.
   D. Changing verbs to the progressive tense forms.
   E. Changing verbs to the perfect tense forms.
   F. The ability to transpose the word order of definitions when this is necessary in order to make a grammatically correct sentence.

47

IV. The ability to use contextual clues in deciding which of several meanings for a verb fits best in a particular sentence.

V. An understanding of the fact that there are synonyms which make a grammatically correct sentence when substituted in context and yet are incorrect from the standpoint of semantics or acceptable usage.

VI. The ability to make the necessary changes in adjectives or adverbs according to degree.

VII. The ability to use words both as different parts of speech and with multiple meanings for each part of speech.

VIII. The ability to recognize prefixes and suffixes and use them as aid in identifying parts of speech.

IX. An understanding of the fact that prepositional words may frequently be used in conjunction with a verb to alter the verb's meaning completely.

X. An understanding of the mechanics of a dictionary, including the following:
   A. The meaning of the numbers, 1, 2, 3, 4, 5, etc.
   B. The purpose of the semicolon in definitions.
   C. The purpose of italicized words and sentences.
   D. The meaning of all abbreviations.
   E. The meaning of the terms synonyms and antonyms.
   F. The ability to use diacritical marks and pronunciation keys as an aid to correct pronunciation of new words.
   G. The ability to use the accent mark as an aid to correct pronunciation.
   H. The ability to recognize and interpret heteronyms.

9. TEACHING CHILDREN TO USE REFERENCE BOOKS

Grace M. Shakin

All those who guide the learning experiences of children agree that the expanding world of knowledge has increased the need for using reference tools easily and skillfully. Language arts handbooks, whether published by state departments or local committees, are likely to indicate the reference skills needed by elementary children. These are flexible outlines giving suggestions on what reference tools should be taught and when to teach them. The unanswered question or the one most frequently discussed is what method of presentation will produce the best habits of research.

In their zeal to help children use reference tools, librarians and teachers alike sometimes teach these tools as separate units. Such artificial lessons are likely to accomplish little unless they are "follow-up" practice periods, and are distinctly recognized as such by the children. To be effective, teaching the use of reference tools—encyclopedias, dictionaries, special reference books, the card catalog itself—must take place as the need arises. Explanation and practice may be necessary, but the only true fortifying of any skill comes in really putting it to use. This should occur both in the library and the classroom.

When fifth-grade Linda uses the card catalog to get the call number for books on Alaska and then, finding those books on the library shelf, uses their indexes for information on her special topic—salmon fishing—an exciting and profitable learning experience takes place. But it doesn't just happen. Linda was a third-grader when the librarian first showed her and her classmates how to use the card catalog. Linda had been surprised to find there were so many books about Indians. In fourth grade, the librarian had taught the class how to use the card catalog to find out more about the countries they were studying. Her teacher had taught her and the class about the importance of using an index. Linda's growing independence in using reference tools thus is the result of careful planning by both teacher and librarian for periods of instruction and many practice opportunities.

The librarian knows and can recommend to staff members effective teaching aids in the field—audio-visual materials and books which may be used successfully in this area of instruction, for example, The Children's Book on How to Use Books and Libraries by Carolyn Mott and Leo B. Baisden (Scribner).

In teaching children to use essential reference tools much repetition, with success, is necessary. Skill in using them is acquired gradually over a long period of time. A fourth-grader, for example, has already learned that many encyclopedias are arranged in ABC order. This is reviewed as his class comes to the library for information about deserts. He learns that Volume D not only has information. There are also related subjects and cross references suggesting many other topics. Whether this is taught by the classroom teacher or librarian or by both working as a team, it is imperative that it be presented as an integral part of a classroom project.

The librarian is constantly alert to take advantage of informal opportunities for clarification and guidance, and the teacher underlines the need for more than one reference and provides many opportunities for children to go to the library.

The ultimate test of the effectiveness of this teaching is what children do and do differently. It is measured by the extent to which children become independent users, not only of their school library but the public library as well.

But, whether it is the classroom teacher or the librarian who helps eight-year-old Kenny learn that the card catalog is the index to the books in the library or who assists Jonathan as he searches for information on a cloud chamber

—both must be mindful that teaching the use of reference
tools is only one aspect of the library program.

The great challenge is to help children discover for
themselves that reading is a stimulating, satisfying experience. One of the greatest gifts the school can give to children is a love of and satisfaction in the habit of reading.

10. TEACHING LIBRARY SKILLS TO
JUNIOR HIGH HONOR STUDENTS

Marilyn Robbins

Although a great deal has been written about the place
of the school library in the curriculum, much still needs to
be done to develop practical methods of coordinating the
school library with the science classroom. Honor students,
especially, can benefit readily from such coordinated programs because of the already highly developed interest in
reading and excellent reading abilities of the honor students.

It is fairly obvious that the library is the key to teaching problem solving as well as investigative skills,[1] and
that if students are to use the library properly, the tools
they need such as the use of the card catalog, reference
books, encyclopedias, and so forth can only be taught when
the student feels a definite need for them.[2]

By intensive use of the library, students develop an
early interest in all phases of science, and it possibly might
be the springboard for future science vocations and avoca-
tions for some students.

The authors experimented with a program of concentrated library work to help develop reading and reference
skills to a higher degree. It was rather difficult to start a

full-scale library program, but once we had the close co-operation of the science teacher, the English teacher, and the librarian, the program went along quite smoothly. This is what we did:

BOOK REPORTS

Method. During the course of the year, each student was required to read three science books from three different fields of science and areas of classification. For example, a student might choose one biography of a famous chemist, one study from the field of biology, and a science-fiction book.

To show the students the interrelationships between subjects, the books were also used to fulfill reading requirements in English. In this way, a science book could be studied from two points of view and be covered in more depth. Biographies took on more meaning when discussed from both a scientific and a literary viewpoint. Students also learned, when reading factual science books, to check copyright dates and the author's background before weighing the importance or meaning of the facts presented in the book. Even science fiction served its purpose. It often allowed the less science-prone student to enter the field slowly (biographies served the same purpose) and to develop his powers of critical thinking.

Results. After a year it was quite gratifying to note that, according to the librarian's records and observations made by the teachers involved, many students were reading science books voluntarily and with pleasure.

LIBRARY RESEARCH AND COMMITTEE WORK

Method: Committee Development and Topic Selection. This part of the program used those general science units that are most amenable to the descriptive case study and/or historical approach; namely, astronomy and meteorology. It was hoped that not only would the research skills already mentioned develop, but also that the students would be given practice in working with others, speaking before a peer group, and organizing a comprehensive report.

The students were divided into five groups, with four to six students in each group. Each group selected a chairman, and the five chairmen, working together and using the textbook as a guide, selected the report topics for their committees. Each of these large topics, such as the solar system, galaxies, storms, and so forth were then broken down into smaller subtopics by the committee members. Each student researched his subtopic, and then all the members of each committee worked together to write one report which was presented to the class.

Library Work. Three committees worked in the library at a time, while the other two committees remained in the classroom. This arrangement had a twofold purpose. First, it enabled the groups working in the library to have access to more books. All books were put on reserve, and none could be taken from the library until the committees were finished with them. It also gave the students more "breathing space" in the library. Second, it allowed the teacher to instruct a small group of only 12 to 15 students at one time in the classroom. It also allowed the class to accomplish more in the way of experiments than is normally possible.

Class Presentation. Before the reports were given orally, each committee met with the teacher and discussed the practical aspects of getting the ideas across to an audience. The students learned by experience how to use visual aids and experiments to clarify difficult concepts and how to speak at a rate that was slow enough for note taking.

As the class listened to each report, it rated the students on their presentation according to a previously set scale of values worked out in both English and science classes.

Exams were given twice during the course of each unit, and all questions were based on the students' reports. Special exams were also given on the material that was studied in the science classroom.[3]

Student Reaction to Library Work. At the end of the term, students were asked to write a 500-word essay stating which of the nine units studied they enjoyed the most. A tally was then kept of the number of students who chose each unit. The results were: Out of 59 students, 42 picked astronomy and weather as the topics that they had most enjoyed studying. Twenty-seven of these students then went on to state that it was because of the library work that they had found these units so interesting, while 15 other students gave no definite reason for picking these units. The remaining 17 students mentioned other units as the ones they had most enjoyed studying. No student expressed a dislike for the library-oriented units.

CONCLUSIONS

After talking with students and consulting both with the librarian and English teacher, we believe that this type of library work deserves a special place in the curriculum for honor-science classes. Its teaching values are numerous. First, the students familiarized themselves with the school library and learned how to use its facilities through actual practice. The librarian is certain that this was many times more effective than trying to learn about the library through lectures that are usually given in English classes. Second, the students learned how to use books, magazines, vertical file material, and encyclopedias as they were needed. Third, they learned how to deal with large topics in some depth. Fourth, they learned how to organize and present science material in an interesting and understandable manner. Finally, they learned how to work together. (Often a student who had finished early helped other students.) These were all-important learning experiences for the student, but the teacher also learned from this project. By working with a small number of students in the classroom for an extended period of two weeks, it was possible to learn many valuable facts about the personalities and abilities of individual students. These facts, which might not have become apparent as soon, if at all, in a normal classroom situation enabled the teacher to establish an excellent rapport with the students and to tailor the science course more effectively to their individual needs.

11. RE-SEARCHING IN THE LIBRARY

Albert Nissman

"Explore our State. Get to know its geography. Learn something about its historical importance. Make inquiries concerning local, state, and federal governments. Learn the big things, the concepts. Of course, you have to know facts before you can develop concepts. But let's not be bogged down by reams of little facts that can always be looked up in reference works." This was my introduction.

"How?" was the expressed and implied collective question of my class, a block (ninth-grade English and social studies) class of twenty-seven pupils on a junior-senior high reading level with an I.Q. range of 113–138.

"By doing re-search. These facts and data have been discovered, explored, and collected by many well-qualified people in the various social studies. These experts were on the prowl for preliminary and original sources of information. Now you are going to discover, explore, and collect these same facts and data again. In other words you will be doing re-search."

55

Questions came furiously, but I did not attempt to answer them at this precise moment. Nor did I think such a modus operandi to be feasible, necessary, or desirable.

In due course, during the process of instruction, I felt that the answers would unfold. Revelations would emerge. There was time, and time is an integral phase of instruction.

Rather, I chose to give the class a skeletal work sheet or guide upon which they were to build. The work sheet, shown on page 57, is not original. No doubt thousands of teachers have made similar sheets, and theirs too are no doubt the result of pedagogical plagiarism, whereby teachers adopt and adapt a multitude of instructional aids. They need not apologize for this. They need only acknowledge the original author, designer, or arranger, where possible. As I tried to point out to my pupils, ideas are universal; it is only the language in sentence and paragraph form in which the ideas are couched that is subject to copyright laws.

Each statement on the sheet was read, explained, and analyzed. Then the most important questions were asked: "What books do we use?" "Where do we get our information?" "Should we use encyclopedias?"

The class was then given a brief but general overview. They were told that all sources—reference books, popular magazines, newspapers, textbooks, almanacs, and so on—were to be used. Any printed material relevant to the subject was permissible. And to make certain that we were all talking and thinking about the same reading sources, I held up examples of each where possible.

The next logical step was to schedule our forthcoming block class in the school's central library. At this time, the librarian, Mrs. Phyllis Arnt, and I in a joint effort refreshed the students' memory of the card catalogue, the location of the books, and the Dewey decimal system. Then the librarian introduced them to an all-important tool—unknown to them until this point—The Readers' Guide to Periodical Literature, an invaluable aid which they later used intensively with much instructional gain.

WORK SHEET FOR LIBRARY RE-SEARCH*
This Is My State

1. I live in the state of . . . .
2. My state is bounded by the following other states:
. . . .
. . . ., and . . . .
3. My state has . . . . square miles.
4. About . . . . live in my state.
5. My state is noted for . . . ., ...,
. . . ., ..., and . . . .
6. It became part of the United States in . . . .
It was the . . . . state to join the union.
7. The state flower is the . . . .
8. The state bird is . . . .
9. My state's nickname is . . . .
10. The state motto is . . . .
11. The capital of my state is . . . .
12. The name of the governor is . . . .
13. The governor and other state officers are elected
every . . . . years.
14. My state has a legislature which meets every . . . . .
. . . . years.
15. The legislature is divided into . . . . parts,
called the . . . .
16. This legislature has . . . . members.
17. My state has two senators in the United States Senate.
Their names are . . . . and
. . . .
18. My state has . . . . representatives in the
United States House of Representatives. The name of
the congressman from my district is . . . .
. . . .
19. Draw pictures of two of the following: state seal, state
flag, state flower, state bird.
20. Draw a map of your state and show where your city or
town is located.

*Adapted from N.E.A. Journal, Jan. 1960, p. 31.

Once the youngsters understood that after completing the
work sheet, they were to build flowing, fluid paragraphs based
on facts and data, they became immersed in searching for
reading materials and re-searching for content within the
sources. They perused every nook and cranny of our library.
By this time the class was aware of the format of the final
project—a booklet replete with writing, pictures, and illustrations. Each booklet was to include a thesis cover, title, table
of contents, good paragraphing, sensible content and construction, maps, charts and a bibliography.

As they worked industriously on their projects in the ample time allotted them in the library, I asked them to think
about what they were learning. I asked them to list items
under two categories, "Library Skills Which I Have Learned"
and "Things Which I Have Learned about the Library." Below is a tabulation of each category. The items are para-
phrased in my own words. Every item was listed at least
once; some were noted as frequently as six times.

LIBRARY SKILLS WHICH I HAVE LEARNED

1. To use the Guide to Periodical Literature.
2. To hunt up magazines.
3. To use fugitive (vertical) files.
4. To use library materials properly.
5. To organize materials.
6. To use reference books.
7. To use different books.
8. To use the Dewey decimal system.
9. To look for certain books.
10. To use the card catalogue.
11. To use different parts of different books.
12. To ask the librarian the right questions.
13. To use the librarian's answer.
14. To use all types of reference materials, not only the
    encyclopedias.
15. To use the almanac, maps, and charts.

16. To get information faster and easier.
17. To note essential facts in outline form.
18. To put these facts into readable paragraphs.
19. To work quietly while concentrating.

THINGS WHICH I HAVE LEARNED
ABOUT THE LIBRARY

1. Proper use of the periodical room.
2. Proper conduct in the library.
3. Intelligent care of books.
4. Contents of the library.
5. Ways of cross references.
6. Divisions and purposes of the library.
7. Function of the vertical file.
8. How to find back issues of periodicals.
9. That many materials discuss similar subjects.
10. That some books cannot be charged out.
11. How to make the best use of time.
12. Proper use of the newspaper rack.
13. That work in the library can be enjoyable.

My conclusions about library work are favorable. I have no reservations about its efficacy provided the teacher considers the abilities and maturation of the youngsters in relationship to the availability of materials in the library. Once these considerations are made, I believe that it is possible to create and motivate a learning experience in research. It is desirable to make such an experience palatable as we provide youngsters with a fundamental functional tool —the intelligent use of the library. All this serves to enhance their re-search skills and broaden their fields of knowledge and understanding. And I further believe that the well-planned use of the school's central library by the teacher will negate the generally low status of the library. Perhaps, all will then recognize it as a vital adjunct to learning, rather than the decorative but dead appendage of the school.

12. "SLIDING" TOWARD PROGRESS

Bernice K. Donehue

The gift of a piece of browsing area furniture, presented to the library through the cooperation of the principal and the Parent Teacher Association at Lindblom High
School in Chicago, resulted in a successful teaching innovation! With the piece of furniture came a scheduled visit to
the library for the PTA, interested in learning how our high
school library served their sons and daughters. In an attempt to achieve a graphic and interesting demonstration
for them, the librarians originated, with the aid of student
photographers, an attractive set of color slides illustrating
all the activities of a busy school library day.

Through this PTA-library occasion came a continuing
realization of the possibilities for on-the-scene slides as
an effective method for teaching library skills. Enticed by
this concept the library advertised in the school bulletin for
student photographers, and then directed selected ones in
photographing all the steps and stages of school library en-
deavor. Now, after many semesters of trial and error fea-
turing both profit and loss, and more recently in response
to the impetus of an accelerated or "blocked" program introduced at Lindblom, the library has achieved complete
sets of kodachrome slides covering all phases of school library instruction and use.

This record on film includes all our service activities,
reference holdings, procedures and methods, catalog records,
shelf arrangement, and special features, with Lindblom students photographed in these many facets of our library scene.
Our reason for the experimentation with slides was based on
a conviction that no library teaching can supersede one that
demonstrates the actual locale of the learning activity. In

the new teaching task now set before us our experimental slides were to prove invaluable.

Repeated requests by teachers for inclusion of a unit on the research paper in our instruction series prompted our latest experiment. This concerns an English VI (last half Junior, 3rd year) blocked class for whom we prepared, for presentation in a three-lesson sequence, a set of slides, photographed from typed cards, explaining bibliographic method, note-taking, outlining, writing the paper, and the correct use of footnotes. This first-bud attempt we used with fair success but not with complete satisfaction so that, having noted the increased emphasis on the research paper in the new Teaching Guide for the Language Arts published by the Chicago Board of Education,[1] and also because we wanted to make our new series a reflection of student opinion, we undertook to expand our pioneer effort into the semblance of a finished product. This is the way in which we brought our hybrid into full and satisfactory bloom.

Arrangements were made through the chairman of the Gifted Student Program at Lindblom to select an English blocked class which had prepared a research paper based on the original set of slides. This class was invited to the library where it was explained to them that they had been selected to assist in enriching and enlivening the slides lecture used with them in their major paper project. Procedures were detailed, with student opinion and criticism invited; questions were encouraged to clarify purpose (one of them being, "Can we really say what we think?"); then, in a group-dynamics approach, student teams were set up under student leaders, and the separate teams "buzzed" for an allotted time as they recalled their experiences in writing a research paper and discussed ways they thought would improve the instruction pattern which had been followed.

Team members then listened as their leaders reported and, as each report was presented, the librarian commented, asked for elaborations, and attempted to clarify meanings. Printed here are verbatim reports as submitted by the students. In reading them, remember that they reflect an overview of both classroom instruction and library activity.

MAJOR PAPER PROJECTS

Student Team I
Outline unnecessary for major paper.
Teacher over emphasized bibliographical index.
Form was not emphasized on the slides.
Need better system for note cards.
Slides were not presented interestingly.
Printed examples to be given to students.
Did not show how to organize paper.
Poor references in school library.

Student Team II
More precise information on footnotes; typing form.
More on bibliography-form; typing.
How to get references.
Teachers should follow one way of writing the paper.
More detail on footnotes.
How to transfer the information from the book to the paper with respect to the punctuation.
Outline of the body of the paper.
The bibliography should be explained more thoroughly.

Student Team III
Elimination of unnecessary information from footnotes.
Example—year of publication, publishers, etc.
Footnotes should be more generalized.
Should be given more specific outline form.
How to take material from a book and put it into your own words.
Contents should be considered more than form. Information on topic is more important than form. After all, what is a term paper for, to learn how to get margins to the precise point or is it to develop one's knowledge on the subject.

"SLIDING TOWARD PROGRESS"

Student Team IV
    Explain how to use the Chicago Public Library (down-
town).
    Explain organization of notecards.
    State that one idea should be on one notecard.
    In bibliography it should state that primary source must
be written by the subject.
    Teachers and librarians should pool ideas and come up
with a combined explanation.
    A college form should be used as teacher lectured.
    Mention exact form of paper.
    Clearly explain footnotes and what is necessary in them.

As a next procedure the librarians studied the student
comments, shared them with the school principal, the gifted
student program chairman, and the chairman of the English
department. From this combined effort came a decision to
establish an inter-departmental pattern for the mechanics of
research paper form, a paramount concern of the student
teams.
    Using a student-assistant artist, our current student
photographer, and selected reference sources,[2] we then
devised a revision of the original instruction lesson based
on the suggestions of the students, and our personal estimate
of the original series. Major changes included re-arrange-
ment of the order of presentation of the slides; the addition
of black-and-white silhouette figures, student-sketched and
photographed, to introduce steps in the research paper process; "live" photographs showing the English blocked class
and their instructor performing the tasks suggested by the
slides, both in the library and in the classroom; plus deletion
of repetitive or extraneous slides and re-photographing of
some slides for corrections or revisions.
    The finished product replete with action photos, black-
and-white sketches, and kodachrome procedure slides,
proved to be a popular, functional, visual tool to use with
students, either "in toto" or sectionally. To demonstrate

this, and to highlight the role of the students in the combined project, we planned an exhibition of our wares, utilizing the following technique to prove our prowess.

With only slight briefing, since time pressures on the blocked classes are so great, the twenty-five students of the original English VI class (who had since become English VII) were brought to the library viewing room where they took seats as previously established teams of five, and were introduced to administrative guests present for the occasion. Our intent was to demonstrate that the blocked class had contributed toward its own educational progress and had concurrently added to the opportunities of other Lindblom students.

Twenty-five slides, selected secretly from the complete research paper set, were flashed on the screen and team members, called on indiscriminately but never more than once, were allotted a carefully timed one-minute interval to discuss: a) the subject matter of the slide; b) the significance of the slide in the set sequence; or c) offer some opinion concerning the research paper as understood by the student.

By calling "OPTION," team chairmen could have an additional thirty seconds to expand each team member's performance. Points were awarded by guests acting as judges, with scoring based on the following three items, plus extra tallies earned by chairmen through optional time.

Tally Point 1. Clarity
(Did the student understand information on the slide and its relation to the entire major paper process?)
Tally Point 2. Completeness
(Were all possible points of information covered?)
Tally Point 3. Originality
(Did the student offer any original opinion, comment, or criticism?)

At the conclusion of this rapidly-paced performance, ratings were tallied, and a candy bar (whose trade name signifies knowledge) put in its appearance in just the right quantity to serve as a prize to be shared by the winning team, and, through their courtesy, by all other team members and guests. The fact that we concluded the demonstration just at lunch was a point in our favor!

In summation we suggest that the interchangeability of all our slides to meet multiplicity of demand serves as one of the greatest assets of this technique. We have found them invaluable not only for instructional purposes, but also in the recognition of grade level abilities and needs, in the presentation of a lesson timed to the demands of the period bell, in the training of student assistants, in the publicity efforts of the library, in library club activities, in "sales" facets of our library effort, and in evidencing to teachers the possibilities of the library function within the school. Over the semesters since we began our experimentation the slides have more than justified the time and expenditure used to produce them.

Specifically, the greatest value of the major paper series rests in the reflection of student opinion in a teaching program of vital concern to them: the interdepartmental exchange is a constructive adjunct; and it may be hoped that the enjoyment of the librarians in planning and working out the project reflected a corresponding enjoyment on the part of the young people for whom it was intended.

13. A HIGH SCHOOL COURSE IN LIBRARY SKILLS

Helen Reed and Maryline Conrey

"I never knew there were so many reference books."
"My book is on the same subject as yours, but it doesn't say
the same thing!" "Wish I'd known about this book last year."
"Look at these fabulous pictures!" "I never knew you could
find things under so many headings." "I'll sure use this bibliography in another class."

These are the comments of students enrolled in the new
"split-week" course at Verdugo Hills High School in Library
Research Skills. Does your school have such a course?
Could one be organized?

A word as to the origin of the new course and a definition of "split-week" seem advisable. Last year, under the
dynamic leadership of our principal, Dr. Gjertrud Smith,
our school increased the number of electives available to
students without lengthening the school day, by setting up a
number of two and a half credit classes which meet on the
average of two and one-half times a week. Aware of the difficulty of getting adequate follow-up throughout the high
school years to our "Library Unit" in Sophomore English,
an English teacher volunteered to plan and teach a split-week
course in Library Research Skills. The librarian eagerly
agreed to work with her. A course of study was approved
for experimental use, and "LRS" was given for the first time
last spring.

The course was planned for eleventh and twelfth graders;
however, some tenth graders have been allowed to take it.
Last February's enrollees were for the most part under-
achievers whom counselors guided into the course in the
hope that it would encourage better study habits. This fall a
higher proportion of academic achievers enrolled, in most

66

cases because they had heard about the course and felt that it would help them.

"LRS" is an English elective and involves some writing and some incidental stimulation of wide reading. Emphasis, however, is upon reference books, and early in the course students are given a list of fifty such books with which they are to become familiar during the semester.

The first few meetings of the class, in the English classroom, are devoted to discussions of the purpose of the course, brief discussion of the history of libraries, a diagnostic test of library skills, and a listing by students of personal interests, hobbies, collections, activities, visits to places of interest, books in their homes, and books which they would buy if they had the money. On the basis of information thus acquired and of teacher-supplied lists of topics, terms, places, people, and movements about which teachers feel students should be informed, the English teacher plans reference lessons. Attractive pictures of people, places, and events are mounted on colored cardboard and displayed in the classroom to stir curiosity.

After the first week or two the class meets in the library. The first activity there centers on use of the card catalog. Then the students plunge into reference work.

The class hits almanacs first with a group of questions on timely topics, many of them suggested by students. Next the group turns to reference materials for geography, history, and literature, and here it is particularly easy to tie in the work with what is being done in other classes. The young people are challenged, furthermore, by the necessity for looking under related headings to find material—a skill stressed also in the catalog lessons.

Students are fascinated by the approach in this course to biographical books. Each member of the class draws from a selected group of pictures of famous persons, and each must find material about "his person." Later, in studying reference books for literature, each must locate information on the lives of one American and one English author.

67

We postpone all but the most elementary discussion of the Dewey Decimal System until the middle of the course. After handling many non-fiction books, students are asking questions about numbers. By this time, moreover, they have observed enough differences between books to be able to see that each number means something, and to understand common form divisions such as 08 and 09.

In the latter part of the term attention turns to college and career guidance materials and to reference books for science, music, and art. The course then concludes with the making of a bibliography on a subject of the student's choosing. We encourage making bibliographies which can be used in other classes.

Ideally, training in the use of library materials should be integrated into the work of all departments in a high school. If each high school had two or more librarians, if all teachers were library minded and well acquainted with resources, and if pressures to cover required textbook material—and classroom pressures in general—were less, there would probably be little need for a special course in library skills. But today such a course seems to meet real needs.

We should like to see more such courses offered, and in more schools.

14. ORIENTATION AND LIBRARY INSTRUCTION

Ralph W. McComb

To open the discussion, the chairman of the group posed
the question: Are orientation programs and instruction in
the use of the library necessary? The group agreed that both
are needed. Orientation was identified as being a limited
program of instruction. Instruction was interpreted to mean
the more comprehensive program offered either in a library
course or as part of other subject courses.

It was pointed out that even those students who have
some prior experience in library use benefit, on entering college, from an introduction to the more advanced materials.
In reply to a comment that students sometime react negatively to such an orientation program, it was agreed that such
negative attitudes should not lead to elimination of these essential programs. None of the librarians present indicated
the use of standard tests, either before or after an orientation program, to determine the effectiveness of such instruction; neither had there been any attempt to divide students into classes on the basis of previous experience in using libraries.

College librarians employ a variety of techniques for library orientation and instruction. The procedure usually includes lectures by library staff members, either in a concentrated period at the beginning of a term or spread out
over a longer period of time. Library tours are normally included in either type of instruction. Locally-devised exams
are sometimes used to test what the student has learned.
Since a student will visit the library only when he feels a
need for its services, the orientation or instruction program
is intended as additional motivation for the student.

There is a general need for library orientation for the faculty, because of the involvement of faculty in library instruction for the student. Encouraging use of the library as a laboratory and offering instruction through course assignments, as a continuing emphasis throughout the undergraduate's career, is the most effective type of library instruction.

This discussion group approved the statements on library orientation and instruction which appear in the Standards. However, it was also agreed that the junior college and four-year college statements should be identical.

15. THE LIBRARY: A WRITING LABORATORY

Robert L. Foose

Thousands of high school students each year produce examples of distinguished creative work, some of it published in one form or other. Of course, not every individual has the innate capacity to become a professional writer any more than every youngster has the ability to become an Olympic athlete. Nevertheless, all students can improve their writing by doing a lot more reading and by writing, writing, writing.

Busy as his life may be, when a typical teen-ager attempts to write, he quickly discovers how limited he is both in ideas and experiences.

He soon discovers also that he must learn to write for a specific purpose in school, college, or his later professional life. This involves a thoughtful and coherent assembling of facts, and the coupling of knowledge with experience. Once he has uncovered facts and organized his thinking, he

THE LIBRARY: A WRITING LABORATORY

must learn how to communicate his ideas in a written form which others will be able to understand.

Waiting to help the student, as he learns to write, is an exciting, fascinating place—the library. One of the teacher's important jobs is to introduce him to this veritable writing laboratory and, jointly with the librarian, to help him learn how to use the wealth that is contained in this storehouse of information.

What are some of the ways that the library can help develop the student's writing skills?

The library can provide ideas. There is no dearth of ideas when teachers bring their classes to the library. As students examine the magazines, displays, and book shelves, and as the librarian begins to reveal the secrets of the Reader's Guide, the card catalog, and the vertical files, ideas come in an avalanche. Now they must be sorted, examined, and selected. Now must begin the reading, which is the essential wellspring of most successful writing.

The library can stimulate critical and analytical writing. From the colleges comes the cry for students who have the ability to think and write critically.

There are devices to help students develop this skill. One senior high school English department requires a critical essay on a literary topic involving the evaluation of a number of books by a single author, the study of works from a particular literary period, or an analysis of some well-known writer's position and beliefs. It is a difficult assignment, posing a tremendous challenge to the student, the teacher, and the librarian, but it provides valuable preparation for college work.

In another project, students select historical novels and nonfiction historical texts covering the same periods from a list prepared by the librarian. After reading widely, they produce written evidence of the accuracy of the historical research done in the novels they read.

The library can provide the laboratory and the tools for research writing. Teachers agree that students need more

71

writing assignments which demand wide reading and digging
for materials. Research projects of this sort are bound in-
extricably to the resources of the library.

As a teacher, I have watched hundreds of youngsters
grow in their familiarity with the use of the library from the
time they start lifting paragraphs from an encyclopedia to
fulfill a written assignment to the time when they become
mature enough to amplify what they have read and present it
in their own words with plausible freshness. This is a transi-
tion, of course, which requires stimulating and skillful help
from teachers and librarians alike.

Both at junior and senior high school levels, the library
can be used to teach writing research. Teachers can take
their classes to the library for an enthusiastic soaking up
of ideas. Librarian and teacher can help them select interesting subjects and then discuss how to limit those subjects
to workable dimensions. Return visits to the library will
provide the opportunity to develop working bibliographies.

After the preparation of outlines, there should be more
visits for reading and note-taking. The technique of taking
notes on cards, with the student's own ideas and brief quotations rather than full paragraphs from the reference book,
must be stressed.

In teaching teen-agers to write, the librarian and teacher make a wonderfully effective team. Few experiences can
be as rewarding as to watch a student grow increasingly familiar with the library until he has developed a confidence
which enables him to say, "Here is gathered together the
wisdom of the ages, which I can use and enjoy."

PART II: TRAINING LIBRARY USERS

16. TRAINING THE LIBRARY USER

B. Agard Evans

INTRODUCTION

'Water, water everywhere
Nor any drop to drink'

This paradoxical, painful and, to many, fatal situation
would not have arisen had the Ancient Mariner and his companions been instructed in the art of making a small distilla-
tion plant or had they had the chemicals for rendering sea-
water potable. The great majority of users are in a similar
position in a library.

So much has been written and so much has been said on
the subject that the Conference may wonder why this hardy
perennial is allowed to come before Aslib once again.

A few will recall the Resolution carried by the Aslib
Conference in 1930, under the Chairmanship of Professor
R. S. Hutton, following a fine paper by Mr. G. F. O'Riordan,
Principal of Battersea Polytechnic, and a discussion led by
Mr. B. M. Headicar:

"This conference, recognizing the vital need for training students in the efficient use of libraries, urges university
and other education authorities to consider the organization
of systematic instruction in this subject in all faculties."[1]

That ought to have done it, but alas and alack! twelve
years later Professor Hutton was impelled to present a paper: "Instruction in library use: a needed addition to the
university curriculum" to the Aslib Conference of 1942.[2]

Six years later the famous Royal Society Scientific Information Conference in plenary session passed Recommendation 11.2: "As part of their education scientists should
be instructed in the use of libraries and information services."[3]

75

In 1949, a working party of the Library Association appointed to consider the recommendation of the Royal Society Conference, reported:
"It is indisputable that instruction in the use of libraries and information services and in bibliography must form an essential part in the education of scientists and it is held that such instruction is no less important than laboratory work."[4]
These remind us that the need for training is recognized as extremely important; and also that precious little is being done about it. In presenting this subject for discussion, I hope to convince the Conference that the need has been amply established, and further, that the things on which instruction is to be given, are also generally accepted. We do not want to recapitulate endlessly matters and views which are not in dispute. Let the discussion concentrate on the practical measures necessary to obtain general recognition of the need beyond the narrow ranks of librarians; to enlist the interest of librarians and others in a relentless campaign of education; and on what weapons should be put into their hands to ensure final victory over the needless ignorance that hampers the work of scientists and renders so much of our own best work abortive.

WHY IS TRAINING NECESSARY?

I have spoken to a number of reasonably well-educated people about their experience at the university and outside in the use of libraries. Most of them reacted that training was not necessary. One used a library: if one had a question, it was a matter simply of referring to the subject catalogue, going through the various books or periodicals most likely to give the answer and eventually discovering it. In time one gets to know the probable source for one's own problems. If something comes along rather outside the normal run, the library assistants are usually helpful and knowledgeable.
I suggest that this is an average attitude and the first task we face in educating library users is to expose the fal-

lacies and dangers of such an attitude. We must convince
them of the need for a wholly different approach. We must
shatter their faith that any library has the world of knowledge so harnessed that one can turn a knob and listen to the
broadcast. We must make it clear that where previously
the library tools, in so far as they existed, consisted of
chisels, nowadays they have the complexity of capstan
lathes, for full and proper use of which instruction is necessary.

I think probably the root of the trouble is failure to
grasp the vastness of the literature. Figures can be quoted
such as 1,800,000 articles of scientific interest per annum
(Unesco figure) and it may be explained that this is 900 articles per hour of working time, but they fail to register.
The reader has touching faith that the twenty or thirty important ones (to him) per month will somehow appear on the
library shelves or in the library catalogue. His mind re-
coils from the reality of the length and breadth and depth of
the spate; just as a child cannot grasp the immensity of the
ocean. Prof. Hutton[2] lists twelve good reasons why instruction in library use is needed. I will not recapitulate them
here, but to me the most cogent are: that university years
are but the preface to the life of learning and the key to further learning lies in libraries; that the complete survey of
past work is essential to the planning of future research or
the establishment of a process; that throughout one's work,
whether as research worker, administrator, student or in
the common day-to-day run of things, information is needed
and however much one may depend on hearsay, consultation
and casual inquiry, there is no more solid and satisfactory
basis for authoritative information than to have it in black
and white, authenticated and confirmed; and finally, the correct citation of references is as necessary to a writer as the
use of clear expression, if he is to convey to his readers the
message he is striving to impart.

In conclusion of this section let me quote from contemporaries:

Dr. Urquhart[5] in 1948: "The majority of scientists and technicians are unaware of their ignorance."

Prof. Hutton in 1942: "The average student and even the majority of teachers are woefully ignorant of the existence and potential service of any wide collection of reference books."

Mr. J. P. Lamb[6] in 1949: "The business community probably provides the worst examples of the disturbing ignorance one finds on all sides about the value of books as records of facts."

Mr. B. M. Headicar in 1930: "These are only some of the things, which, once understood, will save years of his life. It is my argument that instruction on these lines is a necessity for every student, that the librarian is the only person who can give this instruction accurately and thoroughly."

WHAT TRAINING IS NECESSARY?

It is non-controversial that the training should be in successive stages like the teaching of any other subject. Apart from the expanding receptiveness of the student, one must allow for interest. The interest will be more acute when the need for the training is apparent and the opportunity to put it into practice immediately. There should, I suggest, be five stages:

I. Primary School, an introduction to a world of books far in excess of the school text-books; the layout of a public library; and the use of general reference books and alphabetic indexes.

II. High School, an introduction to classified arrangement, subject catalogues, the tracing of references, the existence of pamphlet and periodical material. The proper treatment of books and library discipline generally.

III. Undergraduate (general), introduction to the university library, its resources and tools; bibliography

      generally; the structure and origins of modern litera-
ture.

IV. Undergraduate (subject), introduction to the reference
tools of the subject, the range of periodicals, the
principal contributory sources of new information;
the common information centres, local and national.

V. Post-graduate, a closer review of information centres and clue to their resources; a review of the
literature of the subject, including specialist sources.
Here particular reference should be made to D.S.I.R.
and the Research Associations; Institutions; the national libraries; Aslib; and the whole machinery for
cooperation nationally and internationally.

I have only sketched in the curriculum lightly, but there are
several sources where the matter is expanded in practical detail. The general object should be to widen the horizon in successive stages and to provide the student with maps. It is not
enough to dilate ecstatically on the wealth of knowledge contained in libraries nor the talk of golden keys, though these
may be great truths; but rather let the student know that these
are tools for his use, let him familiarize himself with them
and experience for himself the skill in using them and the
power resulting from knowledge so acquired.

    At all stages it is important that lectures and instruction
should be accompanied by practical application—test problems and the like. It has been suggested that the Science graduate should know something of the structure of scientific literature in the same way as he is expected to know something
about French and German. Dr. Parke has recommended that
final year students should be given a library problem to solve.
It is only by adopting some such method that the true value of
libraries can be brought home to scientific workers at an age
when it will be of the greatest use to them.

WHAT IS BEING DONE?

    For stages I and II, i.e. general introduction at school
level, it is possible that more is going on than has been

recorded or than I have traced in a cursory glance at the position. The lines on which instruction may profitably be given is shown in the books Find it yourself[7] and The back of books[8] and the very practical work of J. P. Lamb[6] in Sheffield. This stage is pre-eminently one for the co-operation of teachers with public librarians, except in the case of schools fortunate enough to possess a living library.

At University level various attempts have been made by librarians well aware of the problem. But no great progress can be expected until the teaching staff are really fully aware of the damage they are inflicting by neglect of this vital part of students' education. As things are at present, professors will not give the necessary lead by insisting upon library instruction as an essential; in fact, many claim that the students' programme is over-full to be burdened further with minor matters that a student should normally pick up for himself!

We cannot blame the student for not realizing its significance. It forms no part of the syllabus; he can pass his examinations comfortably on the set books and the reading lists casually thrown out by lecturers. Unless he is told about it by his advisers; unless the facilities are there and brought clearly to his notice; unless the times and occasion are provided for it; it calls for unusual perspicuity on the part of the student to acquire the instruction.

On their part, the librarians, already understaffed and preoccupied, become discouraged at arranging lectures and instruction, only to be faced with a handful in the audience, made up largely of lonely overseas students with unwanted time on their hands.

Mr. Woledge disclosed to me a system of blackmail which he employed at Belfast. Access to the stacks was only accorded to students who had attended his lectures on the library.

I am only aware of one place where instruction is on a systematic basis, namely London School of Hygiene and Tropical Medicine.[9, 10] The instruction takes the form of three lectures given early in the first term combined with practical exercises. Mr. C. C. Barnard has kindly given me supplementary notes on the talks, but space unfortunately does not permit of their reproduction here. A significant point is that "the lectures are included in the programmes of each of the three classes distributed to students so that they attend as a matter of course, and their attendances are recorded in the same way as for any other lectures." Apart from the instruction the course leads students frequently to consult the librarian at subsequent stages of their studies.

More is being done in the U.S.A., especially where a flourishing library school is part of the university. The successful completion of the course of instruction carries with it credit marks which contribute to the final assessment of a student's education. Conditions in the States, however, are very different from our own and it is important for us to consider how our proposals are to fit into the educational system in this country.

For post-graduate working, many libraries attached to research institutions, government or business organizations, arrange either for lectures to new entrants or for informal discussion with the librarian on the occasion of showing them the library. For the most part, I think that such an introduction is wholly inadequate and fails of its purpose in the majority of cases. There may, however, be frequent opportunities of meeting later; and in the course of assistance in the search for information, the librarian and his staff do gradually educate the user. This is not invariably so, as many of the laboratory staff are content to turn the knob and accept the information dug out for them by the library, without assisting in the search or showing any curiosity as to how the result was achieved.

Many librarians have produced "Notes for new readers" or "Guide to the use of the——library." In general, they are poor little things, uninspired and uninspiring. Perhaps naturally, they do not attempt to instruct their readers in the bibliography of their subject. Nevertheless, when staff are first introduced, it is an occasion on which such instruction might well come in most aptly and opportunely.

Two books which deal systematically with bibliographic instruction are: Crane and Patterson[11] The literature of chemistry, and Soule[12] Library guide for the chemist. Both deal with chemistry, either because chemistry is a nice, tidy subject for such treatment or because chemists are more literature-conscious than other scientists. Probably a bit of both. Both books are very good and may well serve to indicate the ground to be covered and the mode of presentation. It is, however, a matter for consideration whether something a good deal shorter would win readier acceptance by the average library user.

WHAT CAN WE DO ABOUT IT?

Individually and collectively we must make propaganda. We must arouse the conscience of the world of learning to the good food mouldering in the larder, while the world subsists on meagre rations. This should be done for every subject, by series of articles in the specialist periodicals and by lectures to the Institutions, both centrally and in the branches. University librarians should see that suitable articles appear from time to time in students' magazines.

Corporately, Aslib should seek, in concert with the Library Association, Royal Society and others, to make strong representation for a place to be found in students' time-tables for adequate instruction in the use of libraries, both for its importance in education and not least, in the national economy. The training in schools is a matter for the Library Association to foster in co-operation with local education authorities. For the universities, a joint statement might well reinforce the approach by the Royal Society and be issued directly to the Vice-Chancellors or go forward as a recommendation sponsored by the Ministry of Education, University Grants Committee or other appropriate body, such as the Nicholson Committee.

Individual specialist librarians may feel in need of guidance on how to educate their own readers. Aslib Education Committee might compile notes and suggestions on the subjects to be covered and the method of presentation in the form either of lectures or as a guide to the use of the services of the individual libraries.

Let us be clear in our own minds that what is proposed is a campaign against an ignorance; an ignorance that is depriving men of the full enjoyment of life; an ignorance reflected in inefficiency, low productivity and a lowered competitive power.

I realize that the burden of this further education will fall largely on the laden shoulders of the librarian; nevertheless, it is a challenge which we dare not refuse. We should fail of our purpose, if we give our lives to the improvement of bibliographic tools and information services and then allow the benefits to be thrown away by ignorance of the way to use them.

17. WHO SHOULD USE THE SCHOOL LIBRARY—HOW

Robert U. Jameson

Who should use the School Library? The simple and very unoriginal answer to this query is everybody who has any contact with the school: students, faculty, and "patrons" —that is, parents, alumni, and even possibly members of the board of directors.

In any case, what is far more important for the school and particularly for the school librarian, is the question of how the library is to be used. There is nothing very original in what I shall have to say. But I believe very deeply that in an age in which the competition of the television set and the radio and "Hi-Fi" are so stiff, something positive has to be done to insure our young people against the evil of nonreading. Libraries today need promotion. My point is that promotion starts early, continues strongly, and extends itself to a number of improbable people.

How shall people use the school library? First, the students in the school. Boys and girls should start investigating the library before they can read. Teacher must take them to the library and show them books. Who knows what a book is, after all, until he has seen one? At this stage the library is a game—fun. I hope it stays that way for years. Here the most important person in the world is the teacher, and the teacher of the pre-reader has an enormous chore: she must see to it that the library is not an ogre and that the book is not a demon. As children begin to learn to read, the teacher stays important: books must keep their enchantment for the children. You will note that I put the emphasis on the teacher. The teacher knows the children better than the librarian can hope to know them; and thus the teacher must be the instigator of most of the schemes to interest the kids in the books. I need not say also that the librarian's originality in suggesting methods and materials for the teacher will pay dividends. Neither can work without the other.

Beginning with the fourth grade, at the latest, children should begin to learn what is loosely called "library procedure." They should at least be taught something about the arrangement of books on the shelf—to the point, perhaps, when they will understand that it is a fate worse than death to put a novel back "where it belongs on the shelf"—in class 520 or 913. Someone, obviously either the teacher or the librarian, or, better still, both, must point out the facts of library life to these young people. They should know, before they get through the sixth grade, where things are, what the card catalog means, and what browsing means. The last is probably the most important of all. If this is to happen, the teacher must also know all three of these essentials. Do

teachers know these things? More important, do they understand the importance of passing on an enthusiasm for these
things to their charges? The librarian cannot do it alone.

Before children reach the seventh grade they should
know certain other specific things about the library, of which
I should like to mention just three. First, every child entering junior high school should know at least the rudiments of
the use of the dictionary—what a dictionary has in it and how
to find what a dictionary has in it. Secondly, every child entering junior high school should know something about what
can be found in the junior encyclopedias and how they may
be used. And thirdly, every child entering junior high school
should have been taught something about the responsibility
which borrowers of books must assume. Certainly it is not
too radical to suggest that boys and girls must realize at a
rather early age that leaving books on radiators or under
wet bushes, or returning books two months late, whether
they pay fines or not, are anti-social acts.

MORE ADVANCED

In junior high school and high school the use of the library obviously becomes a more complex thing. Boys and girls
have to make "reports" or, later, write research papers or
topics or theses—all based on the materials in the library.
The student must now become aware of more complicated,
or at least more varied materials. He must learn about the
vertical file, the specialized reference books, the periodical
indexes—and how to use them. Again, I make this plea: no
classroom teacher should require any student to carry on
any library project which he (the teacher) could not do. This
requirement indicates that the teacher must know the library
better than his students know it.

At this point, having mentioned the library as an area
for elementary research, I should like to make one very
strong statement about the use of the library in the preparation of "reports" and other such derivative things. It is very
easy for a student to fall innocently into the habit of plagiarism

85

unless we teachers block the habit by showing students how
to use reference material in the right way. I myself have
been increasingly concerned by the amount of unacknowl-
edged copying which I have had to contend with in the last
few years. I am certain that this laziness—to give it a gen-
tle name—is the result of bad teaching rather than of an increase in moral turpitude among our young. I think teachers have been careless.

High school students should, I believe, be shown the
fact that their school library is only one library: that other
libraries, close at hand or far away, may offer them facilities which they may use. In the first place, no high school
graduate should think that all libraries are cataloged alike.
They should know about the Library of Congress system,
whether they see it or not. They should also know that public libraries and local college libraries are usually very cooperative when a young person finds that his school library
does not have more than two pages on the mating habits of
the polyp or the properties of lithium. They should be encouraged also to learn the use of some advanced reference
tools usually found only in larger libraries. After all, there
is no particular reason why the young people who go to college should all be stunned by the college library.

Two other things remain to be said about the students'
use of the library. The first has to do with the library itself.
Any school library worth talking about must have its book
collection geared for real use by the students in the school.
How many libraries have enough books on the hobbies and
the vocations? How many have enough maps and pictures
and other visual material? No librarian or teacher alone
can repair a defunct collection. If the library is not interesting in itself, students will be the first to learn the fact, and
the first to stay away. Since the library in any school is by
far the most important place in the school, it needs attention
by all. And the second, perhaps minor matter is this: the
library is the one place in the school where manners can be
taught most effectively. The word quiet means QUIET, for
example.

Now what about the faculty? I am a teacher and an ex-librarian, and I am somewhat cynical about this part of the subject, from past experience. But I know that what I say has at least some importance.

TEACHERS TOO

In the first place, all teachers must know what is in the library. Particularly, all teachers must know what the library has of interest to their own departments. Every librarian will testify to the number of urgent requests for books which are already nicely on the shelves, but which teachers have not noticed. Perhaps the teacher's first job at the start of every school year is to look over the library thoroughly.

In the second place, all teachers must know what is in the books which they recommend to their students. I shall leave this point without enlarging on it, lest I embarrass some of my friends.

In the third place, teachers must know the library well enough to be able to assist the librarian in that rather esoteric process known as "weeding." This is most important, of course, in the fields of science and the social studies, in which books go out of date very rapidly. But it is also important in a field like English, in which books for background reading may not go out of date but may certainly become dog-eared enough to attract no readers. In this connection, teachers should be happy to serve on library committees of the faculty to assist the librarian in ordering books, in balancing the collection so as to slight no single field, in developing student assistance programs, in suggesting adequate budgets, in fighting off too-eager book salesmen, and in doing all the other important things which no librarian can handle alone. If my experience indicates anything, it indicates that librarians like to run their libraries, but that they like things better if they feel that they have faculty support all along the line.

87

If the school library is in any way complete, teachers may even use it for their own research—at least as a starting point—and for their own recreational reading. It is very curious that so many teachers who like to read, say, fiction or biography hesitate to draw such books from their own school libraries and instead use public libraries or lending libraries at corner bookstores. (This applies, of course, only to those teachers who read books.) It seems obvious that students who see teachers using the library may get the idea that the library is a thing to use.

The third group of potential library users is what can be loosely called "the school family"—parents, patrons, alumni, members of school boards, trustees. In many places, particularly small towns in which there is a good school, the school library may be either the only respectable library within miles or a far better library than the tax-unsupported public library near by. Therefore the community should be urged to use the school library for leisure reading and for reference. The library used in this way is a first-rate public relations agent for the school.

Here the already overcrowded librarian has a fertile field in which to sow good will. I believe that the librarian should circularize the community about the library, either in the local papers or in a library newsletter which would be sent to the patrons of the school. Parents who actually use the school library will certainly have a much better appreciation of the school than they will develop from merely receiving their children's grades and hearing the scores of the latest basketball games. In this area the independent school has the best chance for promotion. From the point of view of the librarian, at least, it is too bad that so many public school libraries are limited in their scope by the tie-in with the local public libraries. Even so, school libraries usually need mouthpieces. Most of them are better than they realize.

At Haverford College some years ago there was formed an organization called the Library Associates. This group of people, many of whom have no connection with the college other than that they live in the neighborhood, pay dues, raise money for books, hold meetings at which distinguished writers address them, and otherwise contribute a great deal, both in funds and in morale, to the library. It seems to me that such an association is a distinct possibility for schools as well as for colleges, and could help the librarian in many ways. In the first place, members of the group would know the needs of the library and would know what is wrong (and might even be able to explain what is wrong) with the alumnus who, in clearing out his attic, decides to present his alma mater with a mint set of The Historians' History of the World or the complete works of Bulwer-Lytton, in half-calf. Library Associates would realize that what a good library needs is a balanced collection in all fields, the right new books, the right audio-visual materials, the right paraphernalia of modern education—not the white elephants out of our forbears' strong rooms. And Library Associates can be a very powerful public relations organ for the school. I think that school librarians, particularly in the independent schools, might do well to consider the founding of such groups.

One last thing has to be said. Whatever is done with a library—whoever uses it, however it is used—the person at the center of the whole process is the librarian. If what I have said here seems to indicate that the librarian has an enormous job, then I have not made a mistake. In many ways the librarian is the most important teacher in any school. Note that I said teacher: the modern school librarian must be a teacher and not just a cataloger of books, pamphlets, and periodicals. The modern librarian must be a teacher, a salesman of the riches of the world's culture, a coordinator of all the work of the school, even, perhaps, a writer or an ad-writer to tell people what the library offers. The librarian in a school, or at least the librarian in a good school library, is a very busy person, and she is, I fancy, happiest when she is busiest. What mainly concerns

me is that other teachers—nay, all teachers—in every
school realize as deeply as the librarian the treasure which
the school library is.

18. WE LEARN ABOUT THE LIBRARY

Leah M. Serck

A library unit for kindergartners? But they can't read!"
These were my sentiments when "The Library" was suggested as a social studies unit possibility. I knew that the
children began their formal reading in the first grade, and
that they started having weekly library periods at that time.
I also knew, however, that the teacher had been reading library books to the children throughout the year, and that the
children already knew and loved many stories. Perhaps it
would be a good idea to acquaint them with the source of
these books, and to give them a little background for using
the library.

Thus, our kindergarten library unit was born. At first
it seemed as though it would be impossible to provide material which would keep a class of small folks interested for
fifteen or twenty minutes each day for two weeks, but as the
unit began to take shape we were amazed at the number of
things which could be taught and understood about the library
on the kindergarten level. Following are day-by-day plans.

GENERAL OBJECTIVES

1. Recognizing the librarian as one of the people who
   help us
2. Acquiring some knowledge of the kinds of books and
   magazines that our library has for little folks

3. Learning proper care of books
4. Learning where to find our books and how to check them out
5. Acquiring some knowledge of library etiquette

DAY-BY-DAY PLANS

Lesson 1: Introducing the Unit
   Specific objectives:
      Review of people who help us
      Introduction of the word librarian and the idea of this
         person as a helper
   Materials:
      Pocket chart and pictures that remind us of community
         helpers (e.g., a saw for the carpenter, a firetruck
         for the fireman)
      Picture of a librarian helping a little girl
   Method:
      Question and answer; discussion
Lesson 2:
   Specific objectives:
      Review function of the librarian
      Acquaint children with various books available to them
      Acquaint children with children's magazines
   Materials:
      Picture of librarian
      Library books for illustrating the variety in subjects,
         kind of matter in book (many words; few words and
         many pictures, coloring of pictures, size of book)
      Copies of several children's magazines: Highlights,
         Wee Wisdom, Jack and Jill, Playmate
   Method:
      Modified lecture, concluding with the reading of a hu-
        morous poem from one of the little magazines
Lesson 3:
   Specific objectives:
      To make children conscious of their reasons for pre-
        ferring a well-kept book to an old, battered one

To point out some of the ways in which books are
abused—dirty hands, large bookmarks, tearing of
pages, breaking of backs, writing in books

Materials:

A nice book

Several abused books

Chalkboard

Construction paper and crayons

Method:

Storytelling. Teacher has made up a story of "The
Happy Books and the Unhappy Books," in which the
books tell their reasons for being happy or unhappy.

Activity:

Making happy and unhappy faces on sheets of construction paper which represent book covers; folding
strips to be stapled on for arms and legs

Lesson 4:

Specific objectives:

To reinforce knowledge gained by children the previous
day regarding the care of books

Materials:

Some new books

Some old, battered books

Book faces made the previous day

Method:

Dramatization. Children work as partners. One child
carries a real book, while his partner carries a
face which shows whether that book is happy or sad
and tells why the book feels as it does.

Lesson 5:

Specific objectives:

To acquaint children with the process of checking books
out of the library

Materials:

A library book and a privately-owned book

Library book card, card pocket and date due slip

Library card box from school library desk

Rubber stamp and ink pad

WE LEARN ABOUT THE LIBRARY

Method:

Demonstration. Show children how library book is different from their own books (card pocket), and then illustrate the checking-out process, acting it out with a pupil.

Lesson 6:

Specific objectives:

Review process of checking books out of library

Materials:

A library book with card in its pocket

Dittoed copies of book card, card pocket, date due slip

Method:

Discussion

Activity:

Pupils cut out the dittoed card pockets, book cards and date due slips and paste them in fronts of bird booklets made in science class.

Lesson 7:

Specific objectives:

To help children learn library etiquette

Points stressed:

Being quiet in the library, and reasons for it

Waiting patiently for book which another child is using, or sharing it with him

Waiting our turn if the librarian is busy

Method:

Discussion and dramatization of proper behavior

Lesson 8:

Specific objectives:

To let children actually see our school library

To give children a chance to use their library etiquette

To display our happy and our unhappy books on library bulletin board

Things to be noticed:

Location of books and magazines for little folks

Wall picture of little boy reading

Tables and chairs—their purpose

Librarian's desk

Card box on desk

Bulletin and chalkboards

93

Method:
>Field trip; experience. After noticing the various things in the library, children sit in a semicircle before the bulletin board and decide, with teacher guidance, how they wish to arrange their books for a display.

Lesson 9:

Specific objectives:
>To have children see a larger library
>To allow children to see a librarian at work
>To re-emphasize library etiquette

Method:
>Field trip to the public library. Librarian will tell children about library hours and will tell them about the library story hour (if it has one).

Lesson 10: Culminating activity

Specific objectives:
>To provide opportunity for children to practice some of the things they have been learning

Materials:
>Books they had made, with cards and pockets in them
>Old date stamp and ink pad from library
>Box for cards on librarian's table
>Table and chairs

Method:
>Dramatization. Teacher becomes librarian, and children check out the books they had made.

19. EFFECTIVE LIBRARY INSTRUCTION IN THE
CREATIVE ELEMENTARY SCHOOL LIBRARY

Beatrice Herrmann and Ann Shaffner

Teaching young children the use of library tools is rewarding for both the pupil and the librarian. To see the
smile of satisfaction on the face of a youngster when he
first learns why those mysterious white letters appear on
the spines of books is an experience that librarians can
treasure.

One of the functions of the elementary school librarian
is to lay the groundwork for lifelong use of the library.
This calls for a well planned program suited not only to the
age levels but also to the interest levels of the groups to be
taught, developed smoothly in scope and sequence. The attitude of the librarian must be one of enthusiastic interest,
because this attitude rubs off. If the approach and the technique are effective, the expense of a little time and effort
will open a whole world of knowledge to the children.

Kindergartners become acquainted with the library as
soon as they enter school and should think of it as a friendly,
enjoyable place, looking forward happily to their visits and
the opportunity to choose their own books. For the most
part they do very well in selecting ones they can read and
enjoy, but the librarian and teacher should always be on hand
too, to help, advise, and encourage them.

Boys and girls in the lower grades must learn library
manners. One technique is to use "library angel" posters,
an idea which appeals especially to the kindergarten age
group. These posters involve no more than a simple line
drawing and a caption (like those by Yvonne Leonard which
formerly appeared in the Wilson Library Bulletin). Typical
captions include: "a library angel has clean hands," "a library

95

angel keeps the table neat," "a library angel turns pages
carefully," "a library angel handles books with care," etc.
Other rules for a library angel might be: he does not crowd
anyone at the shelves; takes the books from the shelves
carefully; replaces them in such a way that the titles can be
read; listens to stories without wriggling and talking; lifts
his chair out from the table without pulling it along the floor;
turns the pages of a book by holding them at the upper right-
hand corner; and returns books on time so that others may
have a chance to read them. In stormy weather he brings
them to and fro in plastic bags, and at home he keeps them
out of reach of baby brother and the family puppy.

This training in library manners continues in the first
and second grades. By then, children are becoming better
acquainted with the book collection; they are giving simple
book reports in their classroom, illustrating stories, and
recommending books to their classmates. First and second
graders discover that the books are put in alphabetical order
on the shelf. They enjoy and learn by just walking from
shelf to shelf, counting and saying the numbers and letters.
They like to know that the numbered books are about "true
things," and the lettered ones are "stories." This is a time
of inquiry. There is a "what is this?" or "why?" for everything, and the questions should be answered. A simple game
of "Can you find . . ." is helpful. The librarian can name a
specific letter or number, then ask one student to find it
while the rest of the class roots for him. With this simple
instruction, future frequent and effective use of the library
may be assured. The unknown is often frightening but can
be made familiar and attractive by simple instruction.

In the third grade, informal instruction can be begun
about the card catalog and the arrangement of books on the
shelves. When a new book arrives, let the class discuss the
ways it can be found in the library, and be sure to capitalize
on timely interest. A snake, a visit to the zoo, a trip, a
classroom unit on Indians, a desire for "another book like
this one"—anything can spark this interest. The call number

and the top line of the catalog card are all the information these youngsters need to be concerned with. Likewise they are interested only in the fact that all books are arranged on the shelves according to what's inside them. This they will grasp, without ever hearing such words as "classification" or "Dewey."

In the fourth, fifth, and sixth grades, the boys and girls learn some of the specifics about the classification system and the card catalog. Memorization of the Dewey numbers may set up a dislike for the library, so the information should be presented to them through visual aids and bulletin boards. Giant catalog cards (purchased or hand-made of white tagboard) are effective in showing the difference between author, title, and subject cards. The children will also learn through their desire to find information, and through practical use of the card catalog. Actual comparison of book card, the catalog card, and the spine of the book will show them the value of the call number and how to use it. Catalog drawers can be put out on the tables, with teams of students locating specific entries. Book jackets of non-fiction books, arranged on a piece of construction paper with the appropriate Dewey numbers printed beside them, make effective displays.

It is in these grades that children are introduced to reference books; their differences, similarities, and use. This instruction should also be informal, the basic purpose being to teach that information can be found in more than one place. Simple alphabetizing games are valuable at this time.

The librarian who keeps herself aware of current happenings, special days and special weeks, through books, newspapers, magazines, radio, television and films will never lack ideas to use in teaching the use of materials in the library. A space flight, a circus in town, a symphony concert, a ballet, a baseball game, a children's play, a television program, a movie—even the local weather can set the background for an introduction to materials in these areas and how to find them. A television show, "Chico the Coyote," created demand in one library for animal and coyote stories, and provided an opportunity to show the children how to locate relevant fiction and non-fiction material.

A current events bulletin board will stimulate children to use the card catalog in locating items of timely interest. A short play or a puppet show is a good means of teaching library skills. When old favorites such as Winnie the Pooh, Pinocchio, Dr. Dolittle, or Mary Poppins are introduced, props can be used; a stuffed toy, puppet, or cardboard figure adds interest.

Use poetry often and share with the pupils the delight of hearing and saying poems. Keep a file of favorite poems about the seasons, the holidays, animals, nature, and birthdays, and keep adding to it. Encourage the boys and girls to recite their favorites, and even to write some of their own. Introduce them to the poetry anthologies in the library and point out to them the qualities of a good poetry book. A librarian who has first-hand information about the people and customs of other countries has much to offer, and mementos collected on travels anywhere can be used to stimulate interest. Examples are picture post cards, travel posters, sea shells, costumed dolls, figurines of book characters, etc.

When a pupil finishes elementary school he should have acquired certain library skills. He should know how to use the card catalog, encyclopedias, dictionaries, and Readers' Guide; what kinds of materials are available in a library and how to use them; the routines for borrowing and returning books. He should have developed discriminating and intelligent taste in the selection of reading materials; be familiar with the works of the best authors and illustrators of children's books; know the library resources in the community through visits his class has made to the public library.

Much repetition is necessary. The librarian's skill as an instructor can only be acquired gradually over a long period of time. She must be constantly alert to opportunities for informal guidance in the use of the library, and must work harmoniously with the classroom teacher. It is

EFFECTIVE LIBRARY INSTRUCTION

the teacher's responsibility to encourage her class in the
use of the library, to help them use the card catalog and
select books, and to encourage book talks or reports.
    These, then, are guidelines we use:
        —Be enthusiastic yourself
        —Plan a sequential program, but deviate from it when
         the need arises
        —Keep all library instruction informal
        —Be prepared to repeat instructions constantly
        —Latch on to any gadgets or props which will create
         or stimulate interest
        —Forget the usual library terminology and adapt it
         to the child's vocabulary
        —Let the main emphasis in the elementary school li-
         brary be on the enjoyment of books

20. LEARNING THE LIBRARY IN GRADES K–6

Leona B. Ayres

    At Jefferson Elementary School, where the library
serves seven hundred students, library instruction begins in
the kindergarten. Each of the four kindergarten classes
comes once a month, according to pre-arranged schedule.
The children listen to stories and then have an opportunity
to select books from the regular shelves and browse through
them. They sit at tables on which the librarian has placed
other books for them to enjoy. During these visits the children learn to appreciate illustrations, to derive pleasure
from looking at pictures, to handle books carefully, to turn
pages properly and to place books on a book cart so that other people can easily read the titles.

99

From the first grade on all classes in the school come to the library once a week for a regularly scheduled half-hour period in which they listen to stories, hear book talks, receive instruction in the use of the card catalog and different types of reference tools, browse, and check out books for recreational reading and classroom assignments. Thus, each week, some twenty classes throughout the school receive special training. Moreover, at any time during the day, even though classes are in session, a child may come to the library to do research, use reference books, check out books or return them.

In the first grade the child continues to gain knowledge of good literature and an appreciation of illustration, develops independence in the selection of books, learns to improve his library manners and practices proper care and handling of books. He also listens to stories, learns how to check out the book which he takes home, reads to his classmates when he has acquired a sufficient vocabulary and dramatizes some of his favorite stories.

Starting to expand

In the second grade the main objectives are to expand the practices of the previous year and, in addition, to promote individual reading choice. So that the child can satisfy his curiosity about nature, science and famous people or his love for fairy tales, Pinocchio, Dr. Dolittle and other favorites, he may each week take two books, one to read himself and one for his parents to share with him.

The aims in the third grade are to encourage wide reading on an easy level; to teach the difference between fiction and nonfiction; and how these classifications are arranged on the shelves; and, most difficult and important of all, to further encourage selection of materials which the child can read and comprehend himself.

Now he may take three books at a time and select them from any part of the library. Through book talks and individual assistance the librarian directs the child's reading.

100

She introduces the youngster to the fiction section by suggesting such authors as Miriam Mason, Ruth Gannett, Hugh Lofting, E. E. White, Frances Lattimore and Laura Ingalls Wilder.

By the time the child has reached fourth grade he is ready to concentrate on technical skills. He should become familiar with the parts of the book, know the meaning of the Dewey Decimal System; master the intricacies of the card catalog and learn how the call number on the catalog cards enables him to locate the books on the library's shelves, and understand how to use encyclopedias.

Getting down to business

The goals for the fifth and sixth grades are the expansion of those presented for the fourth grade with the introduction of additional reference material and the keeping of an individual reading record. At the beginning of the fifth grade a comparison of Compton's Pictured Encyclopedia, World Book, Britannica Junior and Collier's Encyclopedia enables the child to learn that each of these sets has special guides and different ways of arranging material so that he can choose which are best for his needs.

By studying the Dewey Decimal System the student develops an understanding of how books are grouped according to subject material and soon knows exactly where to find those in which he is most interested. For example, he learns that information for social studies is in both the travel and history divisions.

The unabridged dictionary, atlases and World Almanac, come under discussion in these grades when the teacher needs them for a class project.

Our sixth graders usually write a research paper. Part of their material must come from magazines. To make their task easier, the librarian explains The Readers' Guide to Periodical Literature and gives them some practice exercises so she can show them how to interpret the reference correctly.

PINCH

The purpose of the reading record is to have the pupil tackle different types of books in both the fiction and the non-fiction sections. On a sheet of paper he lists author, title, publisher, copyright date, date read and type of book. He gives this book a number which is then placed in the division of a circle that shows the different kinds of fiction books, or in another circle which is divided into the ten categories specified in the Dewey Decimal System. Thus, at a glance, he can tell which groups he has not explored.

The teaching program is only one service offered by the elementary school library. But it is a foundation that must be established if the children are to master knowledge more quickly, know how to evaluate materials and discriminate between propaganda and the truth.

21. WAUWATOSA ELEMENTARY SCHOOLS
TEACH GOOD LIBRARY HABITS

Esther Pinch

The Wauwatosa Public Schools have pioneered in establishing elementary school libraries, the first in 1931. Each school has a library room. The prevalent practice in Wauwatosa is to have classes from grades 2 through 6 make scheduled weekly visits to the library. In the lower grades (2 to 4) a story is usually read by the librarian, or when new books are on display they are introduced to the children, who are then given an opportunity to select books to take home. Both teacher and librarian help each child to find a book to satisfy his interests. Pupils sign up for their books and often stamp the date due themselves.

In the upper grade classes, where a longer period is scheduled, pupils are given planned and individual instruction in the arrangement of books on the shelves, use of the card catalog as an aid in finding books on various subjects and use of the encyclopedia. The general format of a book, emphasizing the importance of the title page, table of contents and index is explained, too.

The Children's Book on How to Use Books and Libraries by Mott and Baisden (Scribner, 1937) has been used extensively in teaching library techniques. The following paragraphs describe present library practices in the Wauwatosa elementary schools:

The Philosophy of the Library: The school libraries are an integral part of the school organization, and library service is considered an essential agency in the modern educational program. The libraries are intended to be service agencies, teaching agencies, book centers, and reading centers. Each library has as its objectives: (1) To enrich the curriculum and supply reference material; (2) To provide for worthy use of leisure time; (3) To train pupils in the use of books and the library.

Library Services to Teachers: Since teachers have closer contact with pupils, it is only through co-operation of teachers and librarians that every pupil can be reached. The Wauwatosa libraries try to make library materials available to teachers by having the library open to teachers at all times during the day, as well as before and after school; by making materials more accessible through organization; and by providing bibliographic service. New library materials are introduced to teachers through displays of new materials in the library, bulletins listing new library materials, book talks and other discussion techniques, and by contacts with individual teachers.

Books, exhibits, magazines, pamphlets, posters, and visual aids are provided teachers for classroom use and for bulletin boards. Teacher-librarian conferences are planned for discussion and recommendation of library materials and for discussion of reading problems to aid in book selection for individual students. The librarians make every effort to participate in curriculum development and to keep informed as to classroom plans and practices. Teachers are urged to use the library for social occasions as well as for professional help.

Library Services to Pupils: The library attempts to create a situation in which the natural interests of the pupils are enlarged, stimulated and directed, and for which materials necessary to satisfy these interests are made readily available.

The elementary librarians meet to discuss their programs of service and to co-ordinate their plans. After much discussion, they have evolved the following objectives, outlined by grade level for the elementary schools. It will be apparent that many of these objectives are continuous throughout the elementary program. They are presented here in detail, since many elementary librarians have expressed a need for this type of material.

Kindergarten
1. Maintain attractive library corner.
2. Develop library citizenship
3. Encourage care for books: (a) keeping books clean; (b) turning pages correctly.
4. Promote habit of going to library to satisfy individual or class interests.
5. Create appreciation and interest in pictures, stories and poems.

First Grade
1. Maintain attractive library corner in classroom.
2. Develop library citizenship.
3. Encourage care for books: (a) keeping books clean; (b) turning pages correctly; (c) opening new books; (d) using bookmarks.
4. Continue to promote habit of going to library to satisfy individual or class interests.

5. Use a definite procedure in taking books for home reading.
6. Create appreciation and interest in pictures, stories and poems.

Second Grade
1. Maintain attractive library corner in classroom.
2. Develop library citizenship.
3. Encourage care for books: (a) keeping books clean; (b) turning pages correctly; (c) opening new books; (d) using bookmarks.
4. Continue to promote habit of going to library to satisfy individual or class interests.
5. Use a definite procedure in taking books for home reading.
6. Develop appreciation and interest in pictures, stories and poems.

Third Grade
1. Maintain attractive library corner in classroom.
2. Develop library citizenship.
3. Encourage care for books: (a) keeping books clean; (b) turning pages correctly; (c) opening new books; (d) using bookmarks.
4. Teach library technique to library groups: (a) checking books in and out; (b) locating books on shelf.
5. Introduce reading circle work.
6. Develop appreciation and interest in illustrations, stories and poems.
7. Continue to promote habit of going to library to satisfy individual or class interests.

Fourth Grade
1. Maintain attractive library corner in classroom.
2. Develop library citizenship.
3. Encourage care for books: (a) keeping books clean; (b) turning pages correctly; (c) opening new books; (d) using bookmarks.

4. Teach library techniques to library groups using reference book: (a) locating books on shelves: (1) information books by call numbers; (2) story books by author; (b) making use of information given on title page.
5. Introduce magazines.
6. Continue reading circle work.
7. Develop appreciation and interest in illustrations, stories and poems.
8. Continue to promote habit of going to library to satisfy individual or class interests.

Fifth Grade
1. Maintain attractive library corner in classroom.
2. Develop library citizenship.
3. Encourage care for books: (a) keeping books clean; (b) turning pages correctly; (c) opening new books; (d) using bookmarks.
4. Teach library techniques to library groups using reference book: (a) understanding arrangement of books in classes according to the Dewey Decimal System; (b) using the card catalog: (1) to find if library has a book with a certain title; (2) to find if library has a book by a certain author; (3) to find if library has books on a certain subject; (c) presenting parts of a book: (1) frontispiece; (2) title page; (3) preface; (4) dedication; (5) table of contents; (6) index.
5. Use of encyclopedia.
6. Guide pupils in use of magazines.
7. Continue reading circle work.
8. Develop appreciation and interest in illustrations, stories and poems.
9. Continue to promote habit of going to library to satisfy individual or class interests.

Sixth Grade
1. Maintain attractive library corner in classroom.
2. Develop library citizenship.

3. Promote respect for books.
4. Continue to teach library techniques to library groups: (a) develop further understanding of arrangement of books in classes according to Dewey Decimal System; (b) drill in using card catalog: (1) to find if library has a book with a certain title; (2) to find if library has a book by a certain author; (3) to find if library has books on a certain subject; (4) to understand cross-reference.
5. Use of encyclopedia: (a) know fact index in Compton; (b) know study guide in World Book; (c) know study guide and Ready Reference volumes in Junior Britannica.
6. Guide pupils in use of magazines.
7. Continue reading circle work.
8. Practice in reference work to develop ability to find information on desired topic.
9. Develop discrimination in book selection.
10. Further appreciation and interest in illustrations, stories and poems.
11. Continue to promote habit of going to library to satisfy individual or class interests.

22. FIRST GRADERS IN THE LIBRARY

Alene Taylor

There's no doubt about it. First graders at the South Newton and Newton elementary schools look forward with much enthusiasm to their library period.

The school board, superintendent, supervisor, principals, teachers, and librarian feel it necessary to make our first graders "library conscious," so we begin their library training with the very first week of school.

Since we have three first grades, each class has one thirty-five minute period a week in the library. The teacher always accompanies her class, since with both teacher and librarian working together the way is paved for many more learning experiences. Our classrooms are equipped with library tables—which are good to a point but are not a substitute for the central library.

We feel that children learn more readily in a relaxed atmosphere, so we try to make our library a pleasant informal place. A visit to the library is an eventful and exciting privilege as we give the children a chance to see, handle, select, and read beautiful books. Stories which have been carefully chosen are read or told by the librarian. No two library periods are alike—surprises galore! The children often share books they enjoyed reading, show pictures made to illustrate their book, or act out favorite stories. These activities do much to stimulate a wide interest in books.

Children quickly learn how to enter the library quietly, what the library is, and what a librarian does. They practice "library manners" which include talking in a whisper so as not to disturb others, walking quietly, and pushing chairs under the tables with care. Three library helpers from each class are chosen by the pupils to serve for the year. Their

duties are to assist with the classroom library table, keep
pencils and books in proper places and leave the library neat
and orderly.

The checking out of books begins with the first trip to
the library. The first books, of course, must be picture
books. Usually, there is someone in the family who will read
to the child. By the beginning of the third month each child
checks out books he can read by himself and takes pride in
signing his name neatly and correctly on the books cards.

You need not fear that permitting six year olds to take
books home will result in loss or damage, for first graders
are more careful with books than any other pupils in our
school!

Each child exercises freedom of choice in selecting his
own books from a group of books previously selected and
placed on a table by the teacher and librarian. Little Tom-
my took his first book home eight times before exchanging
for a different one. "I love this little book; just let me take
it one more time. I don't want another one."

Two first grade teachers had this to say about the library:

"Our library with its attractive surroundings, its many
beautiful books on different levels and its well-supervised
reading activities has greatly stimulated my first grade reading program. My students are extremely interested in reading and I attribute this to their pleasant association with the
library and its books." And, "I have found that our visits to
the school library make my children like to read independently and it increased their reading vocabulary. They often say,
'I know that word because it was in my library book.'"

23. LIBRARY LESSON PERIOD IN THE ELEMENTARY SCHOOL

Elaine Lapidus

"How would you like to select a book for the library?"
I asked my fourth-grade class one morning.

At once, faces brightened, whispers in the far corners
stopped and thirty small children snapped to attention.

I had just finished showing the class a series of publishers' catalogs, and had explained how the catalogs helped
me select books. The children had been interested but, as
usual, were a good deal more interested in waiting for me
to stop talking so we could go on with the important business
of picking out books. Now, however, I had their complete attention.

Pleased, I went on. "I'm going to choose a boy and girl
to act as representatives for the class. These representatives will choose the books they especially like from the catalogs (books for their age groups had already been marked)
and then describe the books to the rest of the class. Then,
you will all vote for the one you want me to buy. Do you like
that idea?"

A loud chorus of yeses.

"Well, who would like to be a representative?"

Every hand was instantly waving. And my Library Lesson Periods were officially started.

I had been planning this step for a long time. It seemed
to me that, while my elementary school pupils enjoyed their
library period, they enjoyed it most because it was a "free
period"—a period where children could relax and forget about
lessons, homework and similar drudgery. Oh, there was a
brief lecture on the card catalog or on the importance of returning a book to its proper place on the shelf. But, by and
large, the library period was a time to have fun.

110

LIBRARY LESSON PERIOD

Gradually, it had become clear to me that haphazard lessons with no follow-up tests were not laying the proper groundwork for the stiff reference requirements of the upper grades.

Furthermore, while I wanted the children to go on enjoying their stay in the library, it seemed a good idea to let them know, even at their tender age, that many people actually work in a library.

From now on, I resolved, my library period was going to be known as the Library Lesson Period. The children were going to receive a full term of systematic library instruction—complete with work sheets and tests. Since this meant I would have to create most of the lesson plans myself—lesson plans for the elementary library being as scarce as they are—I further resolved to make these lessons as interesting as possible.

Letting each fourth- and fifth-grade class select one book for the library seemed a good way to arouse the children's interest in learning about books and libraries. After all, what could be more natural, while we were waiting for the books to arrive, than to discuss the importance of books in our lives? And when their selections did arrive, there were so many things to discuss:

"Before you can check out the book, class, there is a lot of work to do. For instance, we have to decide where to put the book. Is it a fiction book or is it a non-fiction book? Are you sure you know how our fiction books are arranged . . .?

"Then, what kind of marking will be put on the back of the book so we will be sure it goes where it belongs on the shelf? Do you all understand what the call numbers on the books mean . . .?

"Now, let's talk about the cards we should make so that we can find our book through the card catalog . . . .

You could, obviously, base half a term of library instruction on a handful of books that the children were anxious to read.

111

And so I did. The books the children selected were excellent ones since, of course, they were restricted to the catalogs of reputable publishers. (The books chosen included two in the Landmark series, a "Black Stallion" by Walter Farley, the latest "Ginnie" by Catherine Woolley, among others.)

Naturally, when we came to our third library period—which concerned an examination of the title page, with special mention of our new friends, the publisher—the children began to realize that they were being given lessons. You can hide the grim facts of life only so long. There was a certain amount of grumbling, along with plaintive cries of: "When are we going to re-e-ead?" (The most plaintive were from those small boys who spent the entire period looking for—but never finding—the perfect book.)

However, children are philosophical about school. After a few weeks, they had forgotten that library periods had once been "free" and undemanding. They still had ten minutes or so to pick out a book—the voracious readers could also come during Open Periods—and for the remainder of the period they buckled down to work.

The two tests I gave them proved that the majority soon understood clearly how books are arranged in a library, knew how to use the card catalog, and had a fairly good idea of what the Dewey Decimal System was all about.

The second half of the year was devoted to the study of the encyclopedia. Lesson plans are easier to find in this area—Britannica Junior has a fine series of lessons for the elementary grades, for example—and the groundwork had been laid for such topics as "guide words" and "cross references" earlier in the term, so the lessons went ahead at an excellent clip.

There was, certainly, a good deal of work involved in transforming a library period into a Library Lesson Period. Lesson plans had to be devised and then mimeographed. Oversized catalog cards had to be drawn on poster boards. Tests had to be marked and graded.

LIBRARY LESSON PERIOD

But I believe any elementary school librarian who works
out twenty or so short, clear and interesting plans will find
that the Library Lesson Period rewards both the students
and the librarian.

24. TEACHING CHILDREN TO USE BOOKS

D. I. Colley

Fifteen years ago when, as a timid junior, I first crept
into the staff-room of a central library in search of what
was described as "a ten-minute break and a cupper," I listened, hardly daring to breathe, to a discussion among the
Olympians, on whether or not it was a librarian's job to
teach the use of books to children. My attention was somewhat rudely interrupted when it was discovered that by the
greatest of misfortune, I had selected that cup and saucer
which by years of tradition was dedicated to serve only the
Chief Cataloguer; in addition to this enormity, I had drained
the tea-pot.

I retreated in blushing, stammering haste, to the only
place where a very junior could sit in peace until the slings
and arrows of outraged majesty had spent themselves. But
before this strategic withdrawal, I remember an old gentleman silencing the advocates of the "every one to his trade
school" by saying, "I'm a librarian, not a museum attendant,
it's my job to see that my books are used, and if children
don't know how to use them, it's my job to teach them."

Subsequent investigation showed that the methods he
used were those which are now familiar to all of us, and
which were adequately described in a very recent article in
the Record.

113

The procedure may be summarized thus: a class of school children is brought to the library; for many of them it is their first visit; and in one or two forty-minute periods, the librarian and his staff attempt, by means of introductory talks and lists of questions, to explain the arrangement of the library, the use of the catalogue, the local history collection, the skeletons which appear in the basement of every library, and, in addition, how to make use of the commoner works of quick reference.

That the assistants engaged on this work have to be changed frequently is hardly a matter for comment.

I am not suggesting that these visits are entirely without value. As parts of a Civics Project, designed to introduce the child to one of the few remaining offices performed by local government, a modified form of the scheme would have a great deal to commend it. But to describe this paper-chase by the grandiloquent title of "Teaching Children to use Books" is absurd. The visits are little better than glorified conducted tours plus the excitement of a "treasure-hunt" for books that in all probability the child has no particular desire to read, and for information the child does not require to know except to answer the particular question asked of it. It is not surprising, rather it is inevitable, that these visits should degenerate into a mad scramble to be the first to finish a list of questions. What is surprising is that librarians should persist for over fifteen years with a method which is only giving further support to the complaints of the superficiality of modern educational methods.

Let us approach this problem of teaching the use of books from a different angle. One of my first schoolmasters never answered a question concerning a matter of fact. His stock answer to all enquiries of this nature was, "If you want to know a thing, dig for it." And the essential part of this reply was, "If you want to know a thing." Children do want to know things. A normal healthy child is a cornucopia of interest and enthusiasm. Our aim as librarians should be to provide the occasion for a display of these interests, and then to turn, "How does that?" and, "Why is this?" and "What is the other?" into "Are there any books on that?" "Which books will tell me this?" and so on. For the basis of my old schoolmaster's reply was the principle that if you gain knowledge by your own efforts, that knowledge is a permanent acquisition. Provided that, in the first place, you wanted that knowledge sufficiently badly to spend the time digging it out.

How many of us during one of these school visits have seized our question paper from the sticky hand of an excited youngster pursuing the answer to Question Nine, and have asked him to give the author and title of the book he found the map of England in, and have been met by a blank stare mixed with impatience as the rest of the field sweep by him? He no longer has the slightest interest in the book, it contained the answer to question three, and now all he needs is the average height and weight of an Irishman, and the mean temperature at the North Pole, to be first home and top of the class.

If it becomes necessary to use a stunt to arouse the interest of a child, you can be sure that the interest when aroused will be misdirected. And any scheme the aim of which is to teach the use of books is useless unless it is designed to show the child how its own already actively enquiring mind can be satisfied through the medium of the printed word.

I selected a headmaster with whom I had had many discussions on the part the public library could play in the work of the school, and asked him what he would do if his senior modern school was equipped with a reasonably efficient library of some twenty-thousand volumes, including fiction, non-fiction and reference books. His reply, which contained an unprintable description of the existing state of the school library, was, "Give me a library like that, and I'll build the whole curriculum round it." I pointed out to him that the library was already there, three minutes' walk away, not quite as far as the dinner centre, and much nearer than the technical school where the children went for cookery, woodwork and science. When I had convinced him that I wanted him to make use of the whole library, not just the Children's Room, and when we had jointly estimated the amount of displeasure (inevitable as a corollary to such an innovation) we would incur, we started to plan our campaign.

It was obvious to us that a library could not be the centre of all school activity until both staff and pupils were fully conversant with it and with the books it contained. And our first concern was this problem of teaching children to use books.

The head decided that, by rearranging his timetable, each class in the school could visit the library once a week. I agreed to this arrangement and also asked that the first term be considered an experimental one, during which we would have no preconceived plans, but, playing it off the cuff, Peter Cheyney fashion, would start something and wait and see what happened. Provisionally it was left to me to conduct the library side of the project, though each class would, of course, be accompanied by its teacher. The head sold the idea to his staff with varying degrees of success. I found in practice that some teachers preferred to plan the library period, as it was called, themselves, and would only refer to me if they wanted particular books or information. Three classes, however, were conducted along lines which fitted in with my very general and at that time half-formed ideas. Two on more orthodox lines acted as controls. One, the experimental group proper, was run on lines which I can only term "No-plan" system.

The class contained thirty children. In age, they were between twelve and thirteen. Though they were an A stream, their background was poor, and they had all failed to secure entrance to Grammar, Commercial or Technical Schools. I have described their environment in previous papers; it is sufficient for our purpose to say that it was not conducive to intellectual activity. These children had one advantage, they were able to get the maximum enjoyment out of their schoolwork because they were not pursued by the bogy of

116

School Certificate; and untrammelled by this same rigid framework, the staff were able and willing to concentrate on giving them as good an education (in the best sense of the word) as it lay in their power to do.

The class came for their first visit armed with note-books and pencils and gathered timidly in small groups in the children's room. Apart from the fact that they were to visit the library each week, and that they were not to disgrace the school, they had been told nothing. I gave them one of the shortest introductory talks to the library on record. I said, "You will be here till eleven o'clock, you can go anywhere in the building where there are books, look round until you find a book you would like to read, then find a chair and read it. You have notebooks and pencils, use them. Walk about quietly, talk quietly, and put every book back in the exact place you took it from. If you want to know anything, ask me."

Some of the children were already members of the library, and these soon assumed command of the main body of the class in search of Johns, Blyton, Striker and the like. I knew, and the children soon realized, that except on the rare occasions when I had some recent additions to put out, Johns, Blyton and Striker lived in the children's own homes, and were in the library only long enough for us to discharge and re-stamp them. The wandering continued. By accident rather than by design, one of them stepped through the barrier into the Adult Library. Like sheep everyone else followed him, including the teacher and myself. In the larger area, they split up into small groups and were soon hidden behind the shelves. Some wandered into the newsroom, a few lost themselves among the volumes of bound patents, and two, more venturesome, climbed into the gallery to inspect the music storage. On the whole it was a quiet morning, and though we had some difficulty in routing them out at eleven o'clock, the children seemed tolerably well satisfied with the visit.

A day or two later, the class teacher brought in their library notebooks, she had corrected them in the normal manner, marking spelling errors, indicating disapproval of the hand-writing and so on, and finally awarding so many marks out of ten. It was now my turn. I did not mark the books; I commented on them, writing my comments on a separate slip of paper which was afterwards inserted in the book. (The reason for this procedure was that the school was painfully short of writing paper, and its resources had been strained to provide each child with a separate book, for a purpose which did not come under the general heading of Reading, Writing and Arithmetic, and my comments, as you will see, were inevitably lengthy). Most of the children had started off on the first page by writing "Rules of the library," and following this by what they considered to be an accurate rendering of my introductory talk. A few had begun to give an account of the books they had been examining. There was little for me to do. Wherever a spelling error occurred, I wrote, "See dictionary," on my slip; a grammatical error called forth, "See Fowler's English usage," or, "See Teach yourself good English," whichever seemed most appropriate.

On the following week, the notebooks were returned to the children and they were given one final instruction, "Mr. Colley's comments and directions must be followed first; then carry on as you were doing last week." The minute or two necessary for children to read those comments were my last peaceful moments for a long time. The questions all came at once, "Where's the dictionary?", "Where is the book I had last week?", "Where's Fowler?", "How do I find Teach yourself good English?", and so on. For the sake of your peace of mind I will divide them into their component parts and give my answers:

Where's the dictionary?
With the reference books in that far corner.
Where's Fowler?
Look in the catalogue, over there.
Where's the book I had last week?
Who wrote it?
I don't know.

> It would have been a good idea to make a note of the
> author and title in your notebook. What was it
> about?

Cookery.

> Look in the catalogue.

I stood in the middle of the library and acted as a traffic
policeman for about five minutes, and when the last enquirer
had been shunted off in one direction or the other, I reviewed
the situation. About twenty members of the class were hud-
dled round the sheaf catalogue, gazing at it rather disconso-
lately, and making tentative pokes at it with their fingers. I
joined this group and briefly gave them just enough information about it to enable them to answer their own particular
query. This was a deliberate policy. The main business was
to teach the children to use books; the catalogue of a library
is a specialized tool, more used by the staff than the public,
and time spent in trying to explain its mysteries in details
would be not only wasted but possibly harmful to those children whose immediate interest lay elsewhere. Moreover, I
knew that as the weeks went by, there would be a gradual accumulation of knowledge concerning the catalogue, and by
helping themselves and each other, plus the occasional inter-
jections by the staff to help them over the more difficult features, the children would acquire incidentally the knack of
using the catalogue. This proved to be correct, and during
the whole of this trial period the necessity for a formal lesson on the catalogue never arose, and yet in half a dozen
visits the group waiting round the catalogue after my routine
point duty had dwindled considerably, and long before the end
of term, every child in the class was able to handle it with
confidence.

The dictionary users were my next patients, and, here
again, assistance plus the minimum of explanation sufficed
to answer their queries and send them off in search of fresh
material.

By the fourth period, the skeleton of a method began to
take shape. As interests were revealed in the notebooks, I

119

directed the children by my comments to further sources of
information, to encyclopaedias, year books, directories. To
the shelves, to periodicals and the newspapers. Wherever
the child's interest lay, there was printed matter available,
and no group of children at the catalogue, the shelves or the
reference books was allowed to struggle unaided for too long
without a member of the library staff or the class teacher
appearing to give the minimum assistance necessary for the
extraction of the appropriate material.

The following examples will illustrate the method in action.

There was one girl, among many, interested in cookery.
She was rapidly filling her library notebook with recipes
copied from books on cookery. How to make chocolate cake,
how to make meringues and éclairs and so on. I wrote,
"Chocolate cake, meringues and éclairs are all very well in
their place, but you would soon make a family ill if you fed
them on nothing else. What do you know about vitamins,
calories, proteins, carbohydrates, and a balanced diet?"

You might think that this was a little hard on a girl just
twelve years old, and so did the teacher at first. But the
girl, directed to specific dictionaries, encyclopaedias and
cookery books, was as happy as a sand-girl, she found the
library period too short and several evenings spent on her
own account saw her library notebook assume the guise of a
textbook on dietetics.

Another girl, not quite as bright, was on the same tack.
Recipe after recipe of dainties without a square meal among
them. I wrote, "How would you feed your family for a week?
Plan the daily menus, using cookery books, the women's
periodicals, and any other material you can find." We had
bacon and eggs every morning until I pointed out that ration-
ing existed when, to my great joy, we had bacon and eggs,
the joint, and Christmas cake on Sunday, and fish and chips
(from a shop presumably) for the rest of the week.

I hadn't realized before how totally inadequate both in
quantity and quality regarding present-day standards of food

supplies the majority of cookery books are, and as an adjunct to the library period, and entirely on their own initiative, a group of girls began to make a loose-leaf classified collection of recipes clipped from newspapers and periodicals which before I left Liverpool was the most valuable book on its subject in the library.

Greenmantle had been read to them in school, and one boy was fascinated by the book. I suggested he make a list of the Richard Hannay stories in their correct order, and read them. Later, my comments on his notebook suggested that he might like to know something about the author and gave several sources of information. At least three other boys joined him at this stage, and together they went over the ground they had already covered, and then produced quite creditable biographical notes on Buchan. I focused their attention on Buchan's period as Governor General of Canada; their interest separated them at this point, one of them got on to the Colonial development angle and finished up with the Ground Nuts scheme, another toured the American continent and settled on the romance of the moving frontier, and a third was seduced by the glamour of a cowboy's life.

Requests for books additional to those on the shelves began to be more frequent, and when the time appeared ripe, groups of the children were shown how to make application for a book on the exchange service. Again, when the occasion demanded, the regional library system was explained and it was undoubtedly a highlight in one boy's career when he was given a book which had been obtained for him from Burnley (the postage, incidentally, being provided by the teacher).

I had anticipated a certain amount of difficulty with children who were solely interested in sport, football, cricket, boxing and so on. But in actual practice, they were quite willing to be led into related fields of knowledge. The boxing fans, after they had exhausted Ring battles of the Century and the like, and discovered the appropriate sporting records

121

in Whitaker, were directed via articles on Pugilism in the encyclopaedias, to the historical side of their interests, and after satisfying their bloodthirsty instincts on fact and fiction, more often than not finished up with the history of the gladiators in Ancient Rome.

Awkward squads did appear. Two boys didn't want to read, weren't interested. At the first available opportunity, they slunk away behind the bookshelves and just talked. It wasn't until I eavesdropped on their conversation that I hit on a solution. They were keen cyclists, out in North Wales every week-end, and at the moment when I dropped in on their talk were arguing in subdued tones about the name of a village where they had had tea the previous Sunday. I asked them if they took maps on their trips. They didn't. I got one down and traced their route for them, settled the question of the village and left them poring over it. Ten minutes later, in answer to a query from one of them concerning mileage, I gave them an army manual on map-reading; there was no more muttered dissatisfaction from them concerning the library period.

Two other boys presented a different problem. They were willing, but never very happy about the library period. They wanted to draw, the books on art were of no interest, they wanted to be doing things for themselves. I toyed with the idea of allowing them to paint murals on the walls of the children's library, but abandoned this reluctantly. I felt there were limits even to co-operation with the schools. Finally I gave them a hint—the barest hint, mind you.

In quite general conversation I mentioned that it would be very helpful if we had a plan of the library with the positions of the different classes of books marked on it as a guide to other readers. This was done to exact scale; the boys measured up the building themselves, and they were not given the slightest bit of assistance. Later, and this time entirely on their own initiative, they produced a map of the area served by the library.

TEACHING CHILDREN TO USE BOOKS

There came a time when the children themselves demanded an explanation of the classification system. There had been several queries after the style of "Why are there several books with the same number? Why is the non-fiction in order of the book number and not alphabetically like the fiction?" "What does the number mean?" So one morning when they arrived, I suggested that those children who were interested could listen to a series of talks each lasting for fifteen minutes only, about classification. Some of the children, perhaps many of them, were entertained rather than instructed. The three people whose notebooks I have here would appear to belong to this category. The girl, for instance, in her notes has produced this gem, "Another thing for example, is if you got hold of a red-hot poker, you would classify it immediately." I think I agree with her.

At another stage, it became apparent that the dictionary, though easy to use for the correction of spelling errors, was not so simple where pronunciation and derivation were concerned. And as you would expect, though children were directed to it in the first place solely to correct spelling mistakes, it wasn't very long before their curiosity was aroused by the phonetic symbols and the following words in other languages. Here again, when the demand was of sufficiently large order, I gave another series of short talks on the derivation of the English language, and on the phonetics employed in the average dictionary.

Thus individually or in groups, as the occasion demanded, and always governed by the interest of the children themselves, the class was led through the principal reference books, the catalogue, the classification system, and the stock of the library. These interests were wider than any librarian, planning a scheme of instruction in the seclusion of his office, would have catered for. I had, until this experiment started, regarded the bound volumes of patents prior to, say, 1900 as so much wasted shelf space, and so they were as far as use was concerned until two lads on a tour of exploration took down an early volume and were attracted by the title,

"A preparation for the prevention of rust and canquer on armour," and thereafter could be found at the most unlikely times, ploughing their way through patent specifications and the trade-mark journals.

During the second half of this experimental period, the school began an investigation of Merseyside. Its geography, history, its manufactures, industries and commerce. It was encouraging to find that the immediate source of information to which the children turned was the public library. All the material we could obtain, from old prints to Kelly's Directory was made available, and it was used, used with a thoroughness which would not have been possible without the background knowledge of books provided by the library period.

25. THE LIBRARY AND SCHOOL LEAVERS

A. H. Watkins

Teaching the use of the library to school classes is no new thing, and with the head teachers of schools striving to give their "extra-year" classes a view of things in the world outside the school gates, it should be on the increase. There are certain advantages in having the classes at the library which make it preferable to visits to the schools by librarians, the principal one being that, through the schools, compulsory attendance at the library is obtained, the only occasion when this is possible. As the compulsion to attend school is neither irksome nor resented to any extent nowadays, this cannot prejudice the library in the eyes of any child, and when the child from a family of non-library-users is thus brought to the library, we have a great opportunity. At rising fifteen, most children quickly appreciate the signif-

icance of the library and books to their preparation for a
job, and this, as well as leisure reading, is the starting point
of talks on the library service at Bromley which all children
attend shortly before leaving school.

Classes spend two periods at the library, the first talk
showing how the libraries form a part of the municipal services and how the book fund is spent on the different kinds
of books, which leads to a brief survey of the occasions when
they will find books useful, from purely leisure reading,
through hobbies and sports to vocational training, varying the
examples to suit boy or girl audiences. To stress the points
to look for in choosing a book and at the same time to give an
idea of how to make full use of a book, a series of wall-
charts representing the parts of a book are displayed on a
long screen, so that they are all visible at the same time.
Starting with the title-page, the children are shown where
they may find the author's qualifications and the date of publication, and how to distinguish between a reprint and a new
edition. The importance of illustrations in some subjects
and how to check a book's adequacy in this respect is pointed
out and they are shown how, in the preface, an author frequently states his purpose in writing the book and the examination syllabus for which it is suitable. After the body of
the book, the material to be found in an appendix, the use of
the glossary, bibliography and index are explained, and then
follows a pause in the talk, during which the children can examine a collection of attractive books from the adult library
to find the parts mentioned and, if the books are well chosen,
at the same time gain an idea of how closely the books of the
library touch their lives and interests.

The talk continues with a description of the information
to be found in eight reference books, again with wall-charts,
this time representing pages of the books, and also with volumes of the books themselves to assist. The books chosen
are English dictionaries, the Encyclopaedia Britannica, The
Oxford Companion to Music, Chambers's Biographical Dictionary, Who's Who, Whitaker's Almanack and the Statesman's

Year-book, and if, by judicious questions, the children can be induced to tell the lecturer how to use the books, their interest can be kept and enhanced. A collection of reference books, including a number of surpassed annuals and railway time-tables as well as atlases and dictionaries, gives them an opportunity to browse after the talk.

The second visit begins with a description of the arrangement of the books on the shelves and how they may be found. It is pointed out that not only are the non-fiction books arranged according to subject but, as far as possible, related subjects are arranged together, so that the books will be found on neighbouring shelves, and, in addition, each subject has a number; wall-charts of the Dewey classification give them an idea how these numbers are allotted. It is explained that, just as a book has an index, so there is an index to the library, on cards in the catalogue cabinet, with references to the subject numbers. Enlarged reproductions of catalogue entries are shown on wall-charts. Bromley possesses a dictionary catalogue, so it is not difficult to explain that for each book in the library, there is a card under the author's name, one at least under the subject or subjects of the book and, if it is distinctive, another under the title, all arranged in alphabetical order like a dictionary. It then remains to show that the connection between the catalogue and the books is the subject number, to be found at the top left-hand corner of each card, and how the subject numbers can be found on the shelves by using the plan of the lending library and the shelf-guides.

The rest of the period is taken up with a tour of the departments and with finding the answers to a quiz in the reference library, the children usually hunting in pairs, each pair having a different set of questions. The quiz consists of five things to look up, involving, among others, references to the Oxford Dictionary and the Encyclopaedia Britannica; it is not intended as a test but rather as practical work on the subject of the talks, so a librarian is at hand to advise and guide. Requests for seemingly recondite information, such as the name of the Sultan of Zanzibar, or information about a familiar person, e.g., the address of Derek McCulloch, add zest and a feeling of high achievement when found. The quiz ends with a catalogue query in the lending library, each child having a subject to look up and a book on the subject to locate; the brighter children often solve a number of these whilst the laggards are doing one. This is, of course, the most popular part of the two visits, and head teachers have helped by asking a scholar to look up something for them, an address or the time of a train.

The wall-charts, prepared by a member of the staff, are written in India ink with a broad-nibbed pen, usually on half sheets of white cartridge paper, and are easily legible from a distance of twenty feet, which brings them within the range of vision of all members of the classes; we like to limit these to sixteen. A copy of a cyclostyled pamphlet, containing an introduction to the library and an outline of the subjects dealt with in the talks, is given to each child, an attempt to extend and drive home the influence of the library visits.

Librarians are seldom trained teachers, and the help of some of the teachers who accompany the classes has been most useful. One class, in a subsequent English lesson, were asked to write down their impressions of the visits, and their teacher, being frank as well as interested, was able to pass on with her own evaluation, criticisms or signs of lack of appreciation from the compositions. The classes from some schools are graded according to intelligence and in such cases, it is possible to vary the talks to suit the audience, simplifying extensively for the lowest group and getting them to co-operate as much as possible by asking questions. With all classes, however, it has been found that as short a period of talking as is convenient, say half-an-hour, followed by something for the children to do themselves, e.g., looking at the books and works of reference in the first lecture, sustains interest and, we trust, helps to make the visits more memorable. Such is our experience to date; we are still learning.

127

26. NOW I USE THE LIBRARY EVEN MORE: MUSINGS BY A SIXTH-GRADER

Elisabeth Hurd

A small girl tiptoed noiselessly into a cool library room on a warm autumn day in Austin, Texas. A sight awaited that amazed her. Children were hurrying about, checking out books, gathering information, and browsing among the crowded shelves. Two librarians were busy helping children get books, talking to groups, and directing general activities.

When one of the librarians spied the little girl, she came over to the child and pleasantly asked, "May I help you, Elisabeth?"

"This is my first time to come here alone," half-whispered Elisabeth.

"Well, then, you'll want to find your own book and check it out, I know. Do you remember the directions which I gave to your class?"

A slight nod was given by Elisabeth.

"The storybooks you will just love are in the section in that corner. If you have any trouble, come to see me. Good luck!"

The librarian turned to help another child while Elisabeth scampered toward the easy storybook shelves and on her way paused to look at a display window holding model cars and various other collections. While passing the folktales, she enjoyed seeing a tiny model of Paul Bunyan and Babe, his Blue Ox. Elisabeth sat down upon a low stool, and carefully looked at several books before she selected Make Way for Ducklings by Robert McCloskey. She then hastened to the check-out desk where an older girl made the proper records.

Elisabeth walked away jubilantly. During her years at Casis School, she would check out many, many books.

NOW I USE THE LIBRARY EVEN MORE

During the passing of five years, I (for I was that small girl) was in the library for many reasons. One special time I remember particularly. I had come not just for pleasure reading; I had come for information of a special kind. I had a tough assignment which required lots of reference work.

Our class had studied Augustus Caesar's World by Genevieve Foster during December. Now we were supposed to select one of the great personalities in Russian history and write "His World is patterned after Augustus Caesar's World. There were Rurik, Pete the Great, Catherine the Great, Lenin, Stalin, and others to choose from.

Catherine the Great was my choice. I went immediately to the card catalogue to find my subject. There I found references to biographies, one of which was Catherine the Great by Katherine Scherman. After checking that out, I turned to the encyclopedias, referred to my list of countries existing at the time of Catherine the Great, and set to work. And work it was! I had four encyclopedias, a large collection of books, tapes, films, maps, magazines, a vertical file, and a picture file to draw on. Finally, my report was finished and I could truly present people and events which took place throughout the world during the life of Catherine the Great of Russia.

At another time a different scene took place for me. Papers were spread out and pencils were flashing. But it was not reference work that we children were so busily doing. We were filling out our Texas Readers' Club lists. We fourth-, fifth-, and sixth-graders were checking off our requirements for the certificates which were awarded each spring at the grand library program. At this program each year an outstanding author always spoke to us. I remember how excited I was when Dr. McGuire, our librarian, permitted me to present the flowers to Jean Lee Latham, author of Carry On, Mr. Bowditch.

Many times our classes sat fascinated as a slight, gray-haired, gentle-voiced woman wove a web of magic around us. When she finished, we children could hardly pull ourselves

back to reality, so delightful had been our visit with our
Casis"ian" storyteller, Mrs. Brown.

During my sixth grade, Shakespeare also became a special interest of mine. On a sudden impulse I read portions
of Romeo and Juliet. Then I shared them with my class at
literature time and finally began to memorize special parts.
I had gone with my parents to see As You Like It and had
quietly resolved to become a Shakespearean actress. The
girls in our class banded together to perform A Midsummer
Night's Dream. Dr. McGuire was a wonderful resource person and an enthusiastic listener.

Today, on my last day in Casis as I sit in the library,
my wonderful experiences through the years stand out. My
long talks about books and authors with Dr. McGuire and the
happy hours I have spent in the Casis Library come back to
me! I shall miss Casis Library very much!

27. HOW TO MAKE THE LIBRARY FUNCTION:
TEACHING THE USE OF THE LIBRARY

Bernice L. Dunten

Teaching the use of the Library is a matter of orientation. In the long run the student teaches himself; however,
he needs guidance in charting his course. The librarian becomes the teacher and will have to formulate rules for procedure. It goes without saying that she will need a classroom and a scheduled time to meet a large number of students. In addition, there will be many encounters in the library. There is a wide difference between teaching methods
in the use of the library and teaching a course in pharmacy
with library assignments. Whether the two can be combined

or not rests between the choice of the library problem and
the manner of orientation. If the assignment merely requests the location of a certain volume on the shelf with a
report in long hand of an article which has been indicated,
you can say that it will not teach the student to use the library to any great extent. Some may question the necessity of teaching the undergraduate the use of the library at all.
The pharmacy graduate is a professional man, who will meet
a well-informed public, as well as the physician, the dentist,
the biologist, and the veterinarian interested in health problems. He may not have more than a five foot shelf of books,
but he should be trained to use them. He should also have
some idea about journals and the source of current information. The man who goes on to graduate work will be greatly
handicapped without a preformed basic knowledge of library
procedure. His first assignment as an applicant for a degree
may well be, "Cover the literature in the field in which you
are interested to ascertain if the work has been done."
   It is possible to initiate the Junior or Senior student into library work with a minimum of two hours in the classroom and a semester's work in actual practice in the library.
This shortened course does not teach all pharmaceutical literature as we know it, but it does prepare him for the next
step following graduation. The pharmaceutical curriculum
is crowded, and time is at a premium. It is my contention
that three hours of library practice per week per student
for the semester is enough, and might be divided between
two or three subject courses.
   A subject bibliography with annotations does not help at
this point; however, a list of abstracting and indexing journals in pharmacy and in bordering fields should be provided.
It is best not to teach librarianship but to run along with the
science of pharmacy, instruction about the library.
   Of course your library should be in order. Books and
journals should be cataloged and should be found in their
proper places; subject headings which have been used should
be valid; restrictions on books easily understood; rules for
loaning definite and generous.

For the beginner I have found the subject, manufacturing pharmacy, the most interesting as a vehicle for search projects. It furnishes a variety of topics such as ointments, emulsifying agents, suspending agents, antibiotics, or essential oils. The search for this material lends itself to a complete survey of the library. It is best to allow a free hand in the choice of a subject by the individual student. Later, if he wishes to change his subject, one can allow that, but the work should be steered toward production of some pharmaceutical preparation. As the first lecture is given, remember that nomenclature is of prime importance. Words, such as title page, volume, issue, collective index, copy, and classification symbols, should be defined. If you find your student frowning over classification symbols, just remember that this is his first attempt at using them and that he is thinking about them in terms of organic chemistry and structural formulae. Therefore, offer classification simply as a key to unlock the catalog, a code. The explanation can come later by means of a typed or printed card placed above the catalog with definite directions as to its use.

As in many other libraries, my Library has a location chart for journals, although they are classified and recorded on the periodical shelf list card. Beginners are required to use the periodical and current shelf lists, and some graduate students, who have missed library training in their undergraduate schools, fail altogether in the use of the periodical shelf list, the card catalog, and the use of indexes. Monographs are not used at once for the beginner, except a dictionary or handbook for clarification of the subject and the choice of terminology. Instead, he is sent directly to the abstracting journal. A manual which is used has a series of columns for keeping volumes, pages, and their respective guides in order. Twenty minutes with direct supervision prepares the student so that he can proceed on his own initiative. The librarian is available for the ever recurring questions. The end product of this concentrated effort is a series of work-sheets, each showing authority, source, methods, and a résumé in full of the work as found.

HOW TO MAKE THE LIBRARY FUNCTION

What is the best method for teaching the use of a handbook on physical data? I have placed old editions in the laboratory where students are working with melting points, boiling points, and refractive indices. At some time during the semester, the students are requested in a quiz session to give the author, title, and publisher of the books. For the quiz, no one will know the answer, but it is almost a certainty that each will go to the volume at his first opportunity and the information will be retained.

I would like to offer a technique which can be used on a series such as Beilstein's Handbuch der organischen Chemie. I take exception to the "find something question" which so often does not teach the literature. Instead of sending a student on a wild goose chase for one particular compound, state the assignment thus:

Using Beilstein's Handbuch der organischen Chemie, 4th edition, take any synthetic compound to be found in volume 1 (Band 1); find it also in the subject index (Formel register, Band 29); find volume numbers noted in heavy type and pages in light type; the numbers in brackets signify the first supplement (Erstes Ergänzungswerk). Since the second supplement (Zweites Ergänzungswerk) is not covered by the indexes, use the system number (System Nummer) which runs along the top of each page; find this number in the second supplement. This will lead you to your class of compounds in supplement 2. If you have not found any new derivatives of your compound, proceed to Chemical Abstracts 1930 to date. This should be a complete coverage of your compound. Report all original sources in full.

Insist that your students report all title pages from the title page proper. For teaching pharmacological literature I have mimeographed a small manual. This seemed to be the only way to present abstracting services and indexing journals in this field. Here again, the library problem should be stated in such a way that the literature is brought out and not the "pithed rat" for instance. Question 1: "Using <u>Jour-nal of Pharmacology and Experimental Therapeutics</u> and <u>Archiv für experimental Pathologie und Pharmakologie</u>, find three methods for screening drugs." Here you have intro-duced two titles. Although you have not asked for a compar-ison, the student will make one through his volition and the information obtained this way will be retained. Although most students cannot read German, they can read Beilstein with little preparation.

Should one bring the attention of his students to the ab-stracting journals by placing a list in the catalog under the heading Abstracting Services or by using mimeographed lists? There are many useful abstracting periodicals in related fields, such as refrigeration, foods, veterinary sci-ence, and nuclear science, and it is the librarian's job to acquaint the student with these titles.

Pharmaceutical literature covers a wide and varied number of titles, a number of societies, and a long histori-cal past. Library teaching, heretofore, has been carried on with the subject <u>history of pharmacy</u> as a medium; however, this does not lend itself readily to any library method. Dur-ing the past year a method of teaching source material in the course known as Pharmacy Administration was tried. The assignments were made under subjects, such as management and merchandising. The students were given a list of jour-nals which allowed a choice as to subject and journal refer-ence. When it came time to use books, subject headings were given pertaining to economics and business, which the students could choose or discard as they pleased. At no time did this group of students complain or appear disgrun-tled; indeed, they were interested in the work because it was their own.

The matter of teaching subject headings is a thorny one. Many students have never learned the alphabet; consequently, they cannot handle the alphabeting in the card catalog. I have prepared a small readable booklet covering most of the sub-ject headings in our catalog. (Even I make recourse to the list from time to time and find it useful in setting up a long term project or in completing a form to be used for a large number of students.) A card typed daily and placed above the catalog "Subject Heading for the Day," is helpful in calling attention to subject headings.

Do pharmacy librarians have any claim on teaching? It has been said that "Teaching a science lays its claim for existence on the fact that its discipline is based upon its capacity to be different, or to be separated from all other branches of learning."[1] Teaching about the library lays its claim as an entity on its ability to be logically connected with all branches of science, having a function as a coordinating factor, by assembling facts, and so placing science in a new light.

28. THE HIGH SCHOOL LIBRARY AS A
PREPARATION FOR COLLEGE

William H. Osterle, S.J.

To librarians busy about their duties in a high school library, meeting the needs of faculty and students, keeping in close touch with student activities, it happens very often that, with all these obligations to trouble the mind, the big item of "the student's future" receives short shrift; it is shunted to the dusty background with the replaced copies of the Readers' Guide, or shrugged off as a duty of the student counsellor. Yet as librarians—not just as librarians, but as individuals, extremely interested in the intellectual welfare of their charges--they should often dust off that word "future" and set it up as a frequent reminder on their desks, even giving it precedence over such desk items as Publishers' Weekly

135

or the A.L.A. Booklist. For the student's "future" is important; it is a very important item in his education; it is the purpose of education. And the library is an essential to education. Librarians as educators in the real sense of the word (educare, in Latin, meaning to educe from, draw out) must act as guides who draw out the best in their charges and thus prepare them to meet the future. They must gear their work to the accomplishing of this objective.

Statistics have shown that the majority of post-war high school graduates seek higher education and have the prospect of college life before them. Most high school students will go on to either a liberal arts school or an agricultural school or an institute of technology. To carry out their objectives successfully they will need certain "student habits" (using the phrase in its broadest understanding). They will need habits and attitudes of a kind which, if encouraged and developed in high school, can be of inestimable advantage to them throughout their entire college career, habits that will take away some of the unnecessary drudgery of college life and put in its place a real, thorough enjoyment of its varied curriculum.

These habits, these mental attitudes, which can be formed by means of the high school library, are what we wish to consider in this brief paper. If we observe them through the eyes of a college teacher we may find in them new points of view, new lights, that raise questions for thought, and these may in some way help point our duties as librarians in the high school.

One tremendous asset to a student who comes to college is his knowledge of library procedure. A student coming here to Georgetown, for instance, almost the first week he is inside the lecture halls, and even before the effects of hazing have worn off, finds that he has in all his courses "outside assignments," reading projects, research reports, which, if he doesn't want to get "snowed" (as the boys call it) from the very start, demand that he know how to use and to use effectively the university library or the library facil-

THE LIBRARY AS A PREPARATION FOR COLLEGE

ities of the city. For in a college very often the textbook is
just a basic outline of the course, to be elaborated upon and
developed by both the professor and additional outside reading and research. In history, for example, some professors
feel it an absolute necessity, a fundamental requirement for
their course, that the student read at least 2,000 pages of
matter above and beyond his textbook reading. Semester es-
says, or term papers, are almost a "must" in every course.
"It makes men out of them," say the professors.

So off to the library will troop sixty, maybe two hundred,
students, and each will be in search of his own project. No
library orientation course is going to be sufficient to him unless he has learned the "idea" of a library before he comes
to college; unless, in other words, he has acquired the feeling
for a library and its facilities, a sense of familiarity with
library procedure. He should know how to use the card catalog as a bibliography, how to use the standard bibliographical
tools, the encyclopedias, and other reference works to furnish
possible sources of further information on a subject. For
university libraries are frequently closed-shelf libraries,
which require that bibliographical research be done in the
card catalog and other tools available in the reading-room,
not in browsing among the shelves.

These are the methods the student should be thoroughly
acquainted with before he comes to college. It will be the
purpose then of a library orientation course to introduce him
to the intricacies of this individual college or university library, not how to use a library. A further purpose of the
orientation course should be to extend the students' knowledge of the basic reference works acquired in high school to
the more specialized works in special fields of college en-
deavor. We might say, therefore, that the high school library
should teach, not only the "how" of use in the library, but also
the "why." The librarian should always be attempting to inculcate the idea of a library, the purpose and notion of a library. With the "why," the purpose of a library, deeply impressed, students will learn the "hows" and will be more apt

137

OSTERLE

to increase and broaden their knowledge of library services
rather than wear that strange bewildered look we so often
see just a few days before a term paper is due.

This leads us to another very valuable preparation for
college work that can be carried out by the high school librarian: that is, to persuade the student that no matter what
his field of study, no matter whether he is taking Greek, business administration, or playing football, the library is the
place to go to find information on anything. Many a science
major here is amazed that there are charts, tables, fine
plates, and all sorts of information available in "library
books" (as they call them) and that these are very helpful
for their class work or experiments. They often feel that,
since they have to pay such a huge fortune for their science
textbooks, there is nothing more that is worthwhile to be
said on the subject. In this one respect, if the high school
librarian can help to change that mentality, he or she will be
helping the student a great deal. Again, I have seen football
players here who were amazed to find that the library had
some good books on their sport, even down to the detailed
technicalities of it which we laymen couldn't begin to fathom.
In other words, students should be impressed early with the
fact that the library is a university in itself—it is a university within a university—and that all branches of the university,
and minutest ramifications thereof, are represented within
the files and stacks of the library.

With this latter notion, I think, is associated another
basic concept. It is the idea of reverence for books—not
adulation or anything of that kind—but a good, wholesome
reverence for good books. And here again, a high school librarian can go a long way towards instilling this reverence
in the minds of youth—respect and reverence for a great
author, for a profound mind, for a noble idea. As Bernard
of Chartres says, "We are dwarfs who sit on the shoulders
of giants—and if we see further than others it is not because
of our own keenness of vision, but because we have been
lifted up and carried forward by their mighty endeavors."

THE LIBRARY AS A PREPARATION FOR COLLEGE

If we can instill into youth today this notion, we have gone a long way towards giving them the intellectual humility, the firmness of purpose, that will respect the wisdom of the ages and build thereon a more lasting city in their own minds. We have, nowadays, too much of that superficial, cocky (perhaps scoffing) attitude on the part of new and old college students towards the traditions and findings of the past. And if by any means our high school librarians can contribute—whether by their personal attitudes in discussing books with youth, or by their displays and library programs —to the lessoning of this negative attitude they will be doing a great work, a work which, I am sure, will make college a much more profitable place, rather than a place of almost impervious exposure to our forefathers' wisdom.

There is yet another way in which a high school library can prepare for college. It has been touched upon often in other respects than that under which I shall consider it. But the high school librarian can make significant (though often hidden) contributions to the future college life, work, and activities of her students by aiding those students to form good, wholesome habits of reading.

It might be said, in passing, that whatever a librarian does to teach a boy the right techniques of reading, and to correct and direct his facility in reading, will help inestimably the student's future university career. But here I would like to develop the idea of reading not as a skill but as a taste, an art. Habits of good reading started in high school will profit not only the college careers of our charges but also their lives after college, as Christian citizens. The task of developing and encouraging such habits, I admit, is a discouraging one at the present time. We have competition in comic books, the movies, radio, television—everywhere. Yet if, by the grace of God and our own unwearying labors, we gain a convert now and then, it will be worth every bit of our endeavors. For good reading is one of the most healthy signs of true spiritual and intellectual progress. It is a sign that a boy is growing, that his mind is beginning to adapt itself to the good, the true, the beautiful—that he is broadening his outlook. And therefore, whatever we as librarians can do to educate the reading sensitivity of our charges, either by our own personal contacts with students or just by the materials of periodical and book literature that we make easily available to the student, it is part of our work as Catholic educators.

We might, I think be much more effective in this work if we were for an instant to forget ourselves as professional librarians—as the skilled technicians which our library school training might seem to make of us—and become rather more human. We have gradually been becoming too much the professional people, perhaps the falsely professional people. By our profession we have lost a great deal of that warm, human contact necessary for really carrying out what is a very important item in our work.

It is good, it is true, that we have finally accepted a more professional attitude towards our work. We are better catalogers than we used to be; we are much better bibliographers; we have integrated library facilities into the curriculum of the school; we are even better poster-designers and record-keepers. In fact, we have become much more sure of our own capabilities, our own position in the educational set-up. With our training we feel that we—we, the school librarians—can be of much more help to our charges than we used to be. We are now qualified to meet their problems, to guide them.

Yet in this very attitude (for the most part a very wonderful attitude to have), I wonder if we are not losing touch with young minds, a contact that we cannot, must not, lose, if we want to be Catholic librarians, individuals who are helping in our little way God's providential plan for His children. Our courses in library schools, those courses in book selection, work with young people, young people's literature, and such like have encouraged us to be imbued with the idea, "I am equipped to guide youth into good reading, into real taste in reading," when we really mean, "I am equipped to guide youth

into my reading habits, into my reading tastes." In other
words, we have tended to forget the youth before us and
rather concentrate on what book we think is good, what
books we have on our reading lists for young people.

I hesitate to say it, but I have heard it said, that too
often in trying to develop taste librarians have developed
queer taste. They have developed taste too much like their
own, too much dominated by their own personality, rather
than good tastes founded on the basic fineness and often tremendous individual capacities of the young themselves. It
is this boy, this girl, we must help to good reading habits.
And this we must always keep before us: the more our own
ideals, our own likes, are shifted to the background, the better it will be for that boy or girl. For good literature is
good literature. There is a tremendous span of reading
covered by this phrase. Our own little, personal span is not
quite sufficient. When we teach a child to write, for example, we don't try to teach him to write like ourselves. When
we teach music appreciation, do we, for instance, skip
Stravinsky or even Gershwin because we don't comprehend
that type of music?

We librarians must be trying continuously to broaden
our own weak, human minds to see in all good literature the
seeds at least of its greatness and to see in all youth the
fertile soil for noble and good thoughts. And though we
might not appreciate, not even have a taste for, some literature, if we think in our own hearts that maybe this book
might start this boy thinking, might start him reading other
good books, we will use the opportunity well. Good juvenile
books are many, as good mature books are many. We, as
librarians, must be in the most Christian, charitable way be
trying constantly to bring these good books into the hands
of the young. In short, we must be endeavoring continually
to invite our young charges into the swim of good literature,
good taste and good thoughts of all kinds. If college can
carry on that work begun by the high school librarians, we
all will have done a fine service to the young souls given to
our care.

OSTERLE

In summing up, then, the high school library can be a
wonderful preparation for college. It can teach the student
so much that will simplify his college work and assignments
and make them more interesting. You as his librarian guides
can teach him at an early stage the psychological approaches
to books and learning, a reverence that becomes a Christian
gentleman and scholar. By means of a librarian's own personal endeavors a student can acquire that combination of
sound habits of study and good taste in reading that will prove
invaluable to him in his college work. Finally, the high
school library can help to inculcate a truly Catholic approach
to learning, so that the student from a Catholic high school
comes to college with a Catholic view, with a mind which has
been exposed to the good and great in Catholic as well as sec-
ular literature. Having been surrounded with and exposed to
Catholic books, the student gains a familiarity with his faith
and the wisdom of his Church and will carry that into his college life. Under the guidance of a librarian who is a bearer
not only of light and knowledge and technical skills, but a
Christopher, a Christ-bearer in words and charity, the student will be equipped to make college just another stepping-
stone in his Christian formation, and will be led by that help
and encouragement "to the measure of the age of the fullness
of Christ."

29. ORIENTATION OF THE USE OF
                    THE COLLEGE LIBRARY

Mildred Eyres

"As a new student, what did you think about our library?"
asked a library staff member of a new student.

"I was so frightened—it looked too complicated for me—
I'm staying away as long as I can help it," is a typical reply
from those who are still waiting for the library unit to be
taught in their class.

Having observed for some time that the problems relating to assisting freshmen in learning the use of the library
have recently been intensified by the influx of the hordes of
students plus the shortage of professional staffing of the library, I wished to know how other institutions were meeting
this challenge.

Replies to a questionnaire sent to colleges and universities of South Dakota, Iowa, Nebraska, Minnesota and Michigan revealed that many librarians were unhappy with what
was being done for their freshmen.

Some had not been in their new positions long enough to
set up a program; several found that what was done during
orientation week did not have adequate follow-up in the English department; others found that, except for a tour, it had
been crowded out of orientation week; but those who had set
up an audio-visual presentation combined with manuals and
tours were more satisfied with the situation.

Of the 96 questionnaires sent, 61 were returned. Many
of the librarians wrote in detail concerning their situation
and enclosed handbooks. However, there are still many
institutions which have not yet evolved a satisfactory program, and are still groping.

41 colleges distributed handbooks. Two libraries issued
them on demand, and 2 had a fee for the handbooks, feeling

that the student would be more apt to read them if there was a charge.

Of the 61 questionnaires returned from the various colleges in this area, the following data was extracted concerning the ways and methods new students are taught to use the college library.

40 colleges distributed handbooks. Two libraries issued them on demand only, and 2 had a fee for the handbooks, feeling the student would be more apt to read them if there was a charge.

51 out of the 61 libraries replied stating they had library instruction as part of the class procedure.

10 colleges gave a library course for credit hours, and 11 institutions had the informal instructions when needed.

In colleges where class instruction only was carried out:

1 had reading of handbooks in class.

38 read handbooks supplemented by lectures.

In 30 schools the unit was prepared by the English department, in 38, librarians prepared the unit.

56 colleges had a tour of the library preceded with a lecture.

Total number of hours of instruction per student varied from 1/2 to 10 with 3/4 reporting 1 hour. 8 reported from 4 to 7 hours instruction.

Of the teaching devices used:

15 used instructional handbooks;

36 the informational type,

13 had charts,

18 blown up cards,

11 film strips,

10 libraries used commercial slides, and 10 colleges used locally prepared slides,

4 used opieoscope projections,

9 used films,

1 had a taped lecture.

Only 28 out of the 61 questionnaires used any sort of laboratory (that is reference, usage practice, etc.) while 44

had lectures and 29 had tests. 11 schools used supplementary readings on the use of the library.
40 colleges gave library usage aid to Freshmen only.
27 colleges also include transfers in this library program.
2 very large institutions have no program.

Comments from various colleges concerning library instruction include: "When our freshman classes were smaller,
part of orientation week was a tour of the library conducted
by the librarian with a preliminary talk and specific instructions when different vital sections were reached. The size
of present classes makes that impossible—definitely ineffective, so we now have freshmen congregate in the chapel, during orientation week, and the librarian gives them a talk of
about an hour's duration. Emphasis is mainly on awakening
a proper rapport between students and library through telling of its history, its traditions and ideals, bringing out its
rules by statement and anecdote, giving its hours and broad-
ly telling of the various types of books (Reference, Reserve
and Open Shelf) and the ways in which Dewey and Cutter numbers give each individual one its definite place on the shelf."
Another remarks "there seems no valid reason why the
burden of instruction should devolve on the English 1-2 instructors. I think that the social sciences and foreign language instructors should be part of a more general plan of
library instruction. This work could be done with the guidance by the librarians in the use of subject reference aids."
One flatly states "we've reached the conclusion that library tests are a total waste of time because there isn't
proper follow-up on them in the English department."
One college wrote "beginning fall 1961, 2 sections of a
one-hour credit course, Library Orientation, is being taught
for the first time. It is taught by the library science department (a part of the education department) instructor. As you
see we do not reach the entire freshman class. Not all attend the one-hour library lecture (5 sessions) and not all
reached the second semester through the English department.

145

We are using the overhead projector with transparencies prepared by our audio-visual department. This has been quite successful in that the material may be adapted to the situation."

Another says "we use an instructional resources guide —revised each year. A copy will follow. We use a tape adapted to colored 2x2 slides."

Yet another experience, "We are currently involved in a trial program which involves a 2 1/2 hour lecture-tour introduction plus follow-up work from the teachers who are cooperating. We are beginning with freshmen and getting to upper classmen only partially through Honors groups, English major as a group, etc. We are in the beginning stages and have nothing to report here; however, previous experience indicates to me that the library staff must be vitally involved with the process, with full cooperation of a designated part of the faculty.

I have had the sad experience of working with graduate students about to receive degrees who thought the Reader's guide was the only index and did not really know how to use it. One function of an undergraduate program must be to teach the student how to use the research tools effectively."

One college gave encouragement, "Keep up the good work. We need more and better student instruction in how to use the library. Students in my Library Science class in reference often remark that they wish they had had that course years before because it would have helped them in their studies by acquainting them with material they could have used."

The dissatisfaction in library instruction shows in one letter. "We are not happy with the present program. It is a lick and a promise. The former, one-quarter course for one credit was abandoned for three reasons: (1) pressure on staff time. The increasing number of freshmen was too great a burden for even a growing library staff. (2) Pressure on student time. More and more requirements were made of the student. (3) Dissatisfaction of both staff and students with the existing course. Instruction was not suited to the immediate

146

need of freshmen students; they could see no relation to their
freshmen year courses. The occasional senior who wandered
into the course found it very helpful, but late in coming.
Since it had become an exercise in boondoggling, we dropped
it. Now we give them a welcome and invite them to the library, but the policy is essentially 'sink or swim.' Of course,
the individual who needs personal attention and has the gump-
tion to ask for it can and does get help."

At Wayne State the "diagnosis of the problem at this point
is that our concept of 'sophisticated understanding of the library and increasing competence in its use' as a goal of general education is not accepted, perhaps not understood, by
most of the faculty. (The academic world as a whole, of
course, has not achieved anything like consensus about any
of the goals of general education). We conceive of the library
as a highly complicated system, or, better, a network of in-
terrelated systems—which organizes and controls all kinds
of communication. A few instructors understand the conception, but we believe that most conceive of sophisticated library understanding and competence as 'command of the literature of a field of study.' This is what they, themselves,
have acquired in their years of training and experience, and
this is what they hope to stimulate their students to acquire.
Research on student use of the library would indicate that
for the average college student such an expectation is naive.
Perhaps it is equally naive to expect the average college student to grasp the notion of the library as a system of bibliographical organization. Certainly it is difficult to work for
such an objective through faculty members who, themselves,
do not understand it."[1]

While the Wayne State Monteith Library project's ambitious and ideal objectives are beyond the undertaking of many
institutions, it is encouraging to note that here is a pioneer
experiment in educational integration in a new dimension that
could eventually become a trend in unifying integrational education experiences with the library being a dominant force.

For institutions where this kind of planning is still but in embryonic form or non-existent, it is obvious that any kind of library orientation experience must be initiated by dedicated leadership and planning from the library in co-operation with the Educational Policies committee and department heads.

A further study will be made of the handbooks and the audio-visual programs which are proving satisfactory for other schools. If all college librarians of South Dakota, who are interested in this problem, would be willing to pool ideas, contribute information on what has been accomplished so far in their school, outline a unified plan of at least three hours of presentation and three hours of follow-up, we might arrive at a partial solution with considerable avoidance of duplication. Any correspondence relating to this will be most welcome. Perhaps we South Dakotan librarians could pioneer a project in this area which would establish a pattern for others. I believe we should and that we can.

30. FRESHMAN LIBRARY ORIENTATION PROGRAM

Donald D. Ranstead and Sherman H. Spencer

During the past decade there has been a growing interest in the problem of library orientation of college students, yet relatively few reports of working programs have appeared in the professional literature.[1] Although maximum cooperation and coordination with the faculty was not attained at the College of the Pacific in the sense indicated by Knapp,[2] we felt that enough encouragement was received from the teaching staff to make the "experiment." What follows is a discussion of the emergence of the program, a

148

FRESHMAN LIBRARY ORIENTATION PROGRAM

somewhat detailed description of its mechanics, and an appraisal (tentative, of course) of its efficaciousness.
For several years College of the Pacific had given library orientation in the form of a fifty-minute lecture in the library by a member of the library staff. This lecture was given to two groups of students: the freshmen English classes who came section by section just before writing their term paper, and to the students of the graduate course, "Methods and Materials of Research." As the second group was composed of students with more specialized needs, the lecture seemed to work out fairly well. No one, however, was satisfied with the method of orientation for freshmen.
In spring, 1957, a Library Committee, composed of several members of the faculty and library staff discussed the orientation problem and decided on the general outline of how it would be handled. Mrs. Lois Higman, then reference librarian, compiled a twenty-three page handbook, and members of the circulation and reference departments worked out a general outline of the lectures and prepared quizzes.
The plan as it was put into operation this year had each of four library staff participants responsible for two sections of freshman English. The process, to be repeated for the nine speech sections, was as follows: three consecutive Monday lectures, quizzes handed out after the first two lectures to be returned to the library within two days, and a final quiz in class after an abbreviated concluding talk.
The first lecture attempted to cover these points: the floor plan of the library and a discussion of the special collections, the rules of the library, and an explanation of the catalog including treatment of some of the more important filing rules and an explanation of the type of information contained on an individual card.
In planning the first two examinations one major task was to so devise them that all of the students wouldn't have to use the same individual item (in order to preclude the incidence of cheating as well as to keep wear and tear of

149

library materials at a minimum). For example, the longest question on the first exam was one which acquainted the students with tracings and title entries (among other things). In every section each individual was given a different title and had to find the author, a book about the author, and a book on the same subject as the title assigned. Thus, although it complicated the task of grading the papers (there could be no "key" for the answer, of course), we felt the extra work was warranted by the reduced possibility of the students copying from each other—only 8 or 9 having the same title rather than 180. Most of the other sections of the first quiz—a filing problem, one involving Cutter numbers, one using cross-references, and a simple location custom—could be answered by the handbook or the lecture notes.

The second lecture was preceded by handing back the exams and reviewing the questions. The talk dealt with reference materials and special materials kept at the desk such as pamphlets, documents, and college catalogs. As in the previous lecture, it was stressed that notes be taken (especially as over half the questions in this exam could not be answered in the handbook alone). Reference works were discussed by type rather than subject. Thus, Dictionaries, Encyclopedias, Bibliography, etc., were treated in the lecture, but for some categories, e.g. indexes, there was reference made to the handbook. The exam had 22 true-false questions, 5 matching, and a third section in three parts involving the use of indexes. The first (answered in the handbook) asked in which index they would look first to find articles on some 7 subjects, the second gave 6 headings, all but two involving cross references, and asked under what heading (in either the Reader's Guide or International Index of the past five years) they would find the articles, and the third required copying an entry from any index and writing a complete explanation of the citation.

Attention Increases

The final lecture, which again was preceded by a "post mortem" on the previous exam, dealt with the mechanics of

FRESHMAN LIBRARY ORIENTATION PROGRAM

preparing a term paper. The lecturers discussed "back-
grounding" a subject before deciding on a topic; making sure
that in defining broad and narrow topics, the library's holdings be the criterion; and compiling bibliography and assessing material as to its scholarship. We noticed a considerable
increase in attentiveness during this final talk, especially in
the English sections. No doubt the subject being treated no
longer seemed as "academic" as it had previously, since they
were to begin on their term papers that week, with speech
section students giving 15-minute formal talks. The final
quiz which was given during the last 20 minutes of class time,
was really a test as to how well they had absorbed what we
had said the previous one-half hour. They were all given the
same subject, "History and Background of Desegregation in
the United States," and told to indicate the steps they would
take in preparing a paper on that subject, i.e., the steps before the actual writing. The students then returned the second examination and handed in their final test which was
graded and sent, with the other two, to the instructors of
their respective sections.
    The results of the examinations indicated two things to
us at once. First, that the speech sections included the more
serious freshman students and second, that the first quiz was
not taken as seriously or done with the same care as the last
two. It wasn't until they received the jolt of their low grades
in the first exam that they began to apply themselves. Another factor in accounting for the lower curve on the first
exam was perhaps the fact that these exams would count in
the final grade was not stressed enough at the beginning.
    Two or three effects would seem to indicate that the pro-
gram was at least a partial success. One is that the final
quizzes were, on the whole, quite good. Secondly, that the
number of questions of an elementary nature (directional,
deciphering abbreviation in Indexes, etc.) was below that of
the previous year (in spite of an increase in the number of
Freshmen). And, thirdly, that the instructors in English and
Speech noted a rise in the number and caliber of sources
used in the term projects.

151

Even before the project began we felt a number of inadequacies to be inherent in our project. To mention just two: the lectures were spread out over too long a time span (it would have been much better to have done the three in one week rather than three); the lectures on reference materials dealt in too detailed a fashion with too many specific titles. The students found it difficult to take adequate notes and the majority of the titles, no doubt, will never be used or examined by them. We concluded that in the future the amount of information retained would be much higher if we treated fewer specific works and in more detail, with emphasis on Winchell and Shores.

We hope that this report stimulates thinking and re-thinking in what is one of the most important areas with which the college library is concerned. We hope, also, that it might induce other libraries to publish reports of their experiences in this area, thereby aiding all of us in working out programs to orient students to better use of the library.

31. THOUGHTS ON FRESHMAN ORIENTATION

Eleanor Devlin

Every September in college and university libraries all over the United States the library staff prepares to welcome the contingent of Freshman students and to add the library's bit to the full program of orientation arranged for the new students. Every September the Freshmen endure what has been planned for them and every winter and spring the library staff reviews its activities and indulges in some professional soul searching. "Have we done well by our Freshman students? Were we thorough enough? Were we specific enough?

THOUGHTS ON FRESHMAN ORIENTATION

Were they responsive enough? And can they now find their way around the library and in and out of the bibliographical aids with the sangfroid of veteran scholars?"

Well, we all know the usual answers to these and to similar questions and we know that they are a mixed bag. Very few of us, I suspect, would admit to being even moderately pleased with the results of "Library Orientation for the Freshman."

At the risk of belaboring the obvious, I would like to submit the idea that the orientation of the Freshman in the use of the library is only one facet of a larger situation and that such programs of orientation operate in a vacuum if they are not an integral part of the whole collegiate program. The predominant characteristic of the student's situation at the outset of his academic career is that he is one of three responsible and responsive elements. The other elements are the library and the teaching faculty. These three elements, of student, teacher, and book are, of course, the elements of the educative process and each has its peculiar function in the structure of academic activity. In this process each is partially dependent upon the other, or rather each one's contribution is unique and necessary to the whole. The unique contribution of the library is interwoven with those other strands of academic life and is to be considered as part of a larger process of education and intellectual development.

If this idea of the function of the academic community is to be implemented in any practical way the responsibility is threefold. Faculty, students and librarians have the task not only of exercising their own unique functions but also of utilizing and respecting the function of the other parties to the relationship. We like to think that of course the college community exists and operates just by reason of this essential integration and this is in large part true. However, the machinery creaks in certain places and the problem of the Freshman and the library reveals some of the creaks. It is our concern and interest here to examine the peculiar characteristics and distinguishing marks of the three component elements of the academic world in order to understand why it creaks and also to realize what it is accomplishing while creaking and how it can accomplish more.

To the library staff and to the teaching faculty the initial impression of the incoming Freshmen is one of numbers. Except in the very small and highly selective college, integrating the Freshmen is a problem in mass whether the number of new students is one hundred or eighteen hundred or more. We cannot lose sight of this fact. It is essential to an understanding of and a coping with the realities of the collegiate situation.

Freshmen Share Responsibility

Freshmen students are not aware of themselves as problems or as component elements in the great educative process, sharing with the college the responsibility for their education. They do not know that what they are and what they bring to the campus in the way of mental equipment and intellectual achievement will somehow affect the community of which they are about to become a part. Their responsibility to the college community is to arrive with this necessary intellectual equipment and to cooperate with what has been planned by the other elements therein. This indeed is their primary responsibility and their ability to exercise it constitutes the second impression they create. In most of our colleges and universities entering Freshmen vary widely in intelligence, in information, in mental discipline, and in knowledge of the use of books. The variation may be due to differences in individual abilities and talents and/or to the good or poor quality of the secondary education available. The fact remains that Freshmen are heterogeneous in knowledge and ability, needing various degrees of personal attention to achieve their best integration and to become functioning members of their college community. A few teachers believe, and a few students exemplify this belief, that one should not need instruction in how to study and how to use a library, and that this knowledge is acquired in an osmotic and painless fashion as one's years increase. This is the ideal of collegiate and

THOUGHTS ON FRESHMAN ORIENTATION

indeed of all education but this is not the situation we are faced with, especially in our larger colleges and universities and with our present democratic standards of admission to collegiate study. Without pointing the finger at secondary education that does not prepare a person adequately for college and without castigating institutions of higher learning for their eagerness to increase enrollment, let us admit that many, perhaps a fourth, of our entering students are ill-equipped by nature or training to take their responsible place in the academic world. Nevertheless they are in that world as part of its third element. Thus there will be a diversity of talent and response to be considered in planning work with the student element.

Teachers and librarians know this and know too that because of their tutelary position with regard to the students and because of the presumed wealth of their wisdom, learning and maturity, the task of introducing the students to the books is naturally theirs. Teachers have always been concerned that their students should read and librarians have almost always wanted to share their book treasures with their clientele. Within recent times both groups have realized that they are harboring the same ideals and it has become more apparent that teachers and college librarians are working the same side of the street. It is not, I think, necessary to examine in detail the cooperative schemes that faculty and librarians have worked out for the instruction of the Freshmen. They are all geared to the two cardinal points of the size of the Freshman class and the dissimilarity of its components. They include the required course in library resources, with or without credit, the formal tour of the library with all its variations, the film, and the library problem supervised by the library staff or by the members of the English department. These all answer a need and are perhaps better than nothing but they do not fill the hearts of the participants with joy. What can be done to improve on them and make all three groups happier with the process of integration?

Library Orientation Not Integrated

I suspect that one of the primary causes of dissatisfaction lies in the fact that the area of practical cooperation between faculty and library staff is too narrow. Library orientation tends to be presented as a thing apart and not as a vital and indispensable part of the new students' academic environment. The breath of the spirit does not inform the machinery of presentation and thus the students are uninterested, their teachers are impatient and the librarians frustrated. Desired results are not forthcoming and what little is achieved seems hardly worth the effort which is entailed. To correct this state of affairs a far wider field of understanding between library staff and teaching faculty must be created.

It may be well at this point to reiterate that teacher and librarian are two distinct elements in the process of education, each with his own peculiar duty and function and that, though their aims with regard to the student are similar, their methods of achieving those aims are unique and not interchangeable. It is, indeed, out of the activities of their respective and separate disciplines that the need for cooperation between them become apparent and it would be a sad, though most unlikely, day when their two viewpoints should so merge as to become indistinguishable. With this in mind, and knowing the devotion of each to his profession, we may pass to a consideration of their specific aims.

Aims of the Teacher Differ

The teacher is concerned with the intellectual welfare of one or more groups of students. He wants them to learn what he has to teach, to become aware of the depths of the subject and its place in the world of higher learning. He knows the library is an extension of the classroom and he expects the students to use it and to use it intelligently. His classes are usually large, with the usual diversity of ability and attention among the students. He may be the professor

THOUGHTS ON FRESHMAN ORIENTATION

who knows practically every book in the library and thinks
his students should know too, or the one who never goes
near the library and assumes grandly that whatever he happens to mention in class naturally is reposing on the library
shelf waiting for his students to rush over and read it. He
may be the young instructor fresh from graduate school who
treats his Freshmen as though they were graduate students,
or the man who is seeing his own book through the press,
two or three Ph.D. candidates through their orals and several garden variety of classes through their term papers. Whoever he is, he is busy with grades and papers and department
meetings and student conferences when he is out of the classroom. The library is there, of course, especially when he
wants something from it, and it is a fine library, except that
the librarians fuss about overdue books and take an uncon-
sciously long time about getting one's requests bought and out
on the shelves.

The library, of course, is understaffed and the librarians are overworked. There is never enough time or personnel or money or space to do and be all the things that the
campus expects of librarians and that librarians expect of
themselves. The college librarian translates this expectation into a desire to serve completely the needs of the college community, to find every faculty member exactly what
he or she wants and to supply every student with those things
that will widen his horizons or at least get his term paper
written. Fulfillment of this desire is sometimes balked by
the librarian's not being able to find what the faculty member wants, whether it is because the faculty member isn't
sure what he does want or the librarian has exhausted his resources or his skill, and sometimes by the librarian's inability to translate what the student said the professor said
he should read for a class report. The librarian is often immersed in the details of keeping the collection in order and
in circulation, of chasing down missing books, of answering
the telephone and pointing out encyclopedias and periodical
indexes all at the same time, of planning what additions to

make to the reference collection and how to manufacture more space for the map collections, while shepherding two Home Ec students to the books on budget planning and trying to explain to an obdurate professor why it takes the United Nations so long to issue a yearbook. He maintains an elaborate cataloging system which he avers is necessary for the proper recording of the library's collection despite the cries of the braver faculty members that it is confusing and illogical. He will listen to their criticisms and keep right on cataloging, sure of its usefulness, sure of the library's supreme importance on the campus and pretty sure that if professors made a greater effort they and their students would not have such trouble finding what they wanted.

"Good Old Days" Are in the Past

Teacher and librarian both like to think that in the old days when everything was on a smaller scale and everyone didn't go to college, no one seemed to worry about showing the student how to find the library or what to do when he got there. They like to think that all students were superior and understood at once the most subtle pronouncements of their professors and the most complicated bibliothecal systems. If such were the case today teachers and librarians might safely shuttle the students back and forth to the intellectual satisfaction of all three elements and teacher and librarian might continue to regard each other from a considerable distance with a profound respect unsullied by familiarity.

However, the present-day situation demands mutual recognition of the need for closer and more formal connections between the two and an increased understanding of the functions of the one group on the part of the other. Commonsense and self-respect alone require that a system be devised to give a working acquaintance with the tools of scholarship to the hordes of students who present themselves at campus gates every fall. It is true, of course, that some students will not need to have a system planned for them and some, unfortunately, will be unable to coordinate themselves

158

successfully with any. It is also true that some librarians cannot bear to think of their own functions in any new light that may lead toward changing a time-honored pattern, and that some professors regard their own patterns of behavior with the same reverence, and consider planning with the librarian a betrayal of their rugged individualism. There is also however a genuine concern among the people on both sides as to the value and efficiency of the patterns of library instruction now in operation, and at the same time a feeling that whatever the drawbacks to these methods they are at least a tangible grappling with the problem. They are, indeed, and tangible criteria seem to be necessary for measuring progress toward the intangible goal of the intellectual man. Since, however, the goal is intangible and since what librarians and faculty members between them have devised for Freshman orientation in the use of the library does not satisfy any one of the three groups, it is obvious that in this department of academic activity neither faculty nor library staff has found the proper approach to the fulfillment of its aim. Satisfactory progress toward this aim demands a far broader basis of cooperation between the faculty and the library than the week's course in library techniques, the showing of a film, or the reluctant partnership of instructors and librarians in guiding Freshmen.

Just because the human elements are so diverse in both faculty and library, not to mention the students, the pattern of cooperation must include a generosity of outlook, a breadth of vision which encompasses all of the librarian's days and weeks on the job and all of the professor's impact in the classroom. The academic world is a world of individuals: the influence of teacher on student is an individual one and the meeting between librarian and student is also in terms of two individuals. We do not want the student to miss this sense of individual adventure in his college career and we do not want to smother the librarian's urge to individual service or the teacher's feeling of freedom in his dealing with the library. Teacher and librarian must know that they

DEVLIN

should all hang together or else be trampled on separately, and yet paradoxically the hanging together is what will give individual energy its greatest freedom. Therefore it seems to me that when we speak of faculty and library cooperation in the matter of Freshman orientation we are speaking of the most obvious aspect of the general pattern of faculty and library cooperation in the whole process of education. Certainly there must be tangible activities and they may even continue to include group introduction to the mysteries of the large book collection, but these are not the most important manifestations. More important are the tangible activities of the librarian familiarizing himself with the curriculum in order to meet the demands that will be made on his book collection. More important too are the tangible activities of the faculty member familiarizing himself with the book collection and with the special conditions present in servicing and maintaining it. Most important are the attitudes of each group toward the other's activities; the genuine realization on the part of each of the strengths and stresses inherent in the other's role in the educative process. The possibilities in the situation are endless and as various as the personalities of the individuals involved. It is a unity in diversity that is limited only by the abilities and good will—and the strength—of the people involved.

Program to Originate with Librarian

A program aiming toward this wider area of cooperation must, I think, originate with the librarian, perhaps in conjunction with the faculty library committee. It would take the form of an invitation to the teaching faculty to inform the library of the curriculum for the year and what the students will be coming to the library to find. It would offer the services of the staff to organize the required material in the most useful fashion and to be aware of the students' needs and what is on hand to satisfy them. The beauty of a program of this sort is that it is not offering anything new, not starting any additional program. It is merely emphasizing

160

THOUGHTS ON FRESHMAN ORIENTATION

the library's existing services and reiterating the library's
position as a house of knowledge. It supposes a loyal and
capable staff with each member performing his or her particular function.

On the part of the faculty it supposes an interest in and
a knowledge of the library's collections, a willingness to acquaint the library staff with its program and an expectation
that the librarians will work with the teachers and with the
students and thus make classroom and library recognizable
partners in the students' education. Such a procedure does
exist in a partial and fragmentary state on most college and
university campuses. Many professors do use the library
and its facilities in just this way and many librarians do
respond to faculty and student needs. Partial and fragmentary activities, however, are not enough. The program must
be all-embracing, must include the whole of the teaching
faculty and the whole of the library staff working together
and informed of each other's activities.

The responsibility of the students, the third element in
this picture of academic integration, will be to respond to
and make use of this new and improved process of cooperation. Their numbers and their differing abilities will limit
the degree of success of such a program, but with a complete interlocking of effort on the part of faculty and library
staff success should be more familiar than is presently the
case. The new students will not be an amorphous mass to
be herded through a perfunctory schedule that interests no
one; instead they will be members of smaller class-room
groups whose visits to the library will have a purpose
planned by the teacher, expected by the librarian and understood by the students themselves.

Lest I seem to have soared like the lark straight up to
heaven's gate, let me hasten to add that on any campus I
have known or can imagine, I am sure that the human elements engaged thereon will quite definitely set limits to
this program. The fact that performance is bound to be
limited does not, I think, discredit it as a program worth

161

considering. Limitation is, after all, necessary in order to
achieve form. That has been the object of our concern here:
to ascertain the form in which certain aspects of the educative process in a college and university may be clothed.

32. WE CAN USE OUR LIBRARY!

Byrd Fanita Sawyer

While we all wish that our young people might learn to
use the riches of information stored in our libraries through
realistic learning situations, most of us must face the fact
that we can never be present to guide each student through
the library as his need for wider learning demands it. We,
as librarians, do feel that in our complex world everyone
must be exposed to the techniques which will enable him to
be at home in all libraries throughout his life. In the effort
to bring the library to each student, Churchill County High
School teachers have evolved a formal training program
covering four years. This does not mean the librarian does
not work with individuals, but we have found that youngsters
take very good care of their own wants even as second-year
students. We strive to give everyone the fundamentals of
library use which will enable him to adventure far and wide
in the world of books and their related materials. Since
English is required for three years and college preparatory
students usually take the fourth year, we have turned to the
English classes as a field for library instruction.

Our students acquire the skills involved in the use of
encyclopedias, dictionaries, and the catalog as freshmen;
the sophomores add the use of the Abridged Readers' Guide
and pamphlet files to their knowledge. By this time most

162

of the second-year students know their way around the library, so the junior and senior projects include a stress on bibliography, notetaking, indexing, outlining, and footnotes. All the classes come to the library for special assignments throughout the year, but we devote a week of the English course to library understanding in the first, second, and fourth years. The third year people spend two weeks from English and from United States History in the library.

As soon as the English I classes are organized and oriented, they spend a day tracing the history of libraries. Stress is laid on the fact that however inadequate our materials are, they are nonetheless typical of practically all libraries. We emphasize the fact that everyone today should be at home in libraries since the fields of knowledge are so varied. We are now ready to find our way around the library. A guided tour with a Dewey Decimal guide card indicates where the various subject fields are found. Since freshmen come other times during the year to learn the use of encyclopedia and dictionaries, little stress is laid on these matters at this time. We do inspect the card catalog carefully and every student has the opportunity to see a card for the author, the title, and the subject. The catalog is reviewed frequently during the year.

To make this information a part of the student's thinking, we then draw maps of the library, locating the materials they will use during the year. The subjects are located by Dewey numbers on the map and this number is identified in a key. At the end of the week the youngsters range the bookshelves with a degree of independence and assurance. The maps are done on large sheets of drawing paper and a further incentive is offered by displaying them during Education Week to help the visitors find their way around. The map teaches much better than lectures or written instructions.

The sophomores assume the task of making a book on a vocation which interests them. We have found that few people know the resources a book offers aside from its main

body. The process of making a proper book increases awareness of contents in all books and the subject matter of this
assignment gives a fairly intensive look at jobs in the world
today. The "rules" for doing this project show the types of
materials students learn to use:

SOPHOMORE LIBRARY PROJECT

The parts of a book:

Covers	Body
End pages	Appendixes
Title page	Glossary
Copyright	Bibliography
Contents	Index

Arrangement of bibliography:
> General reference: Americana 10:217
> Books
>> Author (last name first), title, publisher, copyright
>> date, 910 p. (At least three)
> Pamphlets
>> (At least two) Same as books
> Magazines
>> Author, title, name of magazine, issue, pages
> Interview
>> Last name of person interviewed, first name, authori-
>> ty, place, date

The book covers are as attractive as the skill of the writer can make them. Every type of material available must be
used and the book is arranged in chapters. Sometimes the
week assigned for this task is not long enough. It takes at
least a day to explain the rules and four days may stretch into five or even six. A few always find a more interesting occupation as they browse and start a new subject which means
lost time. This second-year project is the critical one since
the foundation for the next two projects is laid here.

The materials in this field are found in our vocation
files which are apart from other vertical file materials.

WE CAN USE OUR LIBRARY

Over the years we have found valuable free materials, bought
many items, and service clubs have helped with gifts in this
field. We have books, but here is one subject area where
such materials are so quickly out of date that we do not stress
books on vocations. We have a long spread of bulletin boards,
so our best vocations posters from many sources are put up
a week before the actual work starts to enable youngsters to
look about in many fields. Abridged Readers' Guide is carefully explained. This year we also make "want cards" for
magazines, pamphlets, and books and sophomores learn to
request materials in proper form. The cards make it possible to have pamphlets and magazines ready when the class
arrives after the first day. It will be seen that the instruction sheet has plenty of room for notemaking as the explanation is made.

Sources of free material in this field may be found in
the publishers' list of the Standard Catalog for High School Libraries as well as in the advertising pages of magazines.

Since these projects for the three years include writing,
the English instructor grades the body of the book and I grade
the structure aside from the theme. No library grade is given
until the structure is correct. Since we had some difficulty
with the "books" being passed on to a friend who uses them
the following year, we collect them after the student has seen
his grades and had his questions answered. We return the
projects at graduation. We make the opportunity to display
the projects during the year at clubs and for our own visitors.
This assignment is announced several weeks in advance to
enable youngsters to gather their own materials and the library to borrow materials it may not have.

The junior project is our most ambitious for both the
English III and U.S. history students spend two weeks with
me. Since we do not teach Nevada history in high school, a
review of important items is necessary for the first three
days in history. This same three days in English is devoted
to review of the second year year information and additional
instruction in making notes for which we supply the cards
cut from paper.

NEVADA HISTORY PROJECT

The Nevada History Project for the third-year English and history classes shall cover two weeks of class time, but will undoubtedly take considerable time outside class periods.

The students may study any Nevada subject for which we can secure adequate materials. The work done will be presented in form of a book of 2,000 words or with a map and book of 500 words.

No book will receive a grade until it is in proper form.

Order of book:
- I. Covers
- II. Title page
  - A. Title
  - B. Author
  - C. Illustrator
  - D. Publisher
- III. Back of title page
  Copyright date
- IV. Contents (at least 4 chapters)
- V. Outline of subject (see Frederick's How to Study Handbook p. 353)
- VI. Body of book
- VII. Bibliography (see "order")
- VIII. Index

Bibliography order
    General reference: Encyclopedia and yearbooks
        Volume or year indicated
    Books (at least four)
        Author (last name, first name), title, publisher, copyright, pages used.
    Pamphlets (at least three)
        Same as books
    Magazines
        Author, title, name of magazines, issue, pages.
    Interviews
        Name of person, place, date, qualifications.

WE CAN USE OUR LIBRARY

The more complete the book is and the more outside effort is made, the better the grade.

Note cards (at least 30)

We have done all the above in the sophomore year. This year we learn to take notes and keep them in order. Each heading on the card must be filled out as you read.

We are fortunate in having one of the best collections of Nevada materials in the state. Again, newspaper clippings and pamphlets from many state departments and local chambers of commerce as well as magazine articles offer a wide variety of materials which are not in books.

Many of our students are keenly interested in telling their research story on maps so for these people we cut the words in the body of the book to 500 from 2,000. These maps are uniform in size and done on graph sheets 22"x 36". We have had many interesting local and state maps based on intensive research from this phase of our Nevada work. Any subject concerning Nevada is acceptable if we can find enough material to make research worthwhile. We encourage the writing of a family history if the student is at least a third generation Nevadan. One of the most gratifying by-products of this work is to see the development of family pride when the student and his family discover how important grandfather was in his community.

By this time we have made an attractive looking book, outlined its contents, mastered an unannotated bibliography, and an index, written an interesting story and learned to take notes which will always be a help even though the skill is used only for a paper to be read before the literary club or the neighborhood farm bureau meeting. We attempt to break the habit of copying wholesale from encyclopedia and books at this stage. We add the best papers and maps to our Nevada collection and each year the better ones are sent to other schools and libraries for exhibit.

The English IV project is still evolving. The students wrote a term paper based on the instructions offered by Stanford University. The only skill we added is the use of footnotes. I do not feel that a mastery of footnotes is essential to happiness but most colleges do, so we have footnotes in our 2,000 word book. Our subjects last year were chosen from the many essay contests assailing the English teacher and the better papers selected for the statewide competition. This year we are using English authors as subjects.

Since library skills should have been learned by the fourth year we rehearse the rules for one class period and then adjourn to the library for the rest of the week. Most of these students are college preparatory people who will need the skills as well as the information offered through this project. We have reviewed, through use, each library skill and should be free to roam and find our answers in any library under the Dewey Decimal System.

THE SENIOR TERM PAPER

The term paper will follow the same form used in your second and third year library projects. The body of the book will contain 1000 words. Mr. Wright will grade the theme and Mrs. Sawyer will grade the structure including the outline, bibliography note cards and footnotes.

You have selected as your subject one English author and his work.

No book will receive a final grade until it is in proper form.

A book
    I. Covers
       Title and author at least.
   II. Title page
      A. Title
      B. Author
      C. Illustrator
      D. Publisher
  III. Back of the title page
      Printings
      Copyright dates

    IV. Contents (at least 4 chapters)
    V. The Outline (see Frederick's "How to Study Handbook," p. 353)
    VI. Body of the book
    VII. Bibliography (see below)
    VIII. Index (at least twelve items)

Bibliography
    General Reference: Encyclopedia or yearbooks
        Name and volume number as "Britannica: 10)
        or Who's Who in America, 1956–57
    Books (at least four)
        Author, last name, first name, title, publisher, copyright, pages used.
    Pamphlets (at least one)
        Treat as books
    Magazines
        Author, title, name of magazine, issue, pages used
    Interviews
        Name of person, place, date and authority.

Note cards
    Pick up at desk. You will probably need 30.

Footnotes
    At least ten.

No two schools have the same problems in library instruction and undoubtedly there are many answers to the problem of teaching library skills. It would be of great interest to hear how other high schools are meeting this problem. We realize that our student body of 400 makes it possible for the librarian to work with all the English classes, while large schools might find our plan too complicated. Since we are always seeking improvement we should like to hear other experiences in making the library the center of any community life.

PART III: THE INSTRUCTIONAL APPROACH

33. LIBRARY INSTRUCTION IN THE LIMELIGHT— AND OTHER ASSORTED COLORS

Mary Ann Blatt

Perhaps one of the most remarkable phenomena of our age is the attraction of the lighted screen for its audience— be it cinerama, vista-vision, small-town or home movie screen, the TV picture or the simple overhead projection. Press the button, project an image, and presto—all eyes are there. Do you doubt this? Can you honestly say you have never found yourself watching a TV commercial or even a program merely because the pictures held you spellbound? Have you sometimes found yourself watching the screen (and listening too) when nothing more stimulating than columns of numbers were projected? Was your glance pulled to the screen frequently as a lecturer proceeded or droned on? Isn't there a hint for us in the fact that huge movie audiences are remarkably attentive and that behavioral problems are virtually nonexistent in a school room during showings of films, filmstrips or projectuals?

We all learned long ago that good teaching is reinforced by appeal to both ear and eye. Can a piece of chalk screeching on a green blackboard or the familiar librarian in last year's blue wool hope ever to compete with the glamour and changing nature of the spotlighted projected image? We ourselves may succeed as an attention-getting device at moments, but for a sustained lesson in library instruction I maintain that the teacher or librarian can profit by utilizing a device which flips to a new view frequently.

How has the use of overhead projections for teaching library units operated in actual practice? Specifics of transparencies may vary widely with the unit or subject taught and with the grade level. The extent of what can be done is limited

173

only by the extent of the librarian's imagination. My trial
run in teaching most of the entire unit of library orientation
to seventh graders (five periods for each English class) by
the overhead method issued forth from necessity. One librarian plus twelve seventh grade English classes equals
two solid weeks of library instruction. Result: one tightly
tied-up library at the beginning of a busy school year, and
one librarian with a very sore throat. But, one librarian
plus six large groups (two classes at a time) plus a lecture
accompanied by the use of overhead transparencies (or vice
versa) equals one library used by these groups only half the
time. Result: a more happily accomodated faculty and student body and one librarian who has time for a drink of
water between groups.

What exactly can be shown on the screen? Our seventh
grade unit followed this pattern:

1. Topic—Library citizenship. Patter and discussion
   here were accompanied by six to eight transparencies,
   stick figures in a variety of color similar to Munro
   Leaf's DON'TS or drawings like those in CHILDREN'S
   BOOK ON HOW TO USE THE LIBRARY.

2. Ten simple rules of our library. These were projected
   with a mask, then uncovered one at a time for discussion. No looking ahead was possible.

3. How are books arranged? I simply wrote in purple
   projek pen on acetate while students took notes. They
   were fascinated to see the colored letters appear on
   the screen and equally charmed by the ease in eras-
   ing with a damp toweling. We defined fiction, story
   collection, nonfiction, and biography and explained the
   arrangement of each. Then transparencies in green
   showed books of individual biography out of order so
   students could see clearly to rearrange them. The
   lower half of this projectual illustrated collective biography.

3b. We considered Mr. Dewey, his purpose and work. We
   developed on the projectual together the ten possible

divisions. My transparency (striking cyan blue background with white letters) was masked to reveal each main division as it was remembered or deduced. Another projectual broke down the 500's to show the logical nature of the system. Thus reinforced with knowledge, the students viewed a glaring red image termed "Where do you find it?" And as the pointer designated one of many topics (e.g., the FBI, ballet dancing, poems, an atlas), scattered upon the bright background, students delighted to call out the general classification numbers.

4. Call numbers. One transparency with two overlays showed component parts, the classification number and author letter. Total—a call number.

5. Catalog cards. What can be done with author, title, and subject catalog cards is obvious and will clarify these to students. Colored bands can be drawn to denote phonograph record cards, filmstrips, etc.

We also taught sample bibliography and the indexing of various encyclopedias with simple accompanying projectuals. The few remaining topics were, alas, presented in the fashion of past years.

You may not be satisfied with your first results; I wasn't. The students, however, not so discriminating, rushed for front seats and inquired daily, "Will we see more of those pictures? Oh goody!" There are many of my "firsts" which will need to be improved or altered before next year, but the advantages of the projectual method with accompanying lecture far outshone last year's performance. First, the large groups were more attentive, interested and alert. Second, while I have no accurate measure for this, the learning and retention appear to have increased as we are having more efficient use of library facilities and far fewer questions about topics covered though the ability range of this seventh grade crop is comparable to that of last year. Third, a librarian who can meet the needs of a grade more pleasantly, but in half the time, has increased freedom to work on other projects.

The fact that your school may not yet be equipped is insufficient reason for closing the eyes to possibilities of this technique. Numerous secondary schools in Montgomery County for example have established centers where students as well as teachers are producing the transparencies for use in almost any subject. The necessary equipment, one proto printer and one pickle jar, are simple for all to use. Development centers exist in the central offices of several counties where teachers may use the facilities or where these items may be produced upon request. Projectuals may be shared from school to school within a system since librarians need not all during the same week introduce the READERS' GUIDE or present illustrations to accompany a unit introducing mythology books. Of course, commercial transparencies may be purchased, and while these are extremely professional in appearance, they may not present your information in quite the way you wish. Let all alert librarians investigate now the advantages of transparencies for teaching and help to instigate the installation of a program in the school system.

Now all school librarians give group instruction at a variety of levels on a variety of topics, but what of possible uses of these projectuals for the public librarian? Instruction given so frequently to the individual may not require the use of an overhead projector, but public library sponsored group meetings, great books discussions, poetry hours, story telling, etc.—all learning situations—could perhaps focus some of the ideas in green, blue or magenta highlights. Why not dramatize with rainbow hues the public presentation of fiscal or statistical information for Boards of Directors? And surely an overhead projectual is easier to see than one small illustration in a picture book especially if the story telling group is too large to fold itself at the librarian's feet.

It is a startling and totally new experience to one who (like myself) has lectured the old-fashioned way, using blown-up catalog cards and similar visual devices, to try new-type library instruction while standing beside an overhead projector and facing a group of sixty students, and to observe all eyes focused on the screen—just where you want them.

Librarians of Maryland—Unite! Flip a switch. Turn on the spotlight. Put highlights and lasting color into your library teaching!

34. BEYOND THE DDC: THE TEACHING OF LIBRARY SKILLS CAN BE AN INTELLECTUAL ADVENTURE

Carolyn Leopold

Several years ago, I was informed on rather short notice that I was to teach library techniques to the students at the Holton Middle School (grades seven to nine) in Washington, D.C., to prepare them for high school work. It was a traditional setup, with the girl students taking part of their study hall time to meet in small classes (seven in all) once a week.

Since my teaching was begun without enough advance notice to draw on published material, my first plans read suspiciously like a catalog of courses in library school: "reference tools," "book selection," "the history of books and libraries." And curiously, it was this backdrop to the standard lectures on the DDC, the indexes, and the bibliographies, that gradually revealed to me the enormous intellectual scope of what librarians are really trained to present to their students.

As a librarian, I soon found that I was able to create a special position of authority and discipline within the school framework which still remains outside the limits of the classroom teacher-pupil relationship. As a teacher with the mantle of authority, but without the double sword of grades, I had the psychological freedom to move from specific library techniques into the realm of history of language, and the history of ideas.

177

LEOPOLD

In teaching the format of a book, for example, a standard part of library instruction, the concept of integrity in book revision could be approached. From that point, an examination of the history of books became a platform from which the concept of form as a carrier of ideas emerged.

In such a context, fairy tales became an unusual area of examination, leading two ways. Taking the Caldecott approach, the classes examined variant editions and their type and art work. Using the cultural approach, we separated folk tales from fairy tales and explored the relationship of mythology to religion and to science.

This approach opened wide the entire relationship of books to culture and history, of language to ideas, of bibliographic control to scholarship—and all to history.

We started out with the familiar book talk-book truck format and progressed from there. At the beginning of the year, each girl had filled out a card with age, reading interests, and what whe would like to glean from this course —data that enabled me to stage debates, with the antireaders taking on the readers, or the love-story group challenging the Norse-story clan.

From this fairly traditional beginning, we could jump into a discussion of style, where I used the superbly chosen samples from Eleanor Cameron's article on style in the Horn Book (December, 1962), and on to the idea of critical expertise. "My opinion is as good as anyone else's," filled the air at the beginning. But soon it was answered by, "Yes, but . . ." And we were on the way to discussing critical criteria and book reviewing.

Book reviews, of course, also led naturally into a discussion of reviewing and literary criticism. I would assign very short—three- or four-sentence— book reviews to the students, which were subject to instant correction, dispute, and revision on the part of their classmates and the library teacher. The English department reported improvement in the students' book reports after a few of these sessions, and in the ninth grade they opened the way to a discussion of

reviews, and guideposts for critical judgement. I brought
in the New York Times, Book Week, Time, The New Yorker,
etc., and we read selected reviews from Library Journal in
order to demonstrate the importance of reviews to book
selection. The students got quite argumentative about who
is qualified to judge a book, and how to prevent commercial-
ization in reviewing publications. I used fashion magazines
to bring the problem to their level. Were they qualified to
evaluate?

The lessons sometimes fed into, sometimes led out of,
subject classes. One theme that the English department
asked me to stress was plagiarism. Generally, that sin is
committed unknowingly in these grades. When I gave the
unit on plagiarism, intended to clarify the intellectual contribution required in a term paper exercise, I broadened the
study into an assessment of intellectual responsibility in
general, including that in published works. We reviewed all
kinds of authorship, from corporate authorship to "off the
record" interviews, periodical editors, compilers, and the
proliferation of series books, in order to awaken intellectual skepticism and awareness. As examples, we used the
students' own textbooks, government documents, and periodicals: this led us into the problems of disseminating information. In studying national news, we could also take as
examples the parents of some students.

A simple lesson on the parts of a book evolved into an
exercise for the students in making their own index, and a
clarification of the questions of copyright, new editions, and
revisions (and honesty in revision) of a book. With this kind
of perspective gained in the junior high, ethical textbook publishers may find an aware audience developing!

Working with seventh-grade English classes, I gave a
lesson on locating biographical material in encyclopedias
and biographical dictionaries, after which the English assignment was to locate such materials on authors they were
studying. Not only did the girls learn abstractions, like
"authority" in conflicting sources, but they were able to apply
them to concrete projects in familiar areas.

179

In the unit on biography, I tied assignments in with authors whom the students were studying in English classes, and then with themselves. One day I asked simply, "Who are you?" After some initial astonishment, the girls produced their names. I followed with, "Prove it to me." That beginning led to a discussion of their ancestors, parents, and their own history, substantiated by documents of these from birth certificates to school records. As secondary sources, each student wrote a one-page description of herself or of a friend. These also demonstrated problems in biography and autobiography, and their difference from historical fiction—an approach that could be integrated with either history courses or genre studies in literature.

It was a class on the historical novel and fictionalized biography, in turn, that gave me the opportunity to present not the facts or patterns of history, which is the history teacher's responsibility, but rather the idea and methodology of history. The class theorized about what data would be necessary to support any stated facts about their individual lives. Here in Washington, primary and secondary sources of history are easily dramatized.

The students could now approach their history assignments for the facts, with a greater awareness of the concepts, assumptions, and data-gathering in historical research.

Immediacy is crucial in teaching the use of periodical guides. Shortly after the assassination of President Kennedy, I had students bring in magazine articles on the subject to supplement the library's holdings. When the December Abridged Reader's Guide came in, I duplicated the pertinent pages and distributed them in class. We checked the index against the magazines and discussed the subject headings as clues to the exact contents of the articles themselves. Because of the students' deep involvement with the assassination, the unit became more than a simple classroom exercise.

One of the most exciting units to teach was the one on fairy tales and myths, which opens up the whole world of cultural history. We talked about what fairy tales are, what makes them meaningful, their national characteristics, translations, and abridgements. Seventh and eighth graders are so close to that openly magic world, if not still in it, that their experience provides ready examples and metaphors. We examined the tales of the brothers Grimm—the editions, the etymological origin, and the movie; and Shirley Temple and her TV mutilations, to cite just two illustrations.

The ninth graders were studying Edith Hamilton's Mythology in their English classes. The approach used for them was to enlarge on the idea of comparative mythology, defining a myth as a truth told in an untrue way, and relating myth to science and history. In these classes, fairy tales lost some of their present day stigma of "kid stuff," and many of the girls, pressured by their peers, took the plunge into this world where mysticism and magic illuminate truth. Fairy tales and classics, as well as the Bible, also successfully demonstrate variant editions, translation, textual criticism, preservation of manuscripts, language levels.

Language, indeed, seemed to be the context where young minds might best be excited. The teaching of language skills is the formal prerogative of the English department. But because language is inherent in all subject areas, there is a responsibility for its consideration wherever words are used to teach. The double grade for content and form is a well-known tool. History and science teachers should be aware of this and should, therefore, cooperate in the language education of students. Nevertheless, with the word-poor state of school children today, overcrowded classes, and the present conflicts and ambiguities in the teaching of formal language, the convention is honored in a near vacuum.

In the library, starting with the cliché that words are communication, we could enhance the students' awareness that words have power. (The child who says to the parent of another child, "Jim is a brat," has learned it very soon!) By getting students to set up real-life situations, and then, by working up dialogue for them on different levels of speech, I could make much of the power of words and the nuances of

181

connotation clear to them. In one exercise, the class wrote
"I love you" in all the ways they could think of. Everyone
from the Beatles to C. S. Lewis came into the subsequent
discussion, which ended with one girl carrying off Lewis'
Four Kinds of Love.
  A visiting lecturer, Mrs. Harold Kelleran, of the Virginia Theological Seminary, put the Bible in its historical
context for the students. A young adult librarian in the area
illumined the students' relationship to the public library.
(Thus, I drew on the vast resources of Washington, and often
invited speakers to talk on a subject we were studying.) Following up the lecture on the Bible, I was intrigued by the
multitude of concepts in the area of history of books and language that could be taught by a librarian in a course like this.
In another exercise I had the girls in half of the group write
a sentence on any subject, using the most complicated words
they knew, and the other half translated them into simple English. Then, through mimeographed sheets with three translations of First Corinthians, Verse Thirteen, I traced changes
in the language from the Elizabethan period of the King James
Bible to the contemporary language of the New English Bible.
  In history and geography, I taught research skills, and
the comparison of authorities, through current course work.
When the girls were studying the typography of fiords and
glaciers, I brought in the Life World Library of Books, the
Larousse Encyclopedia of the Earth, Van Nostrand's Scientific Encyclopedia, and other works. These references tied in
with my "reference tools" unit, in which I presented the idea
of varying coverage in encyclopedias by having them check
World Book against Americana and Britannica—the same exercise we used in library school when we were doing original
cataloging and needed authorities. With the ninth grade, different versions of word usage were covered. "Why do we
have more than one dictionary? What is American English?
English English?"
  I do not mean to downgrade traditional instruction in library skills. There is a variety of literature and published

material in the area of formal instruction in "use of the library." Moreover, there are an abundance of audiovisual techniques that seem most natural, and most illuminating, here. The opaque projector can enable clearer presentation than can the blackboard of title pages, the mysteries of Dewey, and subject headings. There are excellent filmstrips available on the use of encyclopedias and the history of the alphabet. Colored slides are ideal for graphic presentation of manuscripts, scrolls, and other subjects related to the history of books and libraries.

But the challenge of teaching comes when the traditional concepts have been expanded through work with teachers, in a kind of on-the-job training, to apply these skills to foster skepticism and a spirit of inquiry.

35. SCHOOL LIBRARIANS AND TEACHERS

Edna S. Macon

"You are not a teacher. You are supposed to take care of the books!" said a self-assured senior boy to his librarian. Of course, this boy does not represent an average attitude of Kentucky's high school seniors. Or does he? Such a statement gives pause for consideration of the teaching role of the school librarian.

Our administrators persist in the conviction that the library is an integral part of the high school program. Our teachers perform a commendable library service as evidenced prominently by the swarms of students searching daily for assignment answers. The administrators are convinced, the teachers are sold, but do the students understand

where the librarian stands? Have we as librarians done our
share of teaching and leading the student into a worthwhile
working knowledge of the use of library materials?

Surely, we as librarians must do no less than present
ourselves as much an integral part of the teaching staff of
a high school as any other teaching member of the faculty.
This teaching need is felt by concerned young people. A
1960 Kentucky high school graduate, now a college freshman,
refers to her high school librarian as always being "so helpful." "How many times she has gone to the shelf, gotten the
book and turned to the right page for information that I
wanted," and then she added, "I didn't know how to begin in
the college library." A Kentucky college librarian observed
that the average college freshman is "so ill-prepared" in the
use of the library. Is the allegation, "You are not a teacher.
You are supposed to take care of the books," in part, then
true?

Oh, but we give library lessons to all freshmen in our
school, we say. Then we try to rationalize that the library
process must begin in the elementary school, and we have
no elementary libraries in our school system. Why, half my
time is spent helping the students find materials for assignments! Rubbish! It appears that we high school librarians
have become so infested with the "helpful habit" that we are
graduating seniors with a full-fledged HELPLESS diploma
in library education. There should be a limit. Where did
this "helpful habit" get the high school graduate who went
helplessly into a college library unarmed with practical
knowledge in the basic principles of library use? Librarians must be helpful, true; but helpfulness is only one phase
of the versatile mission of the school librarian and entails
more than spoon feeding the student with desired information. We are also responsible for the formal and informal
instruction in wise and competent use of library resources.
The formal portion of teaching can easily be fulfilled by a
mere quirk of lesson planning and scheduling, or by integrating projects with the use of the library as the need arises.

However, often formal instruction is limited by student absences and lack of opportunity for immediate application of taught principles, resulting in student library inadequacy.

Informal and individual teaching is just as vital to the library learning process as formal teaching. It is probably the most often demanded, comes at the most inopportune time and, no doubt, is the most time-consuming ration of the instructional procedure.

It is much easier for the librarian to refer the student who wants information about George Eliot to page 334 of the Cyclopedia of World Authors than to invest the time required in explaining to him the trite simplicity of the card catalog and the arrangement of shelves, meagerly stocked though they be. This becomes especially trying if we are already busily engaged in compiling a bibliography for a teacher, or cataloging a back-log of books. But the student deserves this explanation however time-consuming it may be. Even though he may make errors, he learns by the supervised trial and error method, on an individual basis, at his own speed. Thus, the instruction becomes meaningful.

It takes a few steps back to the shelves to look for $\frac{R}{928}$.

The student returns with $\frac{R}{928}$, Twentieth Century Authors.

Lo, and behold, George Eliot is not there. Back to the card catalog and AUTHORS, ENGLISH; but this time the author and title, though previously explained, becomes as necessary as the call number. A long trying process, yes, but how rewarding to hear the student say, referring to the card catalog, "And that's how that thing works. Well, I'll be!"

Not only does the student learn by the informal and individual type of teaching but it is economical because it minimizes the number of students who can not use the library independently. It saves immediate time to trace an article by Jesse Stuart in the Reader's Guide for the student, but what has he learned about using the Reader's Guide? Just think how much time has been wasted because the same time-consuming process must be repeated each time that student must use periodical literature references.

In addition to the economical advantage of individual instruction, it satisfies that intrinsic urge in young people to be independent. The pride displayed by young people upon learning to be independent in the library is sufficient evidence of their appreciation.

Our high school students are young people who read when there are no assignments in reading, they read fiction and non-fiction, anything from mystery stories to Indian Lore. They are also young people, who for the most part, will not go on to college; but they will be frequent visitors in our public libraries. Whether they go to a public, college, or special library they should enter with assurance that they can help themselves.

If we, as librarians, accept our responsibility as teachers and practice the art of teaching our young people to use the library effectively, then our students will see us as teachers. However, more important than this, they may enter any storehouse of knowledge with confidence that their quest for information will be rewarded through their own efforts.

36. DO-IT-YOURSELF TAPE RECORDING
FOR LIBRARY INSTRUCTION

Dorothy Ligda

Combine a teenager with a rock and roll record and something moves. Combine a do-it-yourself librarian, a graduate class needing a demonstration of audio-visual materials in the library, and the problem of instructing one thousand pupils a year in the use of the library, for a similar reaction. There may be a lot of unnecessary motion,

DO-IT-YOURSELF TAPE RECORDING

but there is a lot of satisfaction and fun in tape recording a library lesson.

In Pleasant Hill Intermediate School, we introduce the library to new seventh graders each year, as they enter our schools. Since we have seventh and eighth grades gathered from many elementary schools, the background information of the pupils differs considerably. One constant factor is a lack of assurance as they try to orient themselves to a new school. We try to build a feeling of ease in use of the library facilities at the beginning of each year.

Because of a limited budget, the school is allowed two-thirds of a librarian. To meet the need for a librarian in constant attendance, she teaches library science to all seventh grades in regularly scheduled classes. Thus, one-third of the librarian's salary comes directly from the teaching budget. This plan serves a multiple purpose: it keeps the library within its budget, it insures a person present to care for the collection of 5,000 books, and it helps our seventh graders learn to make good use of their school library.

Since all 17 seventh grades can not be given the library course at the beginning of the year, it becomes important that all new students receive a uniform introduction to the library as soon as possible. To accomplish this, we decided to try a tape recording. Next problem: What, Who, Where, When, and How to record.

A top-notch seventh grade group and a similar eighth grade, with teachers who were interested in creative work, were consulted. They were approached with the idea of writing and producing the script for a tape recording which would give introductory library instruction. Their cooperation was immediate and they carried the idea through to the completed tapes in use now.

Similar methods were used with each group. The problem was presented to the boys and girls by the librarian, who asked for their ideas on what should be explained to the students entering school the next year. From their ideas, collected in an oral discussion session, the script was written,

187

LIGDA

the actors chosen, and the recording made by the pupils in the class under the guidance of their teacher and the librarian.

Interesting facts became apparent as the discussions and work progressed. There was a unanimous feeling that humor must be incorporated into the script (i.e. the classic line, "Come to the card catalog with me.") Connecting musical passages, emphasis on the card catalog as a tool, and a feeling that the librarian should be included to welcome the students to the library, were other ideas. As the script evolved, the characterization of the librarian as a busy and sometimes unintelligible person came from the pupils. They said they had felt lost and confused until they learned to know the library and the librarian. They hoped to show the new students they weren't alone, that this feeling of inadequacy would pass as they became accustomed to library techniques.

When the script had been written and rehearsed by the cast, the mechanical problems of recording were considered. Some things to keep in mind are listed at the end of this article.

With "What To Say" and "Who To Say It" taken care of, "Where, When, and How" to use the tape were considered. Student librarians are trained to take the recording to each new class during the first week of school. The librarian arranges with the major core teachers for use of one half hour of time. As the self-introducing tape is played, the student librarian displays cartoon posters at the strategic moment. After the tape is played, pupils are given a short test to see how much information is retained. The tests can be corrected by each pupil, using a mimeographed page of library information given to keep in his notebook.

We feel we have found a solution to the problem of uniformly introducing the library to our new students. We think we have done it in a way that will encourage them to come to the library.

Now we are looking forward to making another recording to use with the eighth grades. This tape would review

DO-IT-YOURSELF TAPE RECORDING

the library lessons learned in the seventh grade, and point
out a few especially valuable reference materials for use in
the eighth grade.

We are considering other possibilities for use of tape
to vary the pattern of lessons given in the library.

Since this type of lesson must be a do-it-yourself project to fit your own situation, why not try a home-made tape
for some of your library lessons. Choose a lesson that you
are tired of repeating. Ask for help. Young people are
eager to be of assistance, to try something new. Let them
guide you as you guide them. Put on that rock and roll
record, and move.

Mechanics of Recording

Machine: Wollensak Tape Recorder
Tape: Mylar tape. Difficult to break: Withstands wear and
tear.
Controls: Set as recommended in directions for particular
machine. We used Treble setting to give greater flexibility of tone control when playing back.
Background Noise Control: Arrange for room to be as silent
as possible. Things to consider:
1. Notify office you are recording, so incoming mes-
sages will be held.
2. Sign on door, "Recording, do not interrupt."
3. Watch time for bells, change of classes.
4. No paper script pages that need turning.
5. Cast warned about feet, hand movements.
6. Microphone in a stationary position.
Casting: Voices must differ enough to keep the characteriza-
tions separate. Listen for:
1. Pronunciation
2. Enunciation
3. Timing. Be sure cast talks slowly.
4. Spacing. Be sure time is given after humorous epi-
sodes for laughter to subside, without losing an important piece of information.
5. Music—fade in, fade out.

37. A WORKSHOP PROJECT ON USING THE ELEMENTARY SCHOOL LIBRARY

Hilda P. Shufro

How can teachers in the elementary school make use of the school library and the services of a school librarian in planning a unit of study? This was the topic of an in-service workshop in which fifteen teachers from the Paramus, New Jersey, elementary schools participated in the spring of 1963. Its stated purpose was: "To assist teachers to use the various resources in the library in planning class units and student projects; and to develop 'library power' in teachers . . . which would eventually develop in pupils . . . ."

The eight-session workshop was sponsored by the Paramus Board of Education as part of the in-service program under the general direction of the Assistant Superintendent of Schools, and offered points on the salary guide to teachers involved. The system's three elementary school librarians served as leaders, and one of them was chairman. The workshop opened with the presentation of a set of color slides depicting a pilot program that had been carried out the previous spring by a fourth-grade teacher in close cooperation with her elementary librarian.

THE PILOT PROGRAM

The purpose of the pilot program was to show how a unit of study can be enriched when the resources of the school library are tapped and when librarian and teacher work together. The topic of the sample unit of study was India. The librarian and the teacher felt that some children who might not be readily motivated through the usual classroom resources might be reached through the varied materials of the library and the combined efforts of librarian and teacher.

190

WORKSHOP PROJECT

During the six-week period over which the study of India was spread, there were extra visits to the library and a steady flow of books and materials between classroom and library. There were story hours, extra lessons in library skills, new books and sources acquired, and, most important, conferences between teacher and librarian, children and librarian, and children and teacher. A final activity, in the school's multipurpose room, represented Mrs. Kennedy on a trip through India, giving each child in the class an opportunity to contribute the results of his own research.

The outcomes of the pilot program served as motivation for the teachers who were participating in the workshop. Among them were listed:

1. A genuine feeling for the people and the way of life in India.
2. An opportunity to develop critical thinking and analysis.
3. Enjoyment of the library.
4. Increased confidence and skill in using the library.
5. Ability to communicate material to the rest of the class.
6. Ability to incorporate information from several sources into one report.
7. A desire on the part of the children to help India solve some of her problems.
8. The success achieved by individual children, because of the varied resources, the time made available, and the willingness of both the teacher and the librarian to be of help.
9. The enjoyment received from studying a topic in depth.
10. The familiarity with the resource material gained by the teacher, and the discovery that this enhanced and fortified her natural creativity.

After the showing of the slides, discussion centered on the joint role of librarian and teacher in making subject matter come alive for children in third through sixth grades. Some of the questions asked were:

"How will we find time to work in such depth?"

191

"Will slower children be able to handle the research method?"

"How can we avoid their copying from encyclopedias?"

"Will this research reading make it harder to get children to read for pleasure?"

"How can individual library research be successfully shared with the rest of the class in ways other than the traditional written report?"

LEARNING TO USE THE LIBRARY

During the next two sessions the mysteries of the card catalog, the secrets hidden in more than a hundred reference books (not encyclopedias), and the keys to periodical literature were presented, with special regard to their use in the elementary curriculum.

Workshop members were given sets of questions whose answers involved selection, searching, and consequent evaluation of the reference books. They were also given practice in using subject headings in the card catalog, and tracked down specific magazine items in the Abridged Reader's Guide and the Subject Index to Children's Magazines. They examined a variety of indexes to children's literature, anthologies, book-selection aids, and special bibliographies. The role of non-printed materials was briefly discussed.

The fourth and fifth sessions were highlighted by displays and discussion of resources available for three sample units: (1) Middle Ages, for which our libraries are particularly rich in material; (2) the solar system, including both easy and more difficult material; and (3) Russia, for which there is not much obvious material. The librarians also demonstrated the possibilities in more general sources, such as folklore, fiction, poetry, biography, books on arts and crafts, music, games, and food, atlases, and magazine articles.

The teachers found especially interesting, too, a discussion of the use of pamphlets, recordings, filmstrips, realia, class trips, and resource persons. They were enthusiastic over the variety of motivating materials for reluctant learners, the challenging materials for the bright pupils, and the possibilities for all children to make discoveries and contribute to the group.

PUTTING NEW LEARNINGS INTO ACTION

One stipulation of the workshop was that each teacher put into operation a four-week unit in science or social studies with her own class. Some topics selected for such units were electrical principles, an Arabian dinner, a visitor from Egypt, an Israeli water dance, and preparation for planting a tree.

For the next two sessions, the group divided into three sections, each using a different school library under the leadership of one of the librarians. The school libraries were beehives of activity, and the public library was used as well. One fourth-grade teacher reported that sixty-seven books were borrowed for class use, in addition to the many borrowed for home reading.

THE FINAL SESSION AND EVALUATION

The entire group met again six weeks later for a last session to describe and evaluate their experiences. According to reports, the pupils were eager to discover information in new ways. A result frequently mentioned was that children wanted to share information and to help one another find and use material. (The teachers themselves seemed to welcome an opportunity to share professional experiences.)

A questionnaire elicited varied responses. All the teachers reported that because of their own added library knowledge, their pupils were reading more. Ten of the fifteen teachers indicated that individual children had been especially motivated or challenged. In general, the workship participants had found answers to their initial questions, as the potentials of the school library unfolded before them.

They realized that, with the wealth of varied types of material available, they could guide slower children to sources that were rewarding.

They discovered that knowledge of many kinds of reference books lessened dependence on encyclopedias alone, and that learning to extract and understand important information is more relevant than the question of copying.

Their concern about fostering general reading was alleviated as they found that good literature related to units of study can be read for sheer enjoyment.

They were encouraged to devise schemes for coordinating varied individual and group abilities and interests in exciting projects which could replace formal written reports.

Perhaps the most valuable outcome of the workshop was the rapport that it created between teachers and librarians. Keeping the librarian informed about class projects, and drawing on her special training for assistance, became a basic aspect of the total search for knowledge in these teachers' classrooms.

Author's Note: Copies of the slides, narration, and text of the "India Project" are now available on loan from Miss Ann Voss, State School Library Consultant, New Jersey Department of Education, Jersey and Labor Streets, Trenton, N.J.

38. TEACHING LIBRARY PRACTICE TO THE LOW I.Q.'s

Griff L. Jones

The average Librarian and teacher presupposes that
library practice cannot be taught to students in the ranges
70–85 I.Q.
An analysis of the needs of children at this level, their
educational backgrounds, their abilities can enable the librarian, with the help of the teacher of these groups, to
reach these children for they can be taught the fundamentals of library usage, such as using the card catalog, using
reference books, and finding library materials.

Two experimental programs in the teaching of library
usage to low intelligence levels were carried out in Philadelphia at Woodrow Wilson Junior High School by the author,
aided by Murray Karsh, a teacher, and at the Kensington
High School for Girls assisted by Dr. Woodman Huplits, a
teacher.

The junior high school provides an excellent opportunity for the teaching of this low level group. Classes are
generally of the block-roster type and the children may be
assigned a regular day and time to the library.

Planning of the program is important and contributes
greatly to the success of the program. The teaching vocabulary must be revised down to the average level of the group.
The teaching time unit must be revised downward to accom-
modate the average span of attention of this group. Overex-
tension of the teaching vocabulary and of the teaching time
unit can lead to defeat. A general practice is to divide the
units into sublessons of approximately five minutes each,
teaching and practicing each unit until the student grasps
the knowledge offered.

ADAPTING QUESTIONS

The librarian must also recognize the low reading level of the group and prepare test questions that will be understood by the group. It has been found that these students will do better on tests that require a high reading ability if it is administered orally since the inability of the student to read the question will affect the score, and in many cases the students may know the answer.

The librarian and teacher may start in the junior high school with lessons on the use and care of the book and the card catalog. In the senior high school assume temporarily that the student has a knowledge of the use and care of the book, and begin with the card catalog tying it in with use and care and follow up with a lesson on the book.

In teaching card catalog, approach reality, use samples of cards found in your own library. You may use oversize catalog cards prepared especially for this lesson. Teach only the vitally necessary information that can be used by the student such as call number, author, title, subject cards, "see" cards, "see also" cards, information about copyright date, publisher, paging. Analytics are difficult to teach to this group and should be avoided.

On a test on the card catalog by forty-two students at Kensington High School, the following results: Range 32 to 100, Mean 61.9, Median 62, Mode 72, two-thirds of the group had scores between 50 and 80; possible number of points 108; 3 students had scores of 96 or better, 9 scores below 50. The test is the same test that is given to students of higher intelligence, but does not differ greatly in scoring from that of the higher group.

Mr. Karsh uses a research unit at Wilson Junior High School on states in the Union. The students are divided into committees of about five students who work together on one state. A chairman is elected, and this chairman has the responsibility of selecting encyclopedias, using and directing his group to the card catalog, and obtaining books on the state.

For instance, students working on Pennsylvania would be given encyclopedias that contain information on the state. They would also take out books on that state, compiling a booklist of materials in the library of those books.

The students then compare the various encyclopedias as to the information contained in the article such as population, capital, products, area, etc. They use multiple-volume and single-volume encyclopedias. The teacher and the librarian work closely with the group to help them interpret their findings.

The students enjoy looking up information and are particularly thrilled at being able to find it. Laboratory problems should be simple and geared to the educational needs of the students. If the students understand the problem and are given adequate help they are able to solve it easily and are rewarded by their efforts.

Most of these students recognize their own limitations, and the program should be based on this. Reading should be encouraged and students should be made aware of materials available at their reading level and interest. Books should be purchased for this group as part of the total instructional program.

A close relationship of the teacher and the librarian working as a team will help to make this program successful.

39. LIBRARY INSTRUCTION IN THE SECONDARY SCHOOL

Frederic R. Hartz

The disappearance of the "textbook course" has placed an ever increasing emphasis on the adequacy and accessibility of library materials. The secondary school that has both adequate and accessible library facilities as well as a trained professional librarian has two significant assets for learning; but these assets alone will not guarantee that the library will be used to its greatest advantage. In order to get the most out of the whole secondary experience, in order to survive academically, the student must have a knowledge of the use of the library. Unless he possesses this skill before he enters college or concludes his education on the secondary level he may attain it too late.

It is interesting and indeed thought-provoking to note that one third of all that we know came into being before the year 1400; another third of the world's knowledge was discovered between 1400 and 1900; and the final third of today's knowledge is the product of the twentieth century's 65 years. The world has never known such a rapid proliferation of knowledge. It is estimated that every 24 hours enough research papers alone are turned out around the world to fill seven sets of the Encyclopedia Britannica—to say nothing of the books being written and other forms of publications. In fact, information specialists believe that the quantity of information is doubling every 10 years.

The secondary school library that expects to serve its readers, and especially faculty, must attempt to keep up with this geometric growth in facts and ideas and to transmit this accumulation of knowledge to new generations. The library's major concern should be with developing a pattern of habits

198

that will lead the individual to information sources that verify or extend his knowledge. At all levels of education, moreover, new knowledge must be promptly transmitted to students and to the faculty community. It must be verified and made meaningful in relation to existing knowledge. The quickened pace of discovery requires an equally accelerated rate of transmission, unless much of the investment in research is to be wasted through duplication. At best, no single library could ever hope to acquire the written records of all new-found knowledge, there are too many recorded experiences and too many needs to be dealt with, so that the needs of every student can never fully be met.

Regardless of these limitations, there still remains for the secondary-school library the responsibility of meeting most student needs; providing the library instruction necessary to assure the student that he has exhausted his first available source of information before leaving his own school to explore neighboring school, college, public, and research libraries.

The secondary school student should possess several basic library skills to enable him to enter into the natural pursuit of the curriculum. He should be able to locate library materials through the card catalog, periodical indices, and printed bibliographies with a degree of proficiency that will allow him to expand his intellectual horizons through independent study. Secondly, he should have a basic knowledge of encyclopedias, special dictionaries, yearbooks, manuals, almanacs, biographical and geographical sources, and the proper manner in which to use these books for purposes of reference.

Virtually all secondary schools offer their students some type of preplanned instruction in basic library skills. The prime objective of this instruction should be to develop in the student a "self-contained ability to take advantage of the multiple services of the library . . . a competency which permits him to accomplish the independent study and research required of him in his future as a scholar, or, where college experience is not his future, will qualify him to gain lifelong satisfactions through the public library, sometimes called the people's university."

The responsibility for the planning and execution of the instruction is largely the librarian's and can be either formal or informal in its approach. Whatever the form, the following four considerations will influence either method to a great degree: (1) the need for a six-year continuing program, one not limited merely to an orientation in the seventh grade; (2) increased school enrollments; (3) new media of communication; and (4) increased emphasis on the individual student. These four major considerations must be incorporated into the concept of instruction, while still preserving the basic objectives of the program.

Library skills are most often taught completely isolated from the other learning experiences of students. Pupils find themselves assigned to weekly lectures in the library covering such topics as the Dewey Decimal classification, card catalog, and reference books. Devised to give library instruction just once during one's secondary school career, the lectures are burdened with detail and innumerable reference citations, trying to give students in one or two lecture hours what librarians have learned in one or more years of professional training. Students find it difficult to take adequate notes to enable them later to coordinate the lectures into a meaningful experience.

Librarians agree that this type of library instruction is not the most effective and that present formal instruction must be revitalized to include a more realistic approach to course content and presentation and improve the "what, when, and how" of the instructional presentation: What should be taught? When should it be taught? How should it be taught?

If formal instruction is used, the first phase should acquaint the student with the physical arrangement of the library, the rules and regulations, and the special collections, and it should fix in his mind the general location of all major resources. Students should have an opportunity to meet the staff and browse through the stacks, —actually see the vast amount of material available. This first phase of instruction should be a generally pleasant introduction to the "why and what" of the library rather than to the "how to use it."

Phase two, including methodical instruction in the use of the library, could begin when the need arises, logically at the beginning of a specific research project. This would be the time to give detailed instruction on the use of the card catalog, including treatment of the more important filing rules, newspaper and periodical indices, selected reference works and a general introduction to the more important reference sources. This phase can be effectively illustrated by a series of displays, strategically placed throughout the library.

Phase three of a realistic program would naturally be a continuation of phase two, but it would be geared to the needs of advanced students. Juniors and seniors enrolled in accelerated and honors classes are at the peak of their need for advanced reference tools. Courses revolve around the more individual study reported in term and research papers. If instruction is given only once in a student's secondary school career—during seventh or eighth grade— by the time he enters senior high school he has forgotten independent library procedures. Instruction for junior and senior students should include the use of specialized reference tools, not only the more general information sources but also the authorities and their contribution to the field being studied. Advanced library reference instruction, therefore, has a positive place within the current framework of accelerated and honors classes.

Certainly a continuous six-year instructional program is the ideal, but too few secondary school libraries have the staff for this. Giving library instruction to hundreds of students is a monotonous and stultifying experience, consuming staff hours which could be put to more fruitful use. It has been suggested, from time to time, that the faculty could assume some of the instructional responsibility. Teacher instruction taking the form of promoting various degrees of student inquiry; emphasis upon research skills as contrasted to the pedantic required book reports. Librarians are sympathetic to these teacher promoted, research-demanding techniques mainly because they fill the library with students. There is some concern, however, whether teachers and librarians fully comprehend the evolution and consequences of research-demanding activities. Developing investigative competencies in secondary school students raises some questions from teachers and librarians:

1. Are faculty members convinced of the need for having children develop these skills and abilities?
2. Have these skills and understandings been spelled out?
3. Have channels of communication among teachers and between teachers and librarians been cleared so that each knows what the other is doing?
4. Do teachers and librarians have some time and place during the day to work together?
5. Are library materials selected by librarians, after an analysis of teacher and pupil needs and objectives?
6. Is the schedule of the library flexible enough for students to visit it as needed?

There is evidence to indicate that few of these questions concerning investigative competencies are taken seriously by either teachers or librarians.

Only one librarian in four is sufficiently familiar with the classroom activities of her school to analyze the teaching methods employed. Similarly, fewer than one librarian in five visits academic classrooms for planning with students. Also, on the average, the entire faculty in these same schools consumes less than one-half class period per week in curriculum planning with the librarian. Furthermore, librarians, only superficially acquainted with the details of the school's instructional program, have to select the library's supply of new instruction materials because teachers fail to make their needs known.

LIBRARY INSTRUCTION IN THE SECONDARY SCHOOL

Since a majority of the faculty themselves have to be prodded into making better use of the library, it is doubtful whether they could stimulate better student use. In most cases staff, funds, and time for formal library instruction are still provided by the library organization.

The need for a formal six-year program coupled with ever increasing enrollments necessitates a better method of transmission. Larger secondary schools may use closed circuit television for teaching the use of the library. A series of television programs would certainly conserve staff. The librarian presenting the program would have to work harder in preparing the presentation, but several hundred students could be reached in one class hour by one staff member. Additionally, television has a number of advantages as compared to the usual platform lecture and blackboard demonstration:

1. The television screen and the scenes depicted on it tend to draw and hold attention to the exclusion of anything that might be going on elsewhere.
2. Demonstration materials—catalog cards, books, or other display material—can be made clearly visible to every member of the audience by enlarging the object before the cameras to any desired size.
3. The possibility exists, when cost is not prohibitive, of video-taping a complete series of lectures. This would eliminate the yearly preparation for the lectures, thus further conserving staff, time, and funds.

Another concept geared to the formal approach is the use of instructional films and filmstrips on the use of the library. A program based on film media would include:

A set of filmstrips on basic library skills for secondary school students, covering such topics as using the card catalog, classification systems, use of various reference tools, subject heading approach to knowledge, and writing research papers.
A film on the general principles of using college and university libraries for research for high school students

planning to enter college. This film would review the basic minimum library skills and introduce resources and skills needed by college students.

A film to motivate students to use the library, designed for use with secondary school students early in the instructional program. This film should leave the audience with the feeling that the library is an important place for them.

Films suitable for implementing this program are suggested in the annotated bibliography.

Thus far we have concerned ourselves with group instruction, stressing the need for formally presenting instructional material effectively and interestingly to large numbers of students at one time. But is this formal unsolicited instruction as valuable as the casual contacts during which learning may occur? Should the secondary school assume the responsibility for formally teaching the use of the library or should librarians provide the best service to the student who presents himself voluntarily for instruction? So many times we hear students remark: "Why weren't we told sooner?" or "If I'd only known this before I wrote my paper." Perhaps the students would have known sooner or would have known before writing his paper, if he had taken it upon himself to find out.

Lack of staff, limited time for preparation and administration of orientation courses, and diversity of subject matter are going to place more of the burden upon the student. Library instruction will become dependent upon the informal conference between student and librarian. The teaching will be done by conversation and example and by directing the student's attention to the library materials which will have immediate interest for him. By finding and identifying the facts demanded, the student teaches himself the function and limitations of each informational aid. The student engaged individually gains the sense of satisfaction and achievement that comes only through independent effort. The pressure of increased enrollments on librarians and faculty means that students will have to learn to work independently and at a higher level of skill.

Independent student research is not a harsh escape from the dilemma of group instruction but rather a sensible continuation of present secondary school curriculum practices. Tomorrow's secondary school students will have access to better and more adequate library facilities. Hopefully, many students will leave school with at least an introductory knowledge in using the card catalog, dictionaries, encyclopedias, periodical indexes, miscellaneous references, and, in general, in how to use books. The library will then truly become the core of the educational system, the heart of the school, the cultural center of the campus, the citizen's university, or whatever else it may so glibly be called today.

40. TEACHING CORRELATED LESSONS IN THE VOCATIONAL HIGH SCHOOL LIBRARY

Lillian L. Shapiro

When I left the academic division to come into a vocational high school the farewell tendered me by my colleagues was somewhat like a wake. The general impression was that the vocational schools were filled with juvenile delinquents who would rather be dead than caught reading a book!

Nothing could be farther from the truth. We do have, perhaps, a greater percentage of problem students and many more reading problems but, on the whole, these boys and girls are fairly normal adolescents—if that is not a contradiction of terms.

There are at least two factors in the vocational school which must influence the type of library service and teaching

which is to be given. First of all, these students are in an
atmosphere of formal education for the last time in their
lives. Very few of them will go on to college or technical
schools. Secondly, their backgrounds are of that socio-eco-
nomic nature which is not especially bookminded. This is
the last opportunity to instill in them a continuing interest
in books and to teach them some library techniques which
may stand them in good stead as future public library patrons.

RECREATION

I see the role of the vocational high school librarian as
a threefold teaching responsibility. First, we must buy
heavily of those recreational titles in sports, hobbies, and
teen-age romance which will motivate them to read and
which will show our students the profit and pleasure to be
derived from books.

GUIDANCE

The second phase of our teaching—and this is a principle to which I am strongly committed—is one of guidance.
So much of our relationship with the students is on a personal basis. There is no barrier of grades or formal classroom atmosphere between the librarian and student and, for
that reason, you learn much that is wonderful—and heart-
breaking—about many of the boys and girls from their first
year in high school up through the last semester. Possibly
it is more like the Y.M.C.A. or a lonely hearts club than a
library some days—but that's good! With this opportunity
to know the individual well comes the responsibility to guide
him not only in reading but also in his social and educational problems. I do not mean to infer that we may take
the place of the school's guidance counselor or college adviser but we do have the chance to pick up information and
relay it to the expert when necessary.

TECHNIQUES

The third teaching function is, of course, the training in specific library techniques. We try to make this teaching as practical as possible. In the first year our students are given exploratory courses in all the shop subjects available to them. Early in their first term they are given an orientation lesson in the library which presents the library as one of their shops. Just as each shop they visit has its unique tools, so does the library!

Also in this first year we teach our students how to use the card catalog—mainly as a subject index to books needed in their shop classes. The lesson is given in the library during a shop period. In the first part of this lesson the catalog is presented and large sample cards are displayed and explained. The second part of the lesson, which may take place immediately after the presentation or may be scheduled for later in the week, consists of having each student locate a book on the shelf via the catalog. For this laboratory period —and what a mad time it is!—every catalog tray is out on the library tables and each student has a problem. The questions are planned so that each drawer has no more than two students working at it. The student locates a subject in a tray, notes the call number, and then finds the book on the shelf. There is enough activity to keep the librarian and teacher hopping the entire period and some of the better students may also help in checking on the others in the class.

SECOND AND THIRD YEARS

In the second year, when world history is studied, the lesson on the encyclopedia is given in connection with some topic covered in the social studies curriculum, for example, the French Revolution or imperialism. (Every attempt is made to teach our lessons through classes other than English because too often the library is considered simply an adjunct of the English department. It is essential that the faculty and student body both be made aware that the library belongs to the whole school.)

In the third year, when economics is included in the course of study, we feel that the Readers' Guide may be taught to good advantage. This is particularly effective in the unit on consumer education. The classes see the practicality of checking on products in magazines like Consumers' Reports, Consumers' Research Bulletin, and Parents' magazine. So many of the families of the students may be planning the purchase of some household appliance and a large number of the students themselves are prospective buyers—particularly of used cars which they hope to turn into super-special hot-rods.

SENIOR YEAR

In the senior year, either through English or American History, we present sources of biographical information. At this point we review such library tools as the card catalog and the encyclopedia and add to those a few special titles like Who's Who, Who's Who in America, Current Biography, and Twentieth Century Authors. No attempt is made to list every available reference which the library owns. Always, in teaching these lessons, we go beyond the particular topic which motivated the lesson and point out the value of the library tool in connection with their outside interests—vocational or avocational.

These are the so-called traditional lessons, taught at that point in the course of study where they are immediately useful. Parallel with these lessons are those integrated lessons based on some big research topic. For example, a better-than-average class in physics may have some special project involving scientific terms, history, and scientists. For this class a lesson is presented which shows how all the resources of the library may be called into use—books, magazines, and pamphlets from the vertical file. The same kind of lesson has been given to our senior girls. So many of our girls marry at an early age, in fact shortly after graduation from high school, that a course in preparation for homemaking—including budgeting, interior decorating, child care, and so on, has been found to be of great practical value and the integrated library lesson again assembles all the sources of information for the class. What is more, we supply back issues of magazines for the scrapbooks which they prepare for their own future use. In our school we encourage the teachers of all departments to request these lessons as needed with some short advance notice—say, three periods!

There are some problems which militate against the absolutely smooth operation of library teaching. First there is the matter of scheduling. Since our students have no study periods, we schedule a library period for every English class once every three weeks. Therefore, we must program our library lessons for those periods when no English class is already in the library—if it is a lesson which must take place in the library. Whenever feasible, the lesson is taught in the regular classroom. The other major problem is the matter of teacher responsibility. I was being facetious before when I spoke of advance notice of three periods. Actually a library lesson should be planned long enough in advance so that it has its proper place in the development of a topic. The librarian likes to feel that the lesson was requested because it is essential to the subject content and not because some clerical work is due from the teacher that day and the teacher wants to be free to work on her records. Also, the teacher and librarian working together can determine if there is enough material of varying degrees of difficulty available for whatever the size of the class. If the teacher's attitude toward the library instruction is serious the class will be similarly disposed to it.

It is the hope, naturally, of all school librarians that their patrons will also be users of the public library and that aim is always kept in view in working with high school students. It is a source of never-ending pleasure to us that so many of our returning graduates make their first stop to visit the library. It is a constant reminder that we have made some wonderful friendships as well as many avid readers.

41. THE SCHOOL LIBRARY:
                    EACH TEACHER'S RESPONSIBILITY

Dorothy Roche

Recognizing the need for library instruction for all students, Belleville High School teachers assumed the responsibility of planning an effective program of library instruction. Principal and vice-principal gave the signal and it was "full speed ahead" in organizing a feasible course of study.

A committee of teachers representing all departments studied ways and means of helping students make more effective use of the school library. The committee felt, from its personal and classroom contact with the students, that there was a need for a thorough program of library instruction. How this could be accomplished—under crowded conditions and with the services of one librarian—was the problem.

The committee decided that the instruction planned by the librarian would be given in the English classes at all grade levels. The English teachers accepted the recommendation of this committee and made plans with the librarian to develop an effective program of library instruction.

SHARING RESPONSIBILITY

In planning this course, the English teachers felt that they had an opportunity to continue the reading improvement program in which the entire faculty participated last year. Certainly teaching students how to use library tools effectively is important in all subject areas. All teachers share the responsibility for helping students to learn how to use the library tools in their subject areas.

A bibliography of materials and a list of the filmstrips to be used for this instruction were made available to every teacher. The basic course of study was outlined by the librarian and in parentheses after each main topic it was indicated who was responsible for the major teaching of the unit. Of course, this was a suggested procedure only; the teachers were free to arrange with the librarian if they wished any changes in the method of instruction.

The freshman and sophomore classes received a very complete course in the use of the library. This instruction was begun by the librarian and continued by the English teacher and the subject teacher, using the text workbook, Exploring Libraries by Emmet Morris. All ten units in the text were covered in the freshman year. In the sophomore class special emphasis was placed on the uses of the card catalog and the Dewey decimal system and the special references. The junior instruction featured the use of the Readers' Guide to Periodical Literature and those other aids which would help them to prepare their term papers on careers. English 4 classes made extensive study for the preparation of a research paper and its bibliography, utilizing The Research Paper by Lucyle Hook and Mary Virginia Gaver.

At the close of the library instruction, each class made a trip to the public library.

Instruction of this nature will serve to promote good study habits in all subject areas; it will induce "free reading"; above all, it will give the student the "library habit."

<h2 style="text-align:center">LIBRARY INSTRUCTION OUTLINE</h2>

<h3 style="text-align:center">Introduction</h3>

The need for a thorough course in library instruction for each student is most evident. A good working knowledge of how to use the library tools available will benefit the student in many ways:

It will promote better study habits in all subject areas.

It will aid the student to solve his research problems.

It will help him to use these aids intelligently not only
during his high school days, but also in his future life.
It will give the student the "library habit."
It will induce "free reading."
It will promote "reading."
With the cooperation of the English teachers and other
members of the faculty, we hope to train all students in our
high school to make the utmost use of our high school library.

Below is an outline of the basic program of library instruction. In parentheses after each main topic is indicated
who is responsible for the major teaching of the unit. This
is a suggested procedure, only; teachers are free to arrange
with the librarian if they wish any changes in the method of
instruction.

Outline

I. THE BOOK (Classroom teacher)
   A. Origin of the book and early writing and printing
      of the book
   B. Parts of the book
II. DEWEY DECIMAL CLASSIFICATION (Librarian)
   A. Main classes of books—Fiction and Nonfiction
   B. Ten major classifications
   C. Main subdivisions
   D. More specific subject areas
   E. These are again subdivided
III. CARD CATALOG (Librarian)
   A. Subject card
   B. Title card
   C. Author card
   D. Author, title, and subject analytics
   E. Fiction and nonfiction cards
IV. DICTIONARY (Classroom teacher)
   A. Abridged
   B. Unabridged
   C. Parts of the dictionary

THE SCHOOL LIBRARY

   V. GENERAL REFERENCE BOOKS (Classroom teacher)
      Encyclopedias
  VI. ALMANACS AND YEARBOOKS (Classroom teacher)
 VII. BIOGRAPHICAL REFERENCES (Classroom teacher)
VIII. READERS' GUIDE TO PERIODICAL LITERATURE
      (Classroom teacher or librarian at the request of the
      classroom teacher)
  IX. PERIODICALS
     A. Current issues
     B. Back numbers
     C. Newspapers
     D. Bulletins
     E. Reports
   X. GAZETTEERS AND ATLASES
  XI. BIBLIOGRAPHY (Classroom teacher)
     A. Annotated bibliography
     B. Footnotes
     C. Abbreviations
    Classroom teachers are free to request assistance from
the librarian at any time.

42. HIGH SCHOOL LIBRARY INSTRUCTION

Gladys Barreto Spencer

Like Diogenes with his famous lantern, school librarians are continually trotting about seeking a really good way of instructing pupils in the use of library resources. Like Diogenes, too, we are unlikely to find what we want in any one form. What works today, fails tomorrow, and we tend to fall back in discouragement upon some form of the tried-and-found-wanting "library lesson" techniques.

SPENCER

Encouraged by the kind of administration that librarians dream of, we at our school have developed a flexible type of library program that is adapted to almost any situation. These are no formal library lessons. Whenever a pupil uses the library, he uses it as a means to accomplish a purpose which is important to him, and we take infinite pains to see that his work leaves him with a feeling of great personal satisfaction in his achievement. The results have been successful beyond our greatest hope in most cases.

We began this program by making it as easy as possible for the teacher to encourage the use of library resources. Since there is no freshman class in this school, one week had previously been set aside in sophomore English for library instruction. We therefore started our work with second year English students. Material formerly divided into library lessons was outlined under such headings as "Parts of Books," "Dictionaries," "Encyclopedias," "Biographical Reference Works," "Indexes to Poetry and Other Literature," "Geographical Information," "Vertical File," "Finding Magazine Material," "Use of Card Catalog," and "Making a Bibliography." A brief description of each reference book in that class was given, along with points of special importance to be noted. Following each division was listed a number of suggested uses for that reference book in the English curriculum. These suggestions were very definite—for example, under "Geographical Information" it was suggested that the route followed by Ulysses be traced upon a map; that the birthplace of George Eliot be located on a map and a description of the place compared with her description of Raveloe.

The same sort of outline was drawn up for the study of American history, with the suggestions based directly upon the history course. Copies of the material were given to all history and English teachers, and they were asked to keep it in a place convenient for quick reference.

HIGH SCHOOL LIBRARY INSTRUCTION

READING CAMPAIGN

The second large step in our program has been a planned reading campaign. Several of the English teachers have put a great deal of stress upon the reading program. At the beginning of the term, pupils were encouraged to talk freely about their interests and hobbies. It was suggested (not required) that instead of making book reports on whatever book came to hand, they read on subjects in which they were interested. The pupils were sent to the library in groups of three for personal conferences with the librarian, who placed fiction, biography, or nonfiction before them, all the books on that subject suitable for the reading level they might expect to attain. The pupil, after browsing a bit, made a list of books that he planned to use for book reports during the term. Most of them, of course, found that they wanted to read more than the three required.

Each pupil gave the teacher a copy of his list, with the understanding that he might change it simply by notifying the teacher that he had made a substitute choice. In one class that used this planned reading program, about half the group read all the books listed before the end of the first six weeks, only two read the minimum number of required books for the term, and several voluntarily read as many as fifteen books. Our greatest thrill came when a girl who had previously never voluntarily read a whole book, asked for permission to take out four books at once. We had found what she was interested in, and from that point on our only task was to see that her taste and ability matured.

History, science, language, and commercial teachers have been provided with lists of books which would be helpful to their pupils, and have been constantly reminded to bring these to the attention of students. Those instructors who used the lists, based on what they were teaching in history and consisting of the best of new fiction or biography, to encourage vacation reading during Christmas, will testify that the results were well worth the librarian's time in drawing up the lists and theirs in putting over the idea of worth-while reading.

The vocational guidance counselors use the school library widely. When tests show that a student's abilities fit him for certain types of work, the librarian is notified, and the pupil is guided into reading that which will help him make up his mind. Almost every individual problem child ends in the library with all of us trying to help him help himself.

This individual reading program produces a number of "book reviews" modeled on those appearing in Book Review Digest and in popular magazines. Some of these are published over the pupil's signature in our free monthly library newspaper. This newspaper is worth all the work we put into it. To begin with, it gives us library publicity and is a sure way of contacting every pupil in the school at least once a month. Through it we are able to put over our new plans and ideas with a minimum of assistance from faculty and administration. Book reviews, answers to odd reference questions, suggestions for changes in library activities, and a certain amount of library instruction are submitted by members of the student body at large. The paper is put together and edited by the student library staff, but it belongs to the student body as a whole.

RESEARCH PROJECT

The third large phase of our instruction is the most intensive. It consists of a research project assigned by the individual teacher, and may take the form of oral or written composition, round table discussions, or any other device. A favorite subject for the second year English classes is connected with the study of Shakespeare's Julius Caesar. The students select any point which seems particularly interesting, and the subjects may range from the life of Shakespeare to the life of Caesar himself, and usually include almost all phases of Roman life and the Elizabethan theater.

The only requirement about the topic is that it be one which will assist the pupil to obtain background material connected with the play. The student is taught how to find and use the reference books needed. Never, never, never do we have a special shelf reserved for these projects. The child must learn his way about the library. He learns to select material for his own subject, he learns how useful the various indexes may be, and how to use a magazine index; he learns to take intelligent notes on cards, how to outline the material he gathers, how to make a bibliography. All the time he is working in the library he is under the constant supervision of the teacher and the librarian. His difficulties are noted on the spot, and he receives individual instruction just where it is needed. As the play is read in class, each pupil finds himself an expert on some phase of it, and he is important to himself, his teacher, and his fellows.

Before Christmas we had thirty-one such projects in our school of eight hundred and fifty students. The members of the history department seized upon this library project as a major method of instruction. Most of them said that a great deal more interest in classroom discussion arises from this work, and it has become a common thing that no child in a class hands in the minimum requirement of his assignment. Just recently a new teacher, who had been most discouraged about the intellectual possibilities in his class, brought to the library a group of history papers which had resulted from his project. Seven of the thirty-one papers were given grades between ninety-six and one hundred per cent. At least three others were in the nineties. The subjects were of such difficulty that a college professor would not have considered them beneath his notice. The paper on the influence of political parties on American history was positively scholarly, and it was written by a high school junior.

Thus the library program is being fitted into every single activity in this school. We do it the way the teacher wants it done, and the teacher and the librarian work together to obtain every possible good result from the work. The only pressure is to get the teacher really to work at it the first time. One experiment usually makes a convert, unless you have a lazy teacher. The pupil really enjoys doing the work, and we see to it that his accomplishments are recognized and appreciated by his associates. An exceptional piece of work is often passed around among faculty members, who congratulate the writer.

Let me point out that no claim is being made that this program is either easy or perfect. There is never a week that we don't find some little change for the better. The teacher works just as intensively in the library as he would if he were lecturing; the pupil works even harder. The librarian practically never gets a chance to do routine work; most of it is handled by thirty hard-working student helpers who work just for the love of it. Since there is only one librarian for the school and no clerical help for the library, we miss a lot of chances to have a perfect setup. We use printed cards to eliminate cataloging drudgery as much as possible; we subscribe to the Abridged Readers' Guide and other reference indexes and aids, and an understanding school board happily pays for any labor saving device we have located and recommended up to this point. If a choice must be made between fixing up a flossy display or bulletin board and helping a student, the student comes first.

I suppose that is really the heart of our library program: the child and his needs come before any routine dear to the hearts of librarians and administrators. We are busy, we are crowded, and we love it.

43. BLUEPRINT FOR LIBRARY TEACHING

Martin Rossoff

Most school librarians are aware of their responsibility for instructing young people in basic library skills. Few of us, however, are completely satisfied with the kind of instruction we give. We change, adapt, and modify our procedures after each teaching experience yet never quite achieve the ideal lesson. Why?

For one thing, the so-called integrated method of library teaching to be effective requires imagination and resourcefulness. We range over the entire course of study. Here comes a request for a period of library instruction on our Far Eastern policy. The next lesson is a laboratory period on the evils of television. An English class is scheduled for work on the contemporaries of Paul Revere. These are easy. But what happens when a class plans a gazette or journal for the year 1871? Or a science group descends for the relation of plants to the welfare of mankind?

No two teaching situations are ever the same. Even when the topic or unit is repeated, the tempo of the class varies. There is a disparity in the amount of library information possessed by different classes and by the individual members of any one class. There are those who cannot distinguish between a call number and a copyright date. Others are heard to remark not so sotto voce "What—the Readers' Guide again?" and groan.

Each class that comes to us for a period of instruction is new and strange. Not knowing the quality of the group, except in a general way, the idiosyncrasies of the individuals in it, or even their names, we are at a disadvantage. We point, nod, mutter "Yes, miss?" or "No, I mean the boy in the blue shirt," which is certainly not conducive to good rapport. Unlike the classroom teacher, we lack the kind of dexterity in management which comes from handling the same groups, period in, period out, day after day.

One of our greatest handicaps as library teachers is that we do not recognize a common goal or the means by which it may be reached. A recent article in one of our professional journals recommends that we introduce the Cumulative Book Index, the Standard Catalog, and the Book Review Digest to students early in the high school course! Let's content ourselves with objectives less magnificent.

We lose ourselves in wrangles over the merits of the various types of library instruction: correlated, integrated, vertical, horizontal, diagonal. Some schools teach only formal unit lessons. Others have constructed a regular course of study in library techniques, with text, tests, and credits. Still others teach only by request, pitching the instruction to the specific needs of the moment. There are also patterns which combine elements from all these schemes. A recent study shows that it really doesn't matter how we teach, as long as we do teach. The end result will be the same, the means to the end more or less palatable.

Nor do we have a corps of master teachers to whom we may turn for guidance. The literature of the field is meager. Concrete examples of good integrated library teaching with sample drills and devices are rare. Instead, we are afflicted with the same kind of verbal theorizing which characterizes educational thinking in general.

Why can't we have a simple statement of aims and a few suggestions on how these aims may be achieved? In one respect, at least, we have a real advantage. The body of knowledge which we have to convey is small. On the other hand, the number of techniques available for conveying and vitalizing this information is limited.

In general terms, this is our function as teachers and librarians: to assist students in the acquisition of such skills as will enable them to become independent users of the library, in school and out. The library has parallel and sub-

sidiary aims, of course, but they are only indirectly related
to its teaching objectives.

How much information about a library should a high
school graduate possess in order to operate successfully in
his particular social setting?

He should know how to find a book in a library.
He should be able to locate information in magazines.
He should know when and how to use an encyclopedia.
He should know a few of the basic reference books.

Of course we shall teach more than these minimum essentials. But these are the items that will be stressed and
repeated. Schools where newer practices exploit to advantage all the resources of the library will go beyond the minimum. Students who go on to college will receive even more
elaborate preparation. But if this core remains with the
average citizen after the completion of his education, we
have done our job, at least as far as skills go. Attitudes—
that is something else again.

How can these objectives be consummated in an integrated program of library instruction? An alert faculty, a
cooperative administration, and an enthusiastic librarian
are assumed. An orientation period for all new students,
a universal practice handled in one of many different ways,
is also taken for granted. A series of integrated library
periods inserted at strategic spots in the curriculum is
recommended.

A simple procedure is a cooperative arrangement with
some department by which all the students in a particular
grade prepare a special report, a written project, or some
other tangible product. In our school each world geography
class reports to the library at the beginning of its unit on
the Far East. Each student selects for special study a narrow topic within the scope of the unit. The librarian uses
one of these topics—the U.N. in Korea, the caste system in
India, our stake in Formosa, etc.—to demonstrate the tools

and techniques essential for successful research in this
area.

There is nothing unique or unusual about such an arrangement. It works. It can be used with other units and
with other departments. It is particularly successful with
social studies because all the resources of the library are
called into play. The variety makes for increased pupil
participation and interest. Ideally, a series of such lessons should be constructed with a logical progression and
stress on each of the library tools.

Planning the lesson is easy. Here is a formula which
can be adapted to almost any situation. Prepare a table in
three columns. Column 1 will be a list of the tools to be
taught: the card catalog, the Readers' Guide, encyclopedias,
yearbooks, etc. Column 2 outlines the specific information
about each of the tools which will be covered during the
period. Column 3 suggests the various visual aids and
specimens to be used for illustration and practice. Keeping
this simple outline firmly in mind will ensure that the essentials are covered and reduce the natural tendency of
classes to go off at tangents.

Now what are the elements of good teaching which will
help guarantee a successful performance? In the words of
the most enraptured professor of education, quoting the
most recent (or most ancient) text book on method, they are:
the aim, the motivation, the presentation, the development,
the drill, the summary. Let's examine each of these in-
gredients in terms of their application to an integrated library lesson.

THE AIM

In most instances, the aim of the lesson will be "to teach
pupils the library tools necessary for finding information
about . . . ." The exact wording doesn't matter but the
statement should be clear and simple enough to be understood
by every member of the class. In actual practice, the aim is
stated very briefly after the lesson has been motivated.

BLUEPRINT FOR LIBRARY TEACHING

THE MOTIVATION

Of course all integrated library lessons have previously been motivated from the classroom. The class finds itself in the library only because the need for special direction by the librarian has become obvious. Additional motivation by the librarian at the beginning of the library period is beneficial. It brings the attention of the class to the subject at hand and serves as a springboard for the lesson proper. It is accomplished in one of a hundred different ways.

A challenging question or statement arising out of the subject matter proper brings the pupils up sharp. "In the country I am thinking of, most of the people will go to bed hungry tonight. Most of them cannot read or write. Most of them have never seen a doctor, etc."

And the aim follows in natural sequence: "Now we are not going to talk about India this period, but rather how to find information in the library about this country."

THE PRESENTATION

The presentation is a statement of the problem. "Your subject is Radio Broadcasting. What are some of the angles you are going to work on?" Pupils volunteer the particular phase of the subject which they have chosen: history, kinds of programs, effects, etc. If specific assignments have not been made or selected, two or three areas for investigation are elicited or suggested. The presentation then winds up with the query: "Now this is what we want to find out. The problem is how are we going to do it?" The presentation states the problem; the development solves it.

THE DEVELOPMENT

The development of the lesson hinges around a few key questions (known to the trade as "pivotal" questions). The librarian has firmly in mind at least one pivotal question for each of the major tools. "What library tool tells us whether we have any books about the French Revolution?"

223

Or, "What source of information provides us with a short history of our foreign policy?" Auxiliary questions further the discussion and clinch the main points.

DRILL

In the course of the development, opportunities will arise for drill and practice. Sample entries from the Readers' Guide and card catalog are devices which lend themselves to ready dissection and analysis. A real problem for librarians is inventing sufficient and varied practice on general and specialized reference works. An old stand-by is assigning to volunteers in the class written problems previously prepared. The problems are so designed as to bring out the important and pertinent features of each volume under discussion. They are easy enough so that there is a minimum of fumbling and loss of time. The pooling of this pupil research (recitation and discussion) precedes the final summary.

SUMMARY

The summary rounds out the period. It may take any one of a number of forms. A parallel topic may be suggested and a pupil requested to indicate the procedures he would use to investigate it. Or all the tools covered in the lesson may once more be put on the board at a pupil's dictation. The essential facts about each may be elicited from random participants. Or alternate questions along the lines of "Which of these tools would you use to find . . . ?" are all possible and feasible.

It becomes apparent that sooner or later integrated lessons of this type can become as formal and rigid as the old-fashioned unit approach. But there is nothing to prevent librarians from varying and brightening this formula. There is little about this lesson that is original or sparkling. In the final analysis, as people are so fond of saying, it is the personality of the teacher that counts. True. An inventive

224

and ingenious librarian can shed all the trappings and handicaps of this pedagogical straightjacket. But we must begin somewhere. Newcomers to the profession need a guide. And the precepts of good developmental teaching have endured for more than a century.

44. WE USED OUR CAMERA

Loraine J. Kelleher

Our junior high school library has instituted a program which will go into its second year this fall. Colored slides were taken by a member of the science department, who is also the moderator of the photography club, of scenes and materials in the library and school for the purpose of introducing new students to the library. The slides are intended to be primarily introductory rather than teaching.

Two sets of slides have been taken. The first set was on a 36-frame roll of film. We found that we needed to take another set for various reasons: some out-of-focus shots of catalog cards and small print needed to be retaken; other slides suggested themselves to supplement the first set; more pictures of students, especially the new class, were desired. Therefore another set was taken.

The technical aspects of the photography were left completely in the capable hands of our photographer. We were fortunate in having such an interested person willing to undertake the job. The shots were taken during his free periods, lunch hours, after school, and some time was scheduled by the principal to free this teacher from his homeroom duties. The principal offered his support and interest to the program and encouraged it in every way. Financial support was given by the school. The librarian planned <u>what</u> the slides would consist of, the photographer, Charles Disare, planned <u>how</u> to take each shot (lighting, lens opening and speed, etc.). The expense involved consisted only of the cost of the film, developing and flash bulbs.

One problem, a minor one, in taking these slides was the preparation of materials by the librarian and the planning of what was to be taken where and when. This problem was resolved however with a little concentration.

When the program was planned, the literature of education and librarianship was searched to see if any other school had successfully attempted this, so that we might profit in our planning. Very little was found on this phase of audio-visual work. So that others might gain a little from our experience, this is being written.

A list of the slide topics follows:

I. What is the library? (student holding sign)
  1. View of the circulation desk from the entrance (three students, library club member behind the desk)
  2. View of the library from one end of the room (students at tables, shelves, etc.)
  3. Same as above from the other end of the library
  4. View of the location of the card catalog (student)
  5. Dictionary stand (student)
II. Why and when to use the library (student holding sign)
  1. Student reading in a comfortable chair
  2. "Browsing"—students at shelves
  3. Classroom scene with something on the board to lead to library use
  4. Location of encyclopedias, reference books, magazine rack
  5. Shop class
  6. Home economics class
  7. Club group

III. How to use the library (student holding sign)
    1. Close-up of books on the shelf—fiction
    2. Close-up of books on the shelf—nonfiction
    3. Card catalog—outside with guides on drawers
    4. Card catalog—one drawer, close-up showing guide cards
    5. Three catalog cards for the same book—fiction
    6. Three catalog cards for the same book—nonfiction
    7. Close-up of one card with the call number, author, and title indicated
    8. Shot of shelves with children standing with cards (100's, 200's, etc.) to show how the nonfiction books are arranged on the shelves.
    9. Over the shoulder shot of a hand taking a book from the shelf
    10. Inside back of book with card pulled out of pocket to illustrate date due stamped on date slip and card, and signature
    11. Student at desk checking out book
    12. Close-up of book card
    13. Overdue notice
    14. Reserve notice
    15. Neat shelves—"before"
    16. Messy shelves—"after"
    17. Bulletin board display
IV. Where to find information in a book (student holding sign)
    1. Cover
    2. Title page
    3. Table of contents
    4. Index
V. About ten shots of interesting book covers
    Finish with number one again

These slides were well received by the students and seemed to stimulate their interest in the library. Our school has no elementary school libraries so this was their first formal approach to libraries other than their use of the public library. The seventh graders definitely circulated more books than in the previous year. No survey was undertaken to determine why but it is believed that a part of their interest could be traced to their introduction to library services.

Slides were decided upon rather than filmstrips because of their flexibility. Faculty members were present with their classes when the slides were shown to their classes. The presentation can be given in any room in the building or in the auditorium, to large or small groups. We preferred the smaller groups, so showed them to each seventh grade separately and to all new eighth and ninth graders.

The decision as to whether or not to tape or record the lecture was rejected. It was felt that student reaction and student response could be better motivated and sustained with a personal presentation. Speed of presentation could be adjusted to class conditions (discipline, questions, amount of time available). Personal lectures can also be adapted to the age level of the group.

It was felt that these slides taken in our library with our students were more suited to our needs and cheaper than commercial film strips which are for a higher level and are a little too detailed for junior high.

Our program is young enough to be in a temporary form. We hope to enlarge the program to include an introduction to the public library when our students are old enough to use the young people's section of the adult department. Boys and girls move into this section when they graduate to the ninth grade, so an ideal time to show this possible set of slides would be just before their summer vacation.

Our success with these slides has been encouraging. We have found it cheap and profitable.

45. LIBRARY INSTRUCTION "EN MASSE"

Alice E. Johnson

Five years ago Evanston Township High School at Evanston, Illinois, pioneered in a new field of instructional techniques—team teaching. This was designed to utilize teacher time and talent for the improvement of instruction. Although it was initiated by the English Department, by 1960 such areas as social science, mathematics, health education, science, driver education, business, and combined studies were using the method with enthusiasm and success.

The establishment of a "C" room as a community center makes it possible for four individual class sections to meet together for a combined lecture at least once a week. The other days the classes meet in small seminar groups with their individual teachers. This means that the specialist on Greek drama, or Mark Twain or modern poetry or Russia will do the group teaching and give a larger number of students the benefit of his particular talents and study in a given field.

The library, along with the other departments, has discovered that the large lecture room method, once reserved almost exclusively for college curriculums, has definite merit at the high school level. With the use of such audio-visual materials as films and filmstrips, tapes and recordings, the overhead projector with transparencies, it is possible to enrich and dramatize a lesson when it is presented to more than one hundred students at a single class session.

In September of 1960 freshman library orientation was presented by group instruction for the first time. The lecture room then seated more than one hundred and fifty students which made it possible to bring together at one time as many as five sections of I English. This meant that all

229

of the thousand freshmen could be taught in seven periods of one day. (This year the seating capacity of the "C" room has been reduced to one hundred and twelve students so more sections must be scheduled for the group teaching.)

The series of lessons begins with a lecture on the rules and regulations of the library plus a review of the Dewey Decimal Classification system. Special attention is given to certain classification numbers which are used frequently and are not always clearly understood. Such letters as SC for story collections, and FS for filmstrips, the numbers 921 for individual biography, the symbol X for oversize books, the designation Ref for reference books and Pro for professional material from the teachers' reading room, all receive special mention and review.

Since a maximum of three classes (about one hundred students) are all that can be accommodated efficiently at one time within the library, two days are needed to work on individual problems. Half of the classes come one day and the remainder come the next. This means that each group has an extra day in its own classroom for amplification and further study. In the library each student identifies important features of the library on a floor plan and locates books with a variety of call numbers. The latter problem emphasizes the location of certain frequently used subject areas in this particular library.

The group instruction is completed with a second lecture on the use of the card catalog. Again two days of library experience are needed to give practical application to the lecture. Individual problems made from each catalog tray challenge the student to ferret out for himself some of the mysteries of catalog use. An objective quiz of one hundred questions administered by the teacher in the individual classroom completes the orientation program.

The success of the large group lecture method has been due to several factors. Each student is given mimeographed sheets with detailed information on the rules and regulations of the library, on the Dewey Decimal Classification system

and on the card catalog. These give an outline which is explained and supplemented by the lecture. The fact that the
lectures are illustrated and clarified by the use of the overhead projector and transparencies means that the student
can observe in some detail problems he will confront as
he starts to use a new library. The transparencies show
such items as—the location and floor plan of the library,
an attendance slip, a student pass, a book card, a magazine
slip, author, title, and subject cards, author analytic, title
analytic, and subject analytic cards. These and other special characteristics of library usage can be pictured and discussed to help the student in his understanding of basic library knowledge and skills.

Teachers of Freshman English have been pleased with
the methods and results of this program. For the new teacher it is an opportunity for him, along with his students, to
become familiar with the new library he is to use. Experienced instructors who have sometimes taught the unit themselves, prefer to have the library presented from the librarian's point of view. The English teachers give excellent cooperation in assisting with supervision of the "C" room and
in helping with the students as they work on the individual
problems in the library.

Another formal contribution made by the library to the
teaching program has been the development of a four year
English-Library reference project. Beginning at the ninth
grade level, each student is expected to familiarize himself
with about twelve to fifteen basic reference sources each
year. General encyclopedias, dictionaries, quotation books,
play and poetry indexes, biographical dictionaries and literature handbooks are some of the tools a student will need as
he advances in high school and anticipates college. During
the year the English teacher incorporates these sources into his teaching program. In May, each grade level takes an
objective test covering not only his own grade level but also
the books from previous years as well as important features
of the freshman orientation material. This cumulative test

gives the student a chance to review the important reference books he has used to date.

Former high school students testify that this formal emphasis on reference books provides them with valuable background material as they strive for success in college. A librarian is available to help in the presentation of these books to individual classes. Last year all of the Junior English Project was taught in three lecture groups. The junior year reference books were shown and described at some length. Techniques and procedures in the development of term papers were also discussed. Here again the overhead projector with transparencies made possible a more graphic and effective presentation. For example, the student was shown the sources he should consult as he seeks to evaluate the literary worth of a writer. Beginning with the card catalog with its material on biography and literary criticism, he moves on to such reference aids as the Book Review Digest, the biographical dictionaries, the Cambridge History of English Literature, Moulton's Library of Literary Criticism, Cassell's Encyclopedia of World Literature, and the Reader's Guide to Periodical Literature. Sample entries from these sources provide the student with the incentive and assurance he needs as he begins to work on his individual topic. Mass instruction has reduced confusion in the library as several hundred students arrive with their term paper assignments.

Closed circuit television has been in operation at Evanston Township High School for about six years. The program started as a part of a national project sponsored by the National Association of Secondary School Principals with the cooperation of the Fund for the Advancement of Education. Gradually educational television has been absorbed into the total program of the school. It has been used for formal class instruction as well as informally to promote various school activities.

The first two experimental programs were carried on in Beginning Typing and English-Speech. In Beginning Typing, a skill subject, one hundred and forty students were taught at one time by a teacher with a clerical assistant. In English-Speech, one teacher, assisted by student teachers, instructed all the students enrolled in this subject during one class period. This was a subject-matter area which required a close personal relationship between student and teacher and a high level of pupil activity. In both instances two-way audio made possible an inter-change of ideas and the use of questions and answers. The student who desired to ask a question or make a comment raised his hand. The student teacher then pressed a signal button flashing a light at the teacher's table which indicated that a student wished to speak. This procedure also enabled the teacher to ask questions of a student in the viewing room or refer them to another student.

Studies of these experiments have indicated several things. The level of learning was high. Students did well scholastically. They felt they knew their teacher as well and that their teacher knew them as well as in a normal sized class.

The library has had occasion to participate in this program by presenting reference books to the entire group in English-Speech and by suggesting books for recreational reading. Titles from the Richer by Asia list were enthusiastically received. Art objects from the Orient made an effective background in the display of these books. Since the teacher or librarian speaks in a room with one of the classes, he has the benefit of audience response. For most teachers this serves as a stimulation and certainly influences his presentation.

Experimentation is perhaps the key word of a new era in American education. Methods such as these represent a search for and a desire to find better ways to teach this nation's growing student population. The unprecedented increase in the number of boys and girls to be educated plus the acute shortage of able teachers call for imaginative action. The school library as a valuable resource in the enrichment of instruction will want to participate in these programs which add a new dimension to teaching.

46. THE ROLE OF THE RESOURCE UNIT
IN LIBRARY INSTRUCTION

Muriel Bennett

Much has been said and written about the best methods
for teaching secondary pupils how to use the library. It is
the opinion of this librarian that each librarian must work
out a system based on child development and library science
which best suits his particular school and community. The
type of curriculum in each school concerned will determine
the demands made upon the library and the need for particular library skills. Another factor to be considered is the so
called library mindedness of the administrators and faculty.
The demand will be great or small according to these attitudes
and the types of teaching done. However, in addition to this,
a librarian must take a wider view and realize that the child
cannot be kept within the boundaries of the local level, but
must be educated for life in the world with its multiplicity
of problems. It is therefore his responsibility also to formulate a long range goal which will function not only while
the boy or girl is in that particular high school, but will
serve his needs through life in any community.

Pupils for the most part will demand instruction only as
the need arises, and for some the need will never arise. For
this reason it should be the concern of the teachers and librarians to provide library experiences which will lead the
pupil naturally and purposefully into the library and help
him to realize that the library is a social educational center
with lasting and satisfying values.

There is no magic trick whereby this can be brought
about. But it should be associated with some natural process. It is a recognized fact that educational methods and
curricula are undergoing great change. Two global wars

234

and a depression have pointed out the necessity for the adjustment of our educational patterns to fit modern living. The result has been the rise of types of curricula which place emphasis on the development of the whole child rather than on subject-matter. This in turn has produced new methods of teaching and new devices for learning. Among these new devices is the resource unit which is being used widely by progressive teachers.

Since library instruction must keep pace with other types of instruction, if it is going to function in the new curricula, the librarian must acquaint himself with the new educative processes the same as teachers do. He is no longer the custodian of books, but is the co-worker of every teacher and planning committee of the school. It becomes his responsibility to project the library as a source of materials and working tools for every school project.

Librarians have long since recognized the importance of integrated library lessons and have frowned upon the isolated lesson as somewhat equivalent to the old textbook methods of instruction used by teachers of the past decade. The modern methods of teaching recognize the child as an individual. They also recognize the many levels of mentality found in a single classroom and make provision in their planning for materials and activities suitable to meet all these differences. This recognition has led educators to see the usefulness of the resource unit which makes it possible to plan a unit of work which meets the interests and abilities of many pupils in a single group.

Alberty set up the following criteria for the construction and evaluation of a resource unit:

1. The resource unit should recognize the needs and interest of youth.
2. The resource unit should suggest opportunities for student participation in planning, developing, and evaluating the work.

3. The resource unit should provide suitable materials to further the socialization of students.
4. The resource unit should explore the resources of the community that may be utilized in developing the unit.
5. The student activities that are suggested should be based upon sound principles of learning.
6. The various proposals included in a resource unit should be practicable under prevailing school conditions.
7. The resource unit should be constructed in such a way as to stimulate professional growth in democratic methods of working with students.
8. The resource unit should help the teacher to provide experiences for students which call for reflective thinking.
9. The resource unit should be based upon definite educational philosophy.
10. The resource unit should be organized in such a way that it can easily be used by teachers.
11. The resource unit should be developed by several teachers representing as many subject fields as possible.
12. The resource unit should contain many more suggestions than the class is likely to use.
13. The resource unit should be suited to the maturity of the students.[1]

The usefulness and flexibility of such a unit points to a teaching device which has many possibilities for the secondary school librarian interested in improving methods of instruction in the use of the library by secondary school pupils. However, before any real learning process or problem solving, even with a resource unit, can be carried on, each pupil and teacher needs to know certain fundamental techniques for using books and other library materials. Acquisition of this information calls for a period of orientation.

THE RESOURCE UNIT IN LIBRARY INSTRUCTION

It is now the practice in many secondary schools to orient all freshmen and new pupils in the basic procedures of the school sometime during the first few days of the term. This is often done through home room programs, or in the absence of home rooms through the English classes. As a foundation for later work in the library the opening program should include some provision for orientation in the library as it does for all other school departments. Here the teacher, administrator and librarian plan together. The person who is responsible for the group tour of the school plant should orient his group as to what it can expect to see and hear on its first visit to the library as well as to other parts of the school. What happens and what is said on this first visit to the library has much to do with the future attitudes of the pupils toward the library. So it behooves the librarian to make all contacts as attractive and businesslike as possible. When the group arrives at the library, the librarian plays the role of hostess and lays the foundation for future friendships with the group. He points out such items as the arrangement of the books on the shelves, the location of the card catalog, how to charge out a book, and the general behavior expected of a good library citizen. Finally, each pupil in the absence of a student handbook may be given a mimeographed sheet covering library routines such as time of opening and closing, checking out books, returning books, fines and other routine library procedures. This visit should be followed up by a discussion period in the classroom of what has been seen and heard. Such a discussion leads naturally in the classroom into a real orientation period which may be highlighted by a film on the use of the library. This film in most cases will cause some questions to arise which will lay the foundation for another discussion period in which more concrete facts can be examined. At this second discussion meeting the pupils can be introduced by the teacher to filmstrips showing the secrets of the card catalog, Dewey decimal system, the dictionary and encyclopedias which will supplement the remarks made by the

237

librarian on their first visit to the library. Two more periods could be devoted to indexes, reference books and magazines to good advantage. After these orientation periods the pupil should be encouraged to go to the library by himself to browse or check out a book which he has found himself.

It is not expected that every pupil will learn all he could or should know about the library in these brief orientation periods, but many pupils will learn a sufficient amount to free the librarian to help those who need extra help when they return to the library later. When class groups go to the library, the teacher in charge should be expected to go with his group and be so informed that he too can assist in helping those who are not yet independent. All such group meetings in the library should be pre-planned by the teacher and librarian. If this procedure is followed, then when the class comes to the library to develop a resource unit the materials needed will be available and accessible. Again the teacher should brief his group on the care of books and their various parts as well as making suggestions where certain kinds of materials can be found before coming to the library. This will give the pupils a starting point when they arrive. If possible the librarian should attend these briefing periods and offer suggestions also. In this way time and commotion is saved and pupils set to work on their problems as soon as they arrive in the library. At the same time they are being introduced to reference materials and methods of research.

Since no resource unit will require all the resources of the library at the same time, only certain tools can be mastered with each unit. This makes the process seem somewhat slow since only a few materials may be needed at first. However, if teachers and librarians have planned carefully and wisely, many tools and types of material can be introduced and much practice given during the four year period of high school. The results will be gratifying, for the pupils will have found the library a working organization with meaning fitted into their daily needs. The teacher and the librarian will have taught the pupils to know and use again and again the tools which will help them to solve their problems, for as the materials are being used for each resource unit a painless purposeful library lesson will be in process. Pupils may also discover other library materials besides those indicated by the teacher and the librarian, and this will offer an opportunity for the librarian to explain special features of other library resources. This will help to meet the various levels of ability in the group. In this manner the pupil learns library procedures while he is solving his own problems. At the same time he is working in a democratic situation sharing and receiving from his classmates. In this way the resource unit lends itself to the natural approach to the acquisition of library skills. It integrates the library with the curriculum because it is a problem solving process which gives rise to a felt need for library instruction when instruction is needed. It promotes group research as well as individual initiative; it permits teaching on many levels; it can be worked out in a democratic setting. It can be evaluated. It makes it possible for the library to become a laboratory where practices are meaningful and practical. It helps project the library as a planning-teaching center. It places as much responsibility on the teacher as on the librarian. This is a good situation, for it works for better understanding of both the curriculum and the library. To succeed the two elements of the school must blend. By planning and working together each one is working toward a common goal. This takes the library off its pedestal and makes it the cog in the educational wheel that it should be, and, the librarian a teacher.

The effects upon the pupil are worthwhile and wholesome. He has an opportunity to become skillful in the use of library materials because library procedures are no longer isolated facts, but are the tools for solving the problems which interpret his needs. He can learn to discover new materials for himself. He can learn to plan with others, for he, his teacher, his classmates and the librarian make up a planning team which executes its plans after they are made. He is learning how to work with others, cooperatively.

All this adds up to integration at its best. Because this type of approach is democratic, developmental, and satisfying to the individual, both pupils and teachers may profit. Therefore, teaching the use of the library while developing a resource unit which is related to a real classroom-life situation fulfills the modern approach to education. This practical device can be utilized by the progressive educator —the librarian—who would take his place as leader, teacher, and guide in the educative process of all youth; who would see his library as a planning-teaching center; as a dynamo giving vital energy and enriching all educative processes in the school.

47. THE PLACE OF THE LIBRARY IN A HIGH SCHOOL DEVELOPMENTAL READING PROGRAM

Kermit Dehl

I should like to introduce to you this morning my first hour freshman English class. It is composed of twenty-four young people from Oak Park public schools, River Forest public schools, parochial schools from both villages, and miscellaneous schools, both public and private, attended before moving to this vicinity. Their environmental backgrounds range from broken homes, often on an insecure financial basis, to comfortable, secure family situations with every cultural advantage it is possible to have today. And their reading abilities range from seventh grade to fourteenth grade, the equivalent of a sophomore in college. (I might add here that we do have pupils with reading abilities below seventh grade, but they are in our special remedial classes.) How am I going to supply satisfactory reading

materials to a heterogeneous group such as this? Obviously
the library comes in for its share of the responsibility. Its
purpose is not to teach the child how to read, but to teach
him how to find materials that he can read.

The first step is to make the child feel at home in the
library by showing him the fundamentals of its use. And
that is exactly what our librarians do. Within the first two
weeks, a day is set aside for my first period class to visit
the library. As we enter the main door, we are greeted by
one of the librarians, who escorts us to tables reserved especially for us. On these tables are books with attractive
covers, drawers from the card catalogue, and mimeographed
sheets. After I have introduced the librarian to the class,
she gives them a word of welcome and immediately directs
their attention to the mimeographed sheets containing true-
false questions about the library. She carefully explains
that this is not really a test that is going to be graded, but a
kind of game using questions about the library to see how
much they know now about its use. Here are a few sample
questions to be answered true or false:

LIBRARY INSTRUCTION

(Answer with true or false on a separate sheet of paper)

1. The library is open from 7:45 in the morning until
   4:00 in the afternoon.
2. A student who wishes to come to the library during
   a study period should report first to the study hall
   and should arrive at the library late.
3. Students are permitted to do their algebra text-book
   homework in the library.
4. Books lost or damaged must be paid for by the bor-
   rower.
5. All books except "overnight" books may be loaned
   for two weeks and renewed for two weeks.
6. When a student wishes to borrow a book from the library, he takes it without leaving any record at the
   desk.

7. Books labeled "overnight" are charged out after the student's last class and must be returned before A period the following morning.
8. Current magazines may be taken out for one week.
9. On overdue books a fine of two cents a day is charged on each one-week book; a fine of one cent a period on each "overnight" book.
10. Students are expected to respect the rights of others in the library by maintaining a quiet atmosphere and by the proper use of library materials.
11. The only way a pupil could find out whether the library has a book on Florida is to ask the librarian.
12. The cards in the card catalogue are arranged alphabetically according to author, title and subject.
13. The books in the Oak Park Library are arranged alphabetically according to the title of the book.
14. The following call numbers are arranged correctly in the order in which books would stand on the shelves:

917.45	917.47	917.5	917.6
C76p	C21h	K38p	K12d
917.69	917.7	917.78	917.8
T36b	H298i	R21o	C15s

The sheet takes only a few minutes, but it gets everyone to thinking critically about library regulations and adds a great deal of interest to the discussion which follows. Only a few important fundamentals are stressed at this meeting, not enough to confuse these young people and make them dread to try to use the library. The card catalogue system is made clear by holding up a greatly enlarged title card, an author card, and a subject card. Then the pupils are asked to find certain cards in the drawers on the tables. They learn to do by doing, and they enjoy it.

But it is the second visit to the library that really does an English teacher's heart good. I realize that my problem of improving reading ability is well started on the path to a solution when these freshmen really want to read. And so I always look forward to this visit, whose purpose is to present book reading as an enjoyable experience, something which might even compete with the radio and moving pictures! I find that the pupils enter the room with a little more confidence this time. They walk directly to their reserved tables, where they find a most attractive collection of books just waiting to be inspected. The librarian greets them again, this time as old friends, and proceeds to talk informally about specific books of various types as she holds each one up before the class. Biographies and true travel stories take their places beside the novels as she relates tantalizing bits of action as samples of what can be found between the covers of these books. "And now you may browse around among these books on the tables," she tells the class, "as well as the ones on the shelves. When you find a book you want to read, sign the card and bring it and the book up to the desk to be stamped." Before the period is over, everyone has a book and is seated quietly at the table absorbed in a new adventure. Do they really like these books they have chosen? You should see the hands go up the next day when I ask that question.

Now with the pupils acquainted with the general arrangement of the library, interested in getting books that are fun to read, and not afraid to ask questions of the friendly librarians, the next step is to teach the use of the varied materials available for study-type reading. In our school the best opportunity for such instruction in the English department comes in the junior year when the pupils write a long paper on some topic using bibliography, footnotes, and all the various paraphernalia accompanying research papers. The teachers cooperate by handing to the librarians well in advance of the visiting day a list of topics similar to what the class will be using for their papers. The first visit is spent in showing the pupils how to get ready to go to work on their chosen topics. The many different kinds of sources available for use in our library and in the village libraries are pointed out—specific reference books, pamphlets, magazines. The class is told about the fine libraries in Chicago and the regulations for using such libraries as the Crerar Library, Newberry Library, and Chicago Public Library. Furthermore, the pupils are led to see whether there appears to be enough material available on their particular topics to make them worth working on. Some topics are eliminated because of scarcity of accurate information. The class leaves the library after this first visit with a feeling that there are vast areas of source material heretofore unexplored. The intellectual appetite has been stimulated.

A second visit permits each pupil to go to these various sources and prepare bibliography cards. He gets experience in using materials he has never used before; indeed, in many cases, materials which he did not know even existed. As the stack of cards grows, he becomes more and more eager to get into his subject, to read these fascinating books and articles about a limited topic on which he expects to become somewhat of an authority. He has set out to find all he possibly can on this subject, and in many cases the amount of material is surprisingly large—even in the school library. The pupil often finds out for himself after this second visit that his topic is too broad and that he must limit it still further.

The class returns as a group as many times as the teacher feels it is necessary. But the individual pupils continue to come as they work on their topics. The librarians watch with interest, and in some cases actual enthusiasm, the growth of each pupil's project. Real friendship develops between pupils and librarians as every possible source of information is located which even remotely touches the subject. The library is doing an invaluable service in providing this abundance of material, from which the young person must make wise selection, and in teaching him how to use this material.

Now let us consider just where the library fits in to the day-by-day classroom instruction in literature. Let us say that a sophomore class is studying the one-act play, using a text containing some ten or twelve plays representing all the main types being written today. At once the teacher sees how limited the instruction is going to be, how little practice the pupils are going to have in a comparatively unknown field of reading to sophomores. The need now is for extensive reading to supplement the intensive class study. Of course the library is the solution to this problem. All available collections of one-act plays are at once put on reserve for use in classes studying this unit. The librarians help the pupils to find plays suited to their interests and abilities. Certain plays are especially recommended because other sophomores have found them interesting. Every effort is made to help these young people to find satisfying experiences with drama. The teacher then feels as if what he teaches in the classroom is being intelligently supplemented in the library with the aid of trained librarians who understand his aims and his problems.

Similar help is given when the class is studying lyric poetry, the short story, or the essay. In each unit the classroom is extended into the library. Teacher and librarian work hand in hand in the guidance of pupil reading. Of course the librarians are giving similar help to teachers of history, science, and other content subjects requiring supplementary reading. Responsibility for a high school reading program must not be confined to the English department. All teachers of content subjects must be teachers of reading, and the librarians stand ready to help supply the much-needed materials for all types of reading.

And so we come back to our question of the place of the library in a high school developmental reading program. I have tried to show that a high school library can perform four major functions:

1. It can create an atmosphere of warmth and friendliness which makes pupils want to come to the library.

2. It can make leisure reading attractive to modern young people in this age of radio, moving pictures, and commercial entertainment of all types.
3. It can help pupils to learn to use the wide variety of materials available in the library for study-type reading.
4. It can provide supplementary books, pamphlets, and magazines for specific units being studied in class, and thus enrich the study of each unit.

The day of the single textbook is gone. In its place is the organized school library working hand in hand with the classroom to provide a maximum of reading opportunity for every child.

48. INSTRUCTION IN THE USE OF THE LIBRARY

Mary Young Hale

There is a unanimity of opinion among librarians today that instruction in the use of the library is desirable. With school and college librarians it is termed not only desirable but also essential. Yet, with this feeling predominant, in most instances a minimum of time is allowed for instruction of new students at the beginning of a term. There is a tendency, too, with the ever-increasing number of students to curtail a program which was already sketchy.

The very complexities which beset the librarian today have relegated the instruction in the use of the library to the background. One way to deal with this situation is, first of all, recognition by the library staff of the need and importance of a definite program adapted to the objectives of the library. Then a forward step is made by planning a program for overall, long-term use. Finally, take an inventory of present instruction and measure it by the recommended program. This will point up weaknesses and deficiencies and emphasize goals and the line of attack for the future. Having a blueprint of the ultimate objective, it is possible to add gradually to the present instruction until the desired program is attained.

The approach to the problem of setting up a program for instruction in the use of a college library has been twofold: first, by interview and questionnaire to determine current practices in the colleges, similar in size and purpose, in the area; second, by extensive reading in the literature of the subject to cull recommendations and suggestions for instruction programs.

In pursuance of the first objective in March and April 1952 the writer visited libraries and interviewed members of the staffs of Maryville College, the University of Tennessee, Memphis State College, Southwestern at Memphis, Union College, George Peabody College for Teachers, Joint Universities Library, David Lipscomb College, and Middle Tennessee State Teachers College. During the summer she visited Agnes Scott College, Columbia Seminary, and Emory University. In addition to these she has obtained personal interviews with librarians from Harding College in Searcy, Ark., and Georgia State College for Women in Milledgeville. From all of the libraries listed she obtained whatever manuals, teaching aids, handbooks, problems, outlines, syllabi, etc., are in current use in their instruction programs.

On the second approach she has attempted to read and analyze critically the research literature in the field and all pertinent material available. The following observations have been made after consideration of the findings of the survey with emphasis at all times, of course, both in investigation and recommendation, on the needs of the University of Chattanooga Library.

CURRENT PRACTICES

The need for instruction as soon as possible after the opening of the fall semester seemed to be universally recognized. The majority (8) of the colleges contacted gave the beginning instruction during Orientation Week or in an Orientation Course starting at that time. Three colleges extended the instruction throughout the first quarter; only one waited until the third quarter for the first formal instruction.

The amount of instruction given varied from only one hour to eight weeks. The majority gave several class periods, usually handled through the Freshman English classes. The majority (8) centered the instruction in the library, with a special room in the library used in two instances; two colleges held their instruction in classrooms; two used a combination of classroom and library; five libraries gave their instruction on library tours.

In nearly all of the colleges the instruction in the use of the library was handled through the Freshman English classes. In this way all students were reached, and the knowledge acquired could be tested through class problems or the preparation of term papers.

HANDBOOKS

In addition to the classroom instruction and library tours, nine libraries issued handbooks or manuals as an aid in acquainting the students with the arrangement and regulations of the library and as an explanation of the use of the catalog and some of the basic reference tools.

From these consultations with librarians in charge of the instruction programs for their colleges, certain procedures stand out as particularly effective. Memphis State, Middle Tennessee, and Harding College all use a special room equipped with Reader's Guide and other reference tools where an instructor may bring a class for instruction by the librarian, examination of the books by the class, and follow-up practice work by individual members of the class. This is a use-

248

ful arrangement when concentrated instruction must be given in a limited time.

Maryville College attacks the problem of instruction in several ways. During the second week of the fall term a tour of the library by groups at night is scheduled with lectures by the librarian and staff. There is a Freshman Orientation course which meets twice a week for six weeks. The excellent handbook for this course has a splendid chapter on the use of the library, "The Right Book at the Right Time." It was written by an English teacher and it is a good example of effective explanation: well-written, comprehensive, humorous, easily grasped, not too technical. This chapter helps clinch the information given during the library tour. In addition there is a unit in the second semester Freshman English manual. The reserve librarian is the consultant on bibliographic form for the seniors in their special studies program. The program at Maryville has a flavor of its own, a touch of the personality of the college. This is imparted by the handbooks which have been written at Maryville and have become a tradition there.

HARDING COLLEGE

Harding College has a comprehensive and thorough syllabus for Freshman Library Orientation. It consists of three lessons with assignments and a test on the library unit. In the winter term upperclassmen are given elaborate and detailed bibliographic instruction by major fields with comprehensive sets of questions for a follow-up of the instruction.

The reference librarian at Emory University has prepared manuals for upperclassmen. These are selected, annotated bibliographies in four divisions: general, humanities, science, social science. The manuals are distributed to groups by major fields after a general lecture.

The instruction in the use of the library at Union College is given in two required courses for which credit is given: a Freshman Orientation course taught by the Education Department and a later course, Psychology of Adjustment.

The University of Tennessee and Joint Universities Libraries have to cope with very large enrollments. For that reason the instruction has been confined to tours by small groups from the Freshman English classes with lectures by the reference librarians. Manuals are distributed and a follow-up problem is given. Both libraries readily provide lectures for groups from major departments on request.

At David Lipscomb the instruction program is a part of the Orientation course which is required; it lasts eight weeks and no credit is given.

For Peabody College there are two types of instruction necessary: freshman and graduate. For the freshman the librarian goes to the English classes with a tour and a follow-up unit later. In the summer session there is a lecture for groups at night about the second week, covering general tools and the card catalog. Discussions of graduate level research materials are given by request to special groups.

At Southwestern the instruction is given by the library staff to groups in the library as a part of Orientation Week. An excellent handbook is distributed, and a library exercise is given to test the effectiveness of the instruction.

FROM LIBRARY LITERATURE

As the need for instruction in the use of the library is almost universally recognized, there is a great deal of material in library literature on the subject with suggestions, plans, and experiments.

The use of audio-visual material offers a new approach. One of the most original of this type is the present plan for library instruction in Fairmont West Virginia State College. It is centered upon a film, These Three Keys, which stresses use of the card catalog, encyclopedias, and the Reader's Guide. Using a film made on their own campus gives essential information in a vivid fashion, and it is tailor-made, adapted to the needs and situations of Fairmont College. The film was the result of a cooperative effort of several departments: education, dramatics, and the library. The follow-up of the points made by the film is also effectively planned. The freshmen come by English classes for instruction and location of the "three keys." A copy of twelve questions on the library is given to each student before the lecture, thus focusing his attention upon the main points being stressed.

Most instruction programs agree on the basic items for the content of the course. Louis R. Wilson in The Library in College Instruction, published by the H. W. Wilson Company in 1951, gives a comprehensive and detailed outline for a formal course in library instruction. It includes: information about use of local college library, arrangement of books in libraries, the physical book, card catalog, alphabetizing and filing, dictionaries, encyclopedias, reference books, magazines, periodical indexes, audio-visual materials, buying and owning books, bibliography (p. 288–90).

Lucy M. Lamphear, assistant to the librarian, University of Tampa, emphasizes the importance of library instruction in an article, "It Wasn't Sugar Coated," in the Wilson Library Bulletin for January 1950.

> But it could be that time spent teaching students how to use the cards already in the catalog and other library facilities might be more valuable to the students than time spent adding more and more cards to an unused catalog. It is a question of time use which comes perilously close to that two-headed dragon, "Libraries for librarians or Libraries for students?" (p. 366)

William Rainey Harper many years ago underscored the enduring value of acquiring training in the use of books in his The Trend in Higher Education, published by the American Library Association in 1905.

> No more important, no more useful, training can be given men in college than that which relates to the use of books. Why do so many college men give up reading when they leave college? Because in college they have never learned the use of books. The equipment of the library will never be finished until it has upon its staff

men and women whose sole work shall be, not the care
of books, not the cataloging of books, but the giving of
instruction concerning their use (p. 124).

HANDBOOKS AND MANUALS

Fortunately, it is not necessary to blaze a trail in for-
mulating lesson plans for instruction or in planning library
handbooks and manuals. Others have pioneered in these
fields. There are many excellent manuals and well-planned
syllabi which may be consulted very profitably as models.

A library handbook has permanent value and many advantages. It may be used throughout the four undergraduate
years. It is a link with the instruction program for the library. If it is well-designed, informative, and interesting,
there will be an immediate establishment of respect for the
library and its facilities in the mind of the student. It gives
uniform information to every student in a convenient form
for easy reference. It is a useful aid when the librarian is
not available. A handbook answers questions objectively and
concisely.

Handbooks differ according to approach, that is, the
purpose for which they are written and the individual differences in college administration and organization. They vary
from clever, spoofing cartoons to efficient, impersonal text.
The tone of the institution, the appeal that will reach the student groups determine the approach.

Simplicity is the keynote in the text of the handbook of
Georgia State College for Women yet it is adequate for the
needs of the college. Southwestern at Memphis effectively
combines straightforward exposition with simple illustrations. Harding College enlivens its text with a humorous
angle, the experiences of Freddy Freshman, but manages
to impart at the same time much helpful information.

Davidson College Library Handbook has the dual role
of handbook and textbook. It includes a workbook of library
exercises on perforated pages in the back which the student
answers and turns in for a library project.

252

INSTRUCTION IN THE USE OF THE LIBRARY

The Library Instruction Manual of Iowa State College has been prepared as a syllabus for a library instruction course. It is a comprehensive, detailed manual with many illustrations and study and review questions at the end of each section.

The University of Illinois in Chicago Undergraduate Library Handbook may have a cumbersome title but it is well organized and easy to use. It, too, is a handy guide and a textbook and it has been punched for insertion in the student's notebook. The art work, in a humorous vein, is by former students.

The excellent syllabus, The Use of Books and Libraries, prepared by Harold G. Russell and others for the University of Minnesota's course, is superior in every respect, formal, organization, explanation, and annotation. In the preface the author states that the course has been lengthened from twenty-four to thirty-six class periods. "The change represents a demand for more intensive training in the use of the library and its resources and for a more intimate knowledge of reference books." (p. iii)

A RECOMMENDED PROGRAM

I. General introduction to the library for new students.

Purpose: stressing arrangement of the library, hours of opening, rules and regulations, introduction to members of the staff, a brief explanation of the use of the catalog and how to fill out a call slip.

Time: during Orientation Week

Accomplished by: tours and displays. Have as attractive a setting as possible: book displays, flowers, student assistants to take part.

Emphasis: informal, relaxed, colorful—more of an open house.

II. Library handbooks.

Student: a manual carefully written and illustrated; to be used as a permanent library aid during the four years of college.

253

Faculty: a manual explaining reserve system, book orders, stack permits, interlibrary loans, and special information important for faculty members.

Time: distributed at all times, especially at beginning of terms.

III. A formal course of instruction in the use of basic reference books and the periodical guides.

Accomplished by: cooperation of the library with the Freshman English classes, early in the first semester, some six or eight weeks after opening of the term, centered around term papers or library projects. Preferably taught by a librarian in English classroom or library if possible.

IV. A formal course of instruction in bibliography for upperclassmen.

Purpose: to acquaint the upperclassman with the outstanding books in the field of his specialty, i.e., history, social science, literature, etc.

V. Objective library tests for effectiveness of instruction; to be used after program is well-established.

VI. A planned reading program for the future.

Purpose: equipping the student with a reading plan, centered around the subject of his major interest, stimulating and promoting continuing education and adult education after leaving college.

Accomplished by: consultation during latter half of senior year with major professor, adviser, and librarians.

49. TEACHING STUDENTS TO USE THE LIBRARY: WHOSE RESPONSIBILITY?

Virginia Clark

It has always seemed curious to me that the librarian, alone among public servants, eagerly insists on teaching the inmost secrets of his craft to his patrons. This permissive attitude toward the procedural mysteries of the card catalog (so unlike that of the keepers of the couch, the confessional, the prescription pad, or the seal) is of course a concomitant of the public library and the open stack. It has not been always thus; and it might be interesting to speculate on what would happen were we to swathe ourselves in our mysteries instead of working so hard to explain them. But since explanation seems to be called for, this discussion will begin with some definitions.

The three terms of the topic are limited to the areas within which the question of responsibility should be raised. The first is the word "teaching," which may be defined as excluding those casual contacts during which learning may occur and emphasizing the planned encounter during which a conscious teaching effort is made. Second, "to use the library" is defined as "how to use the library," ignoring the general promotional campaigns like National Library Week or Book Week and concentrating on instruction in techniques. Third, by "students" is meant the student body as a whole, not the few who will acquire library skills by their own effort.

There is absolutely no question of "whose responsibility" in these situations that is ruled out of consideration by definition. Any librarian is responsible for giving the best service possible to the patron with whom he finds himself confronted. The school or college librarian traditionally assumes the

further function of making each such consultation a model for
the "next time." It has become a universal expectation that the
librarian in an advertising culture will promote his goods and
services. The question of responsibility for formal, unsolicited
instruction in the use of those goods and services is, however,
debatable.

The offering of such instruction has been assumed to be
one of the objectives of the librarian since the earliest days of
American librarianship, indeed even before the librarians were
undergoing formal instruction.[1] In accepting this duty the
school or college librarian has tried many methods and used
a variety of materials. What do we now know about this instruction?

There has been—as reflected in library periodicals—volu-
minous individual reporting of projects at their conception.
There have been some surveys covering more than one program. The 1951–52 Biennial Survey of Education included one
of these, reporting that separate library courses are offered
in 7.5 per cent of universities and 6 per cent of liberal arts
colleges. There are also courses taught as units in other
courses: in subject courses in 28 per cent of universities and
19 per cent of colleges and as part of a general orientation or
skills course in 22 per cent of universities and 20 per cent of
colleges. Offerings of a combination of a subject course and
an orientation program are made in 21.5 per cent of universities and 37 per cent of colleges. Other combination programs
also occur, but less frequently.[2] Other surveys of the problem
are primarily graduate theses in librarianship or education. A
particularly comprehensive and recent study is Whitten's survey of 72 liberal arts colleges.[3] There has been almost no objective, quantitative follow-up evaluation of the effectiveness of
any of these programs. It is possible, however, to make the
following generalizations:

1. Attempts so far have yielded many more curriculum-
integrated libraries than library-integrated curricula.

2. There is dissatisfaction with the present level of student library skills among librarians, faculty, and the students
themselves.[4]

3. This present skill level is likely to become even more unsatisfactory because of two pressures:

a. The pressure on librarians and faculty of greater numbers of students.

b. The pressure on librarians, faculty and students of the increasing size and complexity of libraries.

These pressures mean that the student will have to work both more independently and at a higher level of skill than he does now, to maintain even his present fractional acquaintance with the world of informational sources.

In the search for means to improve student library skills in the face of these pressures evidence should be considered that points to something that has long been suspected; namely, that the faculty play a more decisive role in determining student library-use habits than many librarians would like to admit. The few studies of student library use available are concerned primarily with amount of use rather than amount of skill. The programs at Stephens College and at the Chicago Undergraduate Division of the University of Illinois, among the programs most analyzed, report in terms of increased circulation and numbers of reference questions.[5] This discussion is more concerned with ability than with quantity. Nevertheless an examination of some of these studies may be relevant.

Harvie Branscomb, in his review of research on student use of several college and university libraries for his Teaching with Books, cited Stephens College and four others as having made particularly spectacular increases in the amount of student library use, as measured by increased per student circulation.[6] At Stephens the library had simply taken over the instructional program when the librarian was made dean of instruction. At Antioch, Lawrence, Olivet, and Southwestern modified tutorial plans had been inaugurated. The same basic type of change had occurred in all five institutions: there had been a change in teaching methods. In one case the change had come about through the initiative of the library, but the campaign had been aimed at the instructional program, through the

257

faculty, rather than at the students directly. The implication of the effect of these five programs on library circulation is echoed in the suggestions of other recent writers on the teaching function of the library that perhaps it is the faculty who are the important element, rather than any program the library can devise directly for the students. [7]

That the faculty should bear the responsibility is easily said. But since even the most library-minded faculty member (and they are few enough) is never library-minded enough for the librarian, should not the librarian do the job? Further evidence that the faculty will remain primary stimulants in student library habits despite teaching efforts by the library suggests the contrary.

In his Teaching with Books, Branscomb reported on his own survey of student library use at a school referred to as "University A." In the section on reserve use he presented an intriguing distribution of student reserve borrowing in four sections of the same history course. [8] Here were students who had been exposed to whatever basic orientation program that university library offered. They were being taught the same course, with the same reading list, and were being offered the same library facilities with which to do their work. In earlier distributions Branscomb had failed to find any correlation between scholastic standing and library use, the most obvious hypothesis; but in his distribution of the borrowers by section the pattern became clear. How much reading the student did depended simply on which of the four professors he had.

All of the findings reported so far deal with quantity of use. Their relevance rests on the assumption that quantity and ability are phenomena each of which suggests the presence of the other. My own experience, which I should like to report to you, deals directly with ability.

The problem was much the same that faced Branscomb—variant performance among sections of the same course. The course was a one-hour-one-semester counseling course which included units on adjustment to college in general, study habits, vocational choice and library skills. All entering freshmen carrying full time programs took the course. (Thus the group of students represented approximates the entering class of a traditional college more closely than would most samples drawn from a community college because of the elimination of the part-time adult students who are the "different" elements in the community college population.) Student assignment to sections was random. The library unit of the program consisted of a one-hour lecture, the issuing of a printed library handbook, and the completion of a written follow-up test done in the library during the week following the lecture and handed in at the next class period. The written test was so constructed as to be a completely individual project; no copying was possible. All papers were graded and detailed records kept for five semesters, 1956–1958. Some of the results are significant.

During this period there were eighty-five sections of counseling with a total enrollment of about 2,550 students. Seventy-eight per cent (1,995 students) completed and turned in the test paper. (This figure tallies nicely with Peyton Hurt's finding that 78 per cent of Stanford graduate students thought library instruction would have been helpful in undergraduate work.[9] It also matches exactly the 78 per cent of a sample of students drawn from the Wright counseling course one semester during the study who rated the library unit "helpful.") The percentage of papers completed increased slightly each semester. The 78 per cent "helpful" rating referred to above was the second highest favorable rating in the student evaluation of sixteen elements of the counseling course. The library unit of the program seemed an established thing, but questions remained. The percentage of returns and the mean and median scores varied widely from section to section. At the end of five semesters a retrospective study was undertaken to determine why this variation occurred.

None of the factors that might have been supposed to correlate significantly with response and performance did so. There was no correlation between performance and which of two librarians gave the lecture. There was no correlation between performance and whether an audio-visual aid was used.

There were a few sections which received direction only from the instructor. A few of these sections did surprisingly well; some did very poorly. An interesting pattern did emerge, how ever, when the sections were distributed, as Branscomb had done, by instructor. Each section was labelled plus or minus according to the relationship of its median score to the median for the group as a whole for that semester. A total of eighteen instructors from various departments taught the eighty-five sections. Two with only one section each were discounted, leaving sixteen. These sixteen instructors taught from two to sixteen sections each. Of these sixteen, seven rated 100 per cent plus (or minus); that is, every section of each of these instructors performed on one side of the median for the semeste The sections of four other instructors performed at a 2:1 consistency ratio. Only three instructors had an inconclusive per formance record, e.g. two sections above and one below. Only two had an even division of plus and minus sections. That is to say, the students of eleven of the sixteen instructors performed so consistently better (or worse) than the norm, over a period of five semesters, despite variations in lecture personnel, methods, and equipment that it is impossible not to conclude that a decisive factor in the attitude and hence the performance of a student on a library assignment in his classroom instructor.

This suggests strongly that the librarian face squarely the fact that in teaching students he has been teaching the wrong people. The responsibility for student library habits belongs to the teaching faculty not only for the type of reason sometimes advanced: that it should for one reason or another; but for the simple and compelling reason that it does. The faculty are responsible probably not only for the amount of student library use but for the level of skill; and we and they might as well realize this and build our library programs from that premise.

This further suggests to me that to be most effective the librarian should concentrate his responsibility on providing the best service he can to the patron who presents himself voluntarily. This service should probably include both personal and printed guidance, and perhaps even the offer of a course in library skills—entirely elective. The librarian should further hold himself responsible for some sort of organized effort directed to make each faculty member of his institution aware of what cooperation with the library has to offer his particular course. This effort should be aimed at the faculty not only because it is easier (there are fewer of them to begin with, and the turnover is slower), but because the evidence suggests that this is the only way to reach the student body as a whole. If his time and his library are not already full, the librarian may still want to storm the fraternity lounges and campus bars for marginal users. But the evidence seems to indicate that unless he approaches these students through their professors his efforts will be largely ineffective.

Faculty members have their responsibilities, of course, to do their teaching jobs to the best of their abilities. This may not always produce the amount and the kind of library use the librarian would like to see; but it may just be possible that the pattern of successful scholarship at certain levels and within certain areas does not demand our kind of library use. We may try, through our work with these faculty members, to convince them otherwise, but in the end they must be allowed to judge. Besides, their feelings will be reflected in their students despite efforts of the library to reach the students directly.

The student also must assume certain responsibilities. The fact is that in most institutions there already are—and in the rest there soon will be—enough "volunteer" library users to keep both faculty and library staff too busy to worry about the others.

My conclusion is not so much a recommendation as a realization of the way things are. The librarian is most effective at making a success of the casual, voluntary student contact. He should, further, feel responsible for "teaching" the faculty. But "teaching students to use the library"—

"formal instruction in library technique for the student body in general" as I have defined it—this is the job of the teaching faculty. The professor should be and clearly is responsible not only for his students' grasp of the subject content of a course, but also for their concept and acquisition of the skills, including library skills, necessary to master that content.

50. THE ROLE OF THE COLLEGE LIBRARY STAFF IN INSTRUCTION IN THE USE OF THE LIBRARY

E. J. Josey

The library undergirds the instructional program of the college. It cannot be separated from the professors or the curriculum. Someone has said that we can dispense with the faculty and rely solely on the college library, and students will continue to be educated, but this is not the prevailing view. In many institutions of higher learning, there is the idea that students will learn without using the library or knowledge of the use of the library. However, it is the firm conviction of this writer that both the faculty and the college library are equally important in the education of college students. The faculty stimulates intellectual curiosity and critical thinking, while the library, through its resources, provides the intellectual sustenance which can be found only in books.

If it is true that intellectual sustenance is housed in the college library, then it is equally true that knowledge of the use of the library is important in the education of college students. The annual output of the world of publishing is enormous. Current publishing, coupled with the scholarship of yesteryear that is found in antiquarian books, as well as information in the old and current periodicals, staggers the imagination. It is sheer folly for college libraries to spend thousands of dollars to assemble these materials, while at the same time no concrete efforts are made to instruct college students in the use of these materials.

PURPOSE OF THE STUDY

Savannah State College moved into its new library in the fall of 1959. The imposing new structure with its spacious reference department and reading rooms stimulated library use. The former cramped quarters had been an impediment to good library service. Now, for the first time in the history of the college, the library staff had adequate space to confer with and offer reference assistance to students. It was soon apparent that many students, including upper-classmen, were woefully unaware of how to use a simple basic tool such as the Readers Guide to Periodical Literature. The stark realization that graduating seniors did not know how to use the card catalog,[1] as revealed from a study conducted by the catalog librarian, also helped to ignite the fire.

The librarian placed the problem before the library committee. It was discovered that the English department was responsible for a unit on the use of the library in Humanities 101. Instructors did their teaching in the classrooms without consultation with the library. After serious deliberations, the committee unanimously adopted the following recommendation and instructed the librarian to inform the chairman of the English department:

> The Library Committee recommends that the library staff be included for one class period in the instruction in the use of the library as it appears in Humanities 101. This instruction should take place in the library so that the students may have personal contact with the reference tools.

The librarian and his staff were not satisfied with the "one class period" recommendation, but in spite of its apparent limited consideration, it was an initial step in the right direction. However, we were not prepared for the tempest in the teapot which followed. The librarian informed the English department of the library committee's recommendation, and the chairman of the English department returned the following reply:

">. . . May I request you to inform the Library Committee that the English Department has already given serious consideration to library orientation in its freshman classes. This consideration is based upon our professional knowledge of the nature of freshman English courses and what constitutes content and procedures in said courses. Accordingly, the members of the department, in light of their experiences, training and background, and in light of individuality in each course, in terms of its constituents and the methodology employed by the instructor, decided that they will work individually with students in their classes according to course outlines in Humanities 101 and 102. And further that members of the Department of English will continue to work with students in their classes in the use of the library in connection with specific assignments requiring such use.

"You will note that the attitude of the department is student-centered and course-centered, not library-centered. As I mentioned to you in an earlier conversation, knowledge of library tools is simply one small phase of information dispensed in Humanities 101 and 102, not the main focus. We are certainly aware of the fact that all students at Savannah State College should have some competence in library usage, but, departmentally, we do not assume the responsibility of bringing light where there may be darkness in this matter, which is college-wide, not merely a matter for the English Department to summarily solve in Humanities 101 and Humanities 102.

THE ROLE OF THE COLLEGE LIBRARY STAFF

"But please be assured, the members of the
department are aware of the problem and will work
on this matter from three points (as indicated
throughout this letter): (1) the individual student
as the need arises, (2) the nature of the individual
course and the teacher's method of conducting that
course, and (3) accepted professional standards and
practices in teaching English in College."[2]

The foregoing letter from the chairman of the English department, and several unsuccessful attempts to confer with
him, led this writer to devise an instrument to determine the
extent of instruction in library use in a group of institutions
of higher education. In addition, an effort was made to assess
the role of the library staff in the process.

METHODOLOGY

In the spring of 1961, the writer sent a questionnaire to
500 college and university library administrators throughout
the United States. The librarians represented institutions of
various sizes and types, i.e., large public universities, large
privately-endowed universities, liberal arts colleges, teachers' colleges, prestige institutions, and less-known institutions.

Eight questions were posed and respondents were requested to check yes or no. (1) The reference librarian or a
member of the staff is responsible for a course in the use of
the library. (2) A member of the library staff gives one lecture or a series of lectures in connection with freshman orientation week. (3) Library instruction is given as a unit in the
freshman English course, and classes are brought to the library for a series of lectures in connection with or one lecture by the library staff. (4) Formal instruction is given by
the library staff to freshman students in a subject area other
than English. (5) If the instruction is not given in conjunction
with the English courses, indicate whether instruction is given
to freshman students by the library staff with class work in
subject courses at a time when the students are most likely

to be using the materials. (6) Instruction in the use of the library is coordinated with the work of the library. (7) Do you feel that freshman library instruction should be given by members of the teaching faculty without the cooperation of the librarian and his staff? (8) Although instruction in library use is handled by the library staff, there is wholehearted faculty planning and participation.

Library literature abounds with descriptions of successful library-staff taught programs, but very little has been done in the area of faculty controlled programs or assessing the role of the library staff in the teaching process. There is no need for a review of the literature, for Bonn has surveyed the literature thoroughly.[3]

FINDINGS

The findings were varied and revealing. Librarians felt so keen about the problem of instructing college freshman students in the use of the library that many were not content to check the questionnaire alone. They also wrote letters to clarify their views. Of the 500 libraries canvassed, 397 or 79 per cent responded. In view of the high percentage of returns, the findings are significant.

Concerning question one, 239 or 60 per cent of the respondents reported that the reference librarian or a member of the library staff was not responsible for teaching a course in the use of the library to freshman students, while 107 or 27 per cent indicated that they offered such a course; 51 or 13 per cent gave no response.

With regard to question two, 177 librarians or 45 per cent indicated that a member of the library staff gave one lecture in the use of the library during orientation week; 75 or 19 per cent presented several lectures during the orientation period, while 145 or 36 per cent failed to check the question. The results of question number two are not too conclusive, in view of the fact that a large number of librarians (36 per cent) failed to check the question, but if we consolidate the 177 librarians who present one lecture during the orientation week and the 75 librarians who provide several, then 64 per cent of the respondents participate in some kind of orientation program. Most of the orientation week programs were no more than guided tours. Therefore, orientation week is used to a large extent to introduce students to the location of the library and in some instances, for elementary instruction.

In spite of this high percentage of participation as reported here, many librarians have misgivings of orientation week programs. This point of view is expressed by the associate director of the University of Nebraska libraries who warns, "We must overcome the general idea that library instruction is something that can be tacked on a one-day orientation program . . . ."[4]

Regarding question three, which is concerned with library instruction given as a unit in the freshman English course, 118 or 30 per cent indicated that one lecture is given to English classes by library staff; 103 or 26 per cent give a series of lectures by the library staff English classes and 176 or 44 per cent did not present lectures in connection with English classes, while 20 failed to respond. Combining the single lectures and a series of lectures given in conjunction with English classes, we find that 221 academic libraries, or 56 per cent of the libraries surveyed, give instruction in the use of the library to English classes.

Teaching freshmen the use of the library in conjunction with English courses seems to be the preference of the majority of the respondents. Nevertheless, librarians are not completely satisfied with this arrangement. The librarian of the University of North Dakota writes, "Our instruction in library use is done in the freshman English course by the instructors in the English department and classes are then brought to the library for a test in library materials and use, which is compiled by the library staff but administered by the English instructor. During the taking of this test the library staff and sometimes the instructor are available to assist the students and offer explanation and further information. We do not feel that this is a very satisfactory means of accomplishing library instruction. In the first place, the responsibility of the individual instructor is met with varying degrees of enthusiasm and competence. Second, the library test seems to be viewed by students rather as a hurdle to be crossed than as a useful adjunct to studies in all fields. Third, because of this student attitude, there seems to be a minimal amount of actual acquaintance with library tools, plus copying of answers from others with similar questions, and other time-saving short cuts."[5]

Although a semblance of cooperation exists between the English department and the library in a large southern university, the respondent writes "This year we changed our program and now have only a thirty-minute televised picture (not enough, but all allowed by the English department) . . . I, personally, am not satisfied with the televised class as it is now handled, but it will be difficult to convince the English department that more time is needed."[6]

Several librarians in their letters indicated that efforts were being made to improve the instruction in English classes. One healthy sign comes from the librarian of Western Michigan University. Miss Stokes reports, "This summer the educational TV staff of the university expects to work with the English faculty and the library staff to prepare a tape to be used for library orientation in English classes. We have high hopes of this being a much better solution than our previous attempts."[7]

Question four sought to elicit whether formal library instruction is given by the library staff to freshman students in a subject area other than English. Answering this query, we find 90 librarians or 23 per cent who responded affirmatively, while 272 librarians or 68 per cent replied negatively and 35 librarians or 9 per cent ignored the question. It appears that for all intents and purposes English seems to be the desired vehicle for instructing freshman students in the use of the library.

Librarians were requested in question five to denote that if instruction is not given in conjunction with the English courses, whether it is given by the library staff, with class work in subject courses at a time when the students are most likely to be using the materials. Their answers revealed that 137 or 34 per cent marked yes, 166 or 42 per cent marked no, while 94 or 24 per cent did not answer. These results pointedly call attention to the fact that the majority of the respondents give the instruction when the students are not using the library for research purposes in their course work.

The answers to questions four and five do not correlate, but the investigator refused to discard question five, for there is the possibility that if busy respondents hastily read question five and ignored the not in the wording of the question, the last question in the preceding paragraph is apropos. At the same time, the low correlation directs attention to one of the great limitations of the questionnaire method, i.e., the respondents do not always interpret and answer the questions in the same context that the investigator is considering.

Turning to question six which attempted to ascertain whether instruction in the use of the library is coordinated with the work of the library, we find that 127 or 32 per cent replied no, 181 or 46 per cent yes and 89 or 22 per cent failed to respond. It is clearly evident that the largest percentage of the respondents felt that there is real coordination between the library and the academic departments in this regard.

Librarians were requested in question seven to answer the crucial question: Do you feel that freshman library instruction should be given by members of the teaching faculty without the cooperation of the librarian and his staff? An overwhelming majority of 379 librarians or 95 per cent answered no, seven librarians or 2 per cent stated yes and eleven librarians or 3 per cent gave no response.

Librarians responded in eloquent, forthright, clear and unequivocal language, in reference to question seven. The librarian of George Peabody College for Teachers stated, "As for myself, I am rather firmly convinced that as our collections grow larger and larger, the library staff must and should be the persons designated to offer a minimum program of instruction in the use of the library."[8] The director of libraries at the University of Notre Dame pointed out that, "I disagree very strongly with a program that would provide

freshman library instruction by members of the teaching
faculty without the cooperation of the librarian and his staff."[9]
Two interesting comments that were included on the questionnaire are the following: Herbert B. Anstaett, librarian of
Franklin and Marshall College, gave a resounding "definitely
no!" In his terse style, Guy Lyle, director of libraries,
Emory University, who answered no, stated, "although it
would be better than non-instruction."

The final question attempted to elicit from librarians
whether there was wholehearted faculty planning and participation if the instruction was handled by the library staff. The
findings showed that 170 or 43 per cent reported yes, 135 or 34
per cent stated no, and 92 or 23 per cent disregarded the question.

Many of the respondents objected to the investigator's use
of the phrase "wholehearted faculty planning and cooperation."
They vividly opposed the use of "wholehearted," striking through
the word and substituting words which did not bespeak well of
their faculties. Some of the more vocal comments on their
questionnaires are as follows: Frank A. Schneider, assistant
librarian of Arizona State University, wrote, "Where we have
stirred interest the cooperation has been high." Joseph T.
Popecki, assistant director of libraries, Catholic University,
stated, "varies with the many freshman English instructors."
Mrs. Mary Watson Hymon, librarian of Grambling College,
wrote "wholehearted planning and participation of those involved. We do not reach the total faculty." And Sarah D. Jones,
librarian of Goucher College, commented, "As new faculty members come, we have to convert them, so that degree of whole-
heartedness wavers."

IMPLICATIONS

The foregoing analysis of the responses from the 397 librarians suggests serious implications regarding the extent of
instruction in library use and the role of the library staff in the
process. Most of the respondents (60 per cent) do not offer a
required formal course in the use of the library. It may be

that librarians have rejected this approach as being academically unfeasible or curriculum committees do not desire the encroachment. The small number (27 per cent) who offer the required course indicated that the course is handled by a member of the library staff.

Orientation week is used by many librarians to introduce the incoming college students to the location of the library. The largest number (45 per cent) offers elementary instruction in the nature of one lecture or guided tour, and a few (19 per cent) present several lectures during this period. A growing number of librarians seem to be doing away with the orientation week approach, because of the large enrollments and the helter-skelter fiesta-type affair that characterize most orientation periods. Concerning growing enrollments, one librarian asserts "We used to give a series of lectures, but due to the rapid increase in student enrollment, the librarians found they had too much to do in such areas as building the collection, etc., to keep up with all of these lectures...."[10] Miss Seaberg writes, "We did have for years, a tour-lecture system. As the enrollment increased and the staff load became heavier, this method seemed to get more and more mass-produced and less effective."[11] Orientation week programs seem to be less palatable. In the words of an English instructor and a college librarian, "clearly, it is not enough to arm the freshman with the floor plan of the library and urge him forward."[12]

On the basis of the findings, it appears that the freshman English course continues to be the traditional course for offering instruction in the use of the library, for 56 per cent reported affirmatively on this question. Many librarians while indicating some degree of cooperation from their English departments are not completely satisfied as reported in the letters referred to above. Cooperation between the library and the English department is essential, if a modicum of progress is to be experienced. This view is cogently voiced by a distinguished reference librarian who states, "I would like to emphasize that the success or failure of any program depends to a

271

great extent upon the cooperation of the English department. We have had our good years and our poor years, depending largely, we feel quite sure, upon the enthusiasm and interest of the faculty member in charge of freshman English instruction."[13]

The majority of the librarians who indicated that instruction was given in courses other than English also pointed out that the instruction was given at a time when the students were not using the library materials. We have no explanation for this situation. There is the possibility that the unit on the use of the library is sandwiched in at the most opportune time without regard for the sound educational philosophy of presenting the instruction when it will be more beneficial to the students.

The results of this study confirm this writer's belief that freshman library instruction should not be given without the cooperation of the librarian and his staff, for 379 librarians (95 per cent) asserted this fact. Librarians are better qualified by their training and knowledge of bibliographical techniques to guide the uninitiate through the maze of materials that are now housed in college and university libraries. As the writer pointed out at the beginning of the paper, it is foolhardy to amass the highly specialized reference tools and collections and, at the same time, fail to provide instruction in the use of these materials. Many of our college freshmen come from areas where there is poor school and public library service; thus, their first experiences in the college library can be foreboding. By and large, members of the teaching faculty are not equipped to cope with this type of college freshman in the college library.

Some college instructors have become so immersed in the educational jargon of "independent study," while they have forgotten that most of our students will continue to be dependent for many years to come until we improve the public schools. A librarian who has a serious concern about instructing the average student in the skills of using the library effectively asserts, "the average or below average student, on the other hand, is likely to avoid the library, having found it a useless if not actually a terrifying place. It is not enough that he be stimulated to use the library, he must be provided with experiences which convince him that using the library is a necessary and meaningful part of education."[14]

It is impossible to evade one of the serious questions raised by librarians who reported that they had dropped library instruction because of growing enrollments and shortages of staff. Increasing enrollments and staff shortages will become more acute as we move towards the 70's. This is a salient fact which every library administrator must consider. A solution to this problem may very well be our turning to automation, as suggested by the director of libraries at Southern Illinois University.[15] In our search for alternatives and in our quest for closer cooperation with the faculty, librarians must be ever mindful that the college library is not an adjunct to teaching, it is at the very heart of the instructional process. Therefore, it is of utmost importance that college students be given the skills to use the library at the beginning of their college education.

The role of the librarian in educating the faculty to this point of view is arduous. College librarians must emphasize the following two inescapable points to their teaching colleagues. First, students' knowledge of using the library strengthens the relationship between the library and the instructional program, and second, professionally trained librarians who teach the skills of library use will not usurp the responsibilities of the faculty, but will supplement their efforts, for librarians alone are aware of the bibliographical and guidance services that the library staff is capable of offering. The essentiality of the times is the need for the integration of college libraries more completely with the curriculum, through a coordinated program of instruction in the use of the library.

51. THE LIBRARIAN AS TEACHER IN
THE COLLEGE LIBRARY

Helen M. Brown

In the instruction of students in the use of the library the librarian becomes himself a teacher and realizes his direct contribution to the educational program of the college.

There are two inherent difficulties in giving such instruction to freshmen. The greatest difficulty is that the subject is not in itself fascinating, like the plays of Tennessee Williams or the burial customs of the Samoans. The ability to use the library is a tool which is appreciated only when the need for it has been felt. The second difficulty lies in the widely varying library backgrounds found among new college students. Great as have been the strides made in library facilities at the elementary and high school levels, many students still enter college with perhaps only the ability to make partial use of the library card catalog. For these two reasons, no instruction can be so successful as the individual guidance given at the reference desk to the student who comes voluntarily seeking help. The library in the college with a small enrollment, which can handle the instruction of entering freshmen on an individual basis, is indeed fortunate. However, many college libraries prefer to give freshman instruction on a group basis, partly to prevent an excessive burden on the reference staff, and partly because they fear some new students may be in ignorance of their own lack of library knowledge.

This group instruction of new students may be given in one of several ways: in connection with an academic course, as part of an orientation program or course, or as a separately scheduled library project. Instruction in connection with an academic course calls for a course which is required of all new students and for which library materials furnish the tools.

THE LIBRARIAN AS TEACHER

An examination of a representative group of college catalogs reveals that many institutions require of first year students a course designed to increase their facility in reading, understanding, writing and speaking the English language. These courses may be listed quite simply as composition, or English, or in the more modern parlance, as communication. The latest Barnard College Announcement rather happily sums up the evident general purpose of these courses:

"The College believes that every student should be able to speak and write good English, and that her mind should be trained to think straight, weigh facts, and seek the truth. Such abilities may be developed in many courses and activities, but specifically the Faculty requires English A as helpful toward this end."

Courses of this type, where they exist, provide an ideal opportunity for library-faculty cooperation in teaching the use of the library. The classroom work, with its emphasis upon themes, shows the student his need for the instruction and provides him with opportunity to put into practice what he learns. The instructor in the course usually plans to bring his class to the library for an hour or two of instruction during regular class periods. We have found that the presence of the classroom instructor, who may enter into discussion with the librarian and who may stay for a few minutes after the formal instruction period to help answer students' questions, aids in establishing rapport. Some of the instructors give follow-up problems which will help fix in the students' minds the important points covered by the library lecture.

In some institutions students may secure exemption from these courses in composition, or English, or communication, by passing an exemption examination. The library then has a choice of giving library instruction as a separate library project to all the students exempted, or of conducting a library test to determine whether some of the entering students may be excused. It is evident that in case the library chooses to administer such a test, it should be given to the entire group of first year students, since proficiency in understanding and writing English does not necessarily indicate proficiency in the use of the library. Some interesting studies of the degree of correlation between the two skills might certainly be made in various colleges, however. Libraries reporting success in the use of these tests have usually made or adapted them to their own particular situation.

The content of freshman instruction in the use of the library and consequently, the material covered in tests of library knowledge, includes the same minimum or core in almost every situation. This minimum is the use of the card catalog as the index to the book material in the library and the key to its location in the stacks, and the use of periodical indexes. To this minimum, we recommend the addition of the use of the Essay and General Literature Index as the guide to material in parts of books. Each library will add to this basic instruction according to the needs most frequently shown by freshman students in the particular college. The teachers of first-year courses and the library service-desk personnel, who meet freshman problems repeatedly, should be asked for suggestions of material to be included in the library instruction. As a starting point for freshman themes the general encyclopedias and the standard English and American biographical dictionaries are frequently included. The value of including any special subject tool is doubtful unless it can be linked immediately to the student's daily experience or to his work in an academic course.

The timing of the instruction is important. Early in the academic year we have to compete with the pressure of many activities and new impressions, and often with homesickness. Yet instruction must be given early if the library staff is not to be unduly burdened with individual guidance. After several weeks, on the other hand, the need for instruction becomes more apparent to the student.

At Skidmore we have arrived at what we think is a happy compromise. Two hours of instruction are given to each section of the freshman English classes. This compromise is the result of a trial last year when some of the entering students

THE LIBRARIAN AS TEACHER

were given both hours of instruction in the first week of the
semester, and others were given only one hour's teaching in
the first week, including the use of the card catalog, the
Essay Index, the standard biographical dictionaries and the
general encyclopedias. The students in the second group
were given their hour's instruction in the periodical indexes
in the fourth week, just before they started work on their
term papers. We found that the students in the first group,
faced with writing papers, were returning in droves to our
service desk to be shown over again how to use the periodical
indexes. Now the first hour's instruction, which is given to
all freshmen early in the second week of the fall semester, includes the use of the card catalog, the Essay and General Literature Index, the general encyclopedias and the standard
biographical dictionaries. The second hour's instruction, in
the use of periodical indexes, is given to each section of the
class just as it begins work on the term paper. This practice
has met with noticeably greater success. Since the work of
the classes has been planned so that the sections begin work
on the paper in successive weeks, the library instruction periods have been spread out and the weekly teaching load on the
library staff lessened.

Some college library staffs give formal credit courses to
students in the use of the library, the courses continuing in
most cases throughout one semester or term. In the past
these courses have usually consisted of lectures covering the
use of library tools, beginning with the general group and then
continuing through the major subject fields.

Now we are coming to recognize that such courses are
basically unsatisfactory in that they force students to study
subject bibliography for which they have no immediate need,
and in the use of which they will have no early practice. Various attempts to offset the difficulties inherent in such instruction may be traced through current college catalogs. One
modification is the placing of more emphasis on the history
of books and libraries, thus giving the course substance and
dignity in its own right. Other courses stress the sources of

277

BROWN

information on present day problems; some give more attention to the method of working and permit the student to concentrate on an independent project, frequently a bibliography to support a paper in another course.

I think you may be interested, in this connection, in a recent decision we have made at Skidmore. We have been offering a one-semester, one-credit course known as Bibliography 301, open to juniors and seniors with the permission of the instructor. This permission clause has given us the opportunity to ask each student, before enrolling her in the course, why she wanted to take it. Several impressive reasons have been offered, but only one student had the innate honesty, or courage, to admit to me that it was the only one point credit course that fitted her schedule. Of the 18 students who attended classes during two years at Skidmore, it appears that only seven English majors and six chemistry majors had sufficient motive for electing the course. The other students, who obviously had needed one credit to round out their programs, were correlating the work of the course with work in art, physical science or philosophy courses.

Each student showed interest in, and was ready to profit by, several classes during the semester: the hours during which we discussed the theoretical aspects of bibliography, the card catalog, general aids and government documents, and the classes which covered particular fields in which the student was studying. However, each was forced to spend several hours considering groups of tools in which she had no interest. This seems to me a great waste of time for both students and instructor.

With the concurrence of the Curriculum Committee, which is yet to be consulted, we are planning to drop this course and offer instead to extend our teaching of class groups in the bibliography of their subject. Members of the chemistry department, upon being approached for their reactions to the proposal, proved so responsive that they are planning to include the literature of chemistry in the department seminar, the bibliography to be taught jointly by a member of the department and the librarian.

THE LIBRARIAN AS TEACHER

Members of the English department, also approached as being the other group chiefly concerned in the change, have replied favorably. This year we met informally with a group of students from the English seminar for a discussion of the tools of special importance to them in the preparation of their papers, but the time allowed was too short and attendance voluntary. The staff had to follow up with hours of individual instruction. Next year, we shall meet the students during regular class periods. We are already following this plan successfully with the history seminar.

We are going on the theory that it is better to spend our time in teaching the use of subject tools to class groups who will have immediate use for them, than in giving more extensive instruction to the few students who elect Bibliography 301 and have no practical use for about half the course.

In making our plans to drop the course rather than to transform it into another type of course, we have been influenced by the college curriculum and by the size of our staff. Much as we should enjoy giving a two or three credit course combining the historical background of printed sources of knowledge with a survey of the basic general and subject bibliography, we think there is little place for it in our college program which encourages the combination of vocational with liberal arts courses. The college believes that a girl may take a generous amount of work in any of the vocational departments of the college and still be eligible for the Bachelor of Arts degree and conversely, "that the physical education teacher, the nurse, the dietitian, or the commercial artist, is a better professional woman and a better citizen if at least half of her college course is made up of the familiar liberal subjects." Such a philosophy in practice leaves little room in any student's program for non-essentials.

Our second consideration is that our comparatively small staff must spend available instruction time in the way which will most benefit the greatest number of our students.

This teaching of students in class groups involves preliminary discussion with the instructor regarding material to be covered and regarding individual projects of the students in

the class. It is essential that the library staff not only understand the plan of the course, but be kept informed of assignments involving special use of library materials. The library
should maintain, as a matter of routine, complete files of class
outlines, reading lists, and assignment sheets.

Unquestionably it is the informal teaching of individual
students by the reference staff which meets with the greatest
measure of success, because the instruction is given in answer to a specific personal need that has just been felt.

The peculiar contribution of this individual teaching done
by the reference librarian is his part in helping students to
clarify their problems and to go logically about solving them.
The member of our staff in charge of readers' service said
to me the other day, when we were discussing this point,
"Whose responsibility is it to help these girls think through
their problems?" Perhaps the responsibility lies largely with
the classroom instructor, but he certainly shares it with the
library reference staff. Some students, confused in defining
their projects, will seek a conference with their instructor;
others will go directly to the library, requesting information
as to where to find material on a startlingly broad subject or
on a fuzzily defined subject. In dealing with these students,
it is essential that the reference librarian acknowledge, accept and enjoy his own role of teacher; it is essential that he
refuse to state the problem for the student, but that by patient,
tactful and understanding questioning he lead the student to
think it through for himself.

The teaching activity of the reference staff will always
reflect the educational program of the college. Institutions
which emphasize the type of instruction in which students
work out individual problems of interest to them will naturally provide to the library staff the greatest instructional opportunities.

It is important that library staff members continue to
regard themselves as teachers in their relations with their
student assistants. The full educational possibilities in student assistantships will be realized only when the staff super-

visors take pains to assign jobs so far as possible in accordance with the students' interests. They should also interpret to them the place of necessary routine jobs in the work of the library as a whole, and finally insist on a satisfactory standard of performance.

There will always be two limitations to the educational potentialities of student library jobs. The primary purpose in employing student assistants is to get the work of the library done. Since students are for the most part untrained, short-term help, many of them must be assigned to routine work. The second limitation is the degree of receptivity and imagination of the student himself, which will govern the extent to which he will profit by the educational possibilities of his job. A Skidmore student shelving just three hours and twenty minutes a week was assigned to reading shelves in the section where the books in her major field of interest were located. She emerged from the first week's work in a glow because she was finding out about books which she did not know existed. Another student would make dull routine of the same job. Let us not forget that education is a two-way process!

Student assistantships of educational value will fall roughly into four classifications. First are jobs in which the student works in the subject field of his interest or has the opportunity to practice what he has learned in the classroom. In this category are assistantships in divisional or departmental reading rooms, poster making, checking orders for foreign language books, etc. In a second group are positions which open up to the student a new field of knowledge. Examples of this class are the acquisitions department job which gives the student assistant an introduction to the book trade, or work in the mechanical preparation of books which involves an understanding of book construction and may lead a student, on suggestion from his supervisor, to read McMurtrie's The Book or a similar title. Then there are jobs through which students may incrase their knowledge of present day problems and of the sources of information on them. Work on exhibits is particularly fruitful in this respect. A student assistant in the Skidmore Library

BROWN

looks up material for the exhibit which is maintained in connection with our weekly Open Forum radio program on vital issues of the day. The exhibit is supposed to present authoritative material, in not-too-lengthy form, which will provide background information for intelligent audience participation. Part of the exhibit consists of four or five questions which are suggested as fundamental to the problem. Although a staff member assumes final responsibility for the exhibit, the student assistant obviously must scan the material available to make a preliminary selection and to suggest pertinent questions.

Finally there is the large class of student jobs which are of educational value chiefly because they help develop good personal qualities, sense of responsibility, habit of carrying work through to completion, ability to organize work, etc. These should, of course, accompany anything else the student learns. There are some types of work which are particularly helpful in this respect—for example, service at a reserve desk where the student may be left in charge at certain periods. The development of these qualities in the student assistant depends upon good personnel practice in the library and the teaching ability of the staff member who supervises the student's work.

The opportunities open to the librarian as a teacher in the library are almost limitless. It remains only that he accept and welcome these opportunities and participate actively in this role.

52. UNIVERSITY LIBRARY ORIENTATION BY TELEVISION

Edward G. Holley and Robert W. Oram

"Can instructional television solve the problem of library orientation for large numbers of students?" This is one of the questions which many librarians in larger colleges and universities are beginning to ask themselves as they face the task of coping with increasing enrollments. For most institutions of considerable size the time has passed when individual class lectures and guided library tours provide adequately for library orientation. When one speaks of first-time degree-credit students, five to ten thousand of them in fourteen institutions, or even of three to five thousand students in thirty institutions,[1] it becomes fairly obvious that a more efficient means of familiarizing these students with the library must be found than the traditional method of conducting students through the library in groups of twenty to thirty at a time. Moreover, there are numerous institutions with first-time degree-credit enrollments of one to three thousand which will undoubtedly double or triple their enrollments in the next five to ten years. Some institutions are already overwhelmed by trying to provide even a basic introduction to library services, and content themselves with offering each entering student a library handbook and bidding him Godspeed.

The problem of orientation is highlighted at an institution like the University of Illinois, which has both a large total enrollment and a sizeable complex of colleges and schools whose library needs are supplied by an equally extensive library system (over three million volumes in some thirty-four separate locations). Prior to 1961, most orientation for freshmen took place through means of the personally conducted library tour. There was a general tour for students in the beginning English course (Rhetoric 102) and, in addition to this basic introduction,

283

some departmental librarians serving the various professiona colleges provided instruction in library use for their specific fields—occasionally in formal courses and upon invitation fror specific faculty members, but more often through personally conducted tours of their own special libraries.

In the case of the education, philosophy, and psychology library, the librarian and his assistant provided tours for thre hundred and fifty to five hundred students in Education 101 (the basic introductory course), for forty to eighty students in som sections of Education 240 (the methods course), and for one hundred to a hundred and fifty students in the children's litera ture courses offered by the graduate school of library science a minimum total of some five hundred students per semester.

The amount of staff time spent on these tours, plus the time the librarians devoted to more formal lectures, began to be a serious burden, to say nothing of the limitations in effec- tiveness when a staff member has delivered fifteen lectures a semester on the same subject for the last ten years.

The problem of orientation for all incoming students, par- ticularly those in rhetoric or similar courses in the division of general studies, was much the same as that for the college of education, although general orientation had to cover a large physical area and had to be both more general and, in some ways, just as specific. The tours of the main library building had always been directed at students writing term papers in rhetoric; no tours were offered for any other groups unless an individual instructor wished to conduct a tour of his own. Pro fessional librarians from the reference department and the undergraduate library gave the rhetoric tours, which took fifty minutes, a large part of which was devoted to moving groups of twenty to twenty-five students from one place to another in a building which covers the better portion of a block. Often the students ended the tour by being more familiar with the corridors than with the card catalog. Although the tours did have the advantage of giving the student a feeling for the phys- ical arrangement of the building, even though his attention might wander if he were on the fringe of the group, the tours were highly unsatisfactory from a library viewpoint. Large blocks of staff time were involved, only half the rhetoric instructors took advantage of the opportunity, the tours disturbed other students studying or using the card catalog, and it was often difficult for all members of any one group to see the cards in the tray or even the large mock-ups used. Sometimes the size of the group and the height of the rooms prevented even the strongest-voiced librarian from being heard properly.

Under these circumstances, many librarians came to question the effectiveness of an operation so time-consuming and so obviously ineffective. As increasing enrollment compounded the problems, it was apparent that the small, well-organized, personally conducted tour had outlived its usefulness. In the fall of 1960 a number of interested staff members visited Illinois State Normal University in Normal to observe their experimental orientation program using television as the medium, and to see if there might not be implications for a much larger and more complex university.[2]

Although the group was impressed with the program at ISNU, they generally believed that TV facilities at Urbana might call for a different type of program. Initially, the library could experiment with one unit, learn from the mistakes, and possibly eventually develop a comprehensive program of library orientation by television.

The need for a better orientation program was discussed formally in the College of Education Library Committee for the better part of a year. While the committee believed that orientation was needed at all levels, e.g., undergraduate, graduate, and faculty, no one program would be likely to serve all groups equally well, and the undergraduates certainly constituted the most pressing problem. Many students coming to Illinois for the first time were completely bewildered by the size and complexity of the library system, and from their first frustrating contact resolved to have as little to do with the library as possible. The unusual student doggedly persisted until he knew his way around the system and could find what he wanted. Neither attitude was conducive to adequate preparation for teachers. To discover what kind of program would serve student needs most effectively, the committee sought answers to these specific questions: when does the student need orientation most, upon what course should the program be built, and through what medium can such orientation most efficiently be provided? Other faculty members, librarians, and students themselves were queried in an attempt to find the answers. While various points of view were expressed, the tendency seemed to be to use TV in preference to film, personally conducted tours, or handbooks. The course which provided the logical basis for experimentation was Education 101, an introductory course. After discussion with the office of instructional television and upon the offer of Charles J. McIntyre to assist in the program, the committee decided to go ahead with a video tape. Once the program had been taped, it could be rerun as many times as necessary, and production costs were definitely lower than those of film. A subsidiary advantage, which later proved illusory, lay in the coordination of the library orientation program with the general university-wide use of instructional television for orientation.

Once the decision had been made, the Education Library Committee drew up a complete list of what was to be included in the program, including the format, the number of photographs of the library, etc. On one point the committee was clear: the program should include certain very specific types of information and concentrate upon these rather than give the student a panoramic view of everything in the library. Particular attention should be given to the reserve book system, use of the card catalog, and instruction in the three basic reference tools in the field of education: Education Index, Buros' Fifth Mental Measurements Yearbook, and the Encyclopedia of Educational Research. Subsidiary information might be presented upon special materials such as periodicals, curriculum publica tions, and educational and psychological tests, but the main emphasis (subsequently reinforced by various devices throughout the actual program) would be on location data and the three reference tools. To assure this essential focus, the program was framed with only the needs of Education 101 students in mind, though the committee recognized that the program might be useful for other classes as well.

In the summer of 1961, the librarian narrated a 39-minute tape, "Education Library Tour," incorporating the above suggestions. Although the tape was filmed in the TV studio, ample provision had been made for the introduction of slides and diagrams showing the actual parts of the library, the various procedures for checking out books and locating data, and other devices demonstrating items the student would probably use in this library. Since the office of the dean of students was working on a general orientation program for freshmen at the same time, the committee agreed to give the program its trial run in that framework. To provide the proper introduction and stimulate interest, the dean of students, Fred H. Turner, and the dean of library administration, R. B. Downs, taped a six-minute preview to the main program. On September 26, 1961, "Education Library Tour" was broadcast over the university's television station, WILL-TV, for the first time. All organized houses and dormitories had set up stations to receive this and other programs in the general orientation series and had provided specially designated students as discussion leaders for each program.

Prior to the broadcast the librarian met with the instructors of the various sections of Education 101 to discuss ways in which they could make the orientation program more effective by emphasis on its main points before the program and a follow-up project afterwards. As a rough measure of the tape's effectiveness, each student who viewed the program was to be given the same simple ten-question quiz which had been given to students who took the tours the year before. Thus there would be some basis for comparison of the two methods of orientation, though such test results could obviously not be interpreted too strictly.

Although the test results were not spectacular, they did
reveal that the students had at least obtained as much information from the tape as they had from the tours. Furthermore, it was the general consensus that this program on
a specialized library had suffered from its inclusion within
the framework of general university orientation. House conditions were not always favorable to attentive viewing, the
confusion of large groups made retention difficult, and a
number of students reported difficulty in seeing the program
at all. Criticism and comments from both faculty and students favored broadcasting "Education Library Tour" to
specific class sections during the second semester. Despite
some mechanical difficulties and the need to improve certain technical details in the tape, all agreed that the program
was worth continuing. The revision of the tape could await
further trial under different conditions with the expectation
that the revised program could be undertaken in the summer
of 1962.

Since the library staff was in agreement with the judg-
ment of faculty and students, Dean Downs appointed a committee composed of the circulation librarian, the reference librarian, and the undergraduate librarian to develop a TV program providing a general introduction to the entire library
system. This program could replace the rhetoric tours and
might well serve as a basis for a subsequent series of programs for the specialized libraries.

The new committee viewed the education library tape
and agreed that the TV presentation was a satisfactory solution to the problem of communicating details of library routines to large groups of students. This committee believed
the ideal solution would be a complete sound-track movie,
but the complications involved in such a program, plus the
expense, made such a step impossible, at least until an experiment with TV tape had been made. The education library
tape was a good learning device for this committee, and without it more time would have been wasted in experimentation,
both by the librarians and the TV production personnel. None-

theless, the format did not seem to fit too well the general orientation picture. Designed as it was for a very special audience, the "Education Library Tour" had used the librarian as a sort of host-narrator who was seen as well as heard. When the camera was not focused on a title-page, catalog card, or slide of the library, it was directed to the narrator. The committee decided to abandon this format in favor of an unseen narrator. The camera could, under the new proposal, always be on the title or the card or the index being discussed. Moreover, the committee decided to use as many motion shots as possible with a silent camera. These shots would substitute for the physical presence of the student, avoid confusing floor plans, and help pinpoint locations.

For this new tape, a definite time limit of 30 minutes was suggested to conform to the over-all orientation program. Presumably, the same material which had been presented in the tours could be condensed if there were no problem of moving students from one spot to another. Later this proved to be a false assumption since the committee found itself adding more material in order to give depth. The program covered the same area as the tours had covered and had to be designed so that it gave orientation not only to rhetoric students but to any other group of potential users. This marriage of the specific and general, the simple and the complex, had its drawbacks and later led to some student complaints that it was too slow for those who knew the library[3] and was much too compressed for those who had never seen a library of the complexity of Illinois. The latter criticism was countered by providing a previously prepared handbook, Your Library, to every undergraduate. Since the TV program was viewed as a supplement to the handbook, the script referred to the handbook several times and assured the students that any details missed in the film could be found by an investigation of this booklet.

To give continuity to the tape, the committee decided to use one subject as its basis and carry this subject throughout the program. The subject, "Space Flight," proved an appropriate one since the first showing of the program coincided with

the John Glenn orbit. The program was designed to begin
with the general (the card catalog), and progress to the specific (circulation desk routines, reference department materials, and undergraduate library routines). All three librarians worked on sections of the program but the final draft was
edited by one person for the sake of continuity. Areas stressed
by the committee were the university's main card catalog, the
Reader's Guide, and other reference materials which provided
keys to the material on "Space Flight."

Once the committee had finished its task and the program
had been approved, it was submitted to the rhetoric department for suggestions. Aside from stylistic corrections, the
main objection was that the script was library-centered rather
than rhetoric-centered, an objection mitigated by showing the
student how to transcribe library information on cards in correct bibliographic form. The script was then submitted to TV
production personnel to make the necessary 181 slides and
130 feet of film.

The program, "Your Library," was broadcast on March 13
and 14, again within the framework of general university orientation. As had been true of the education library program,
there were many problems: bad listening conditions, confusion
caused by large groups and inability of individual instructors
to follow up the program. Presumably, with closed-circuit
TV, as had been used at Illinois State Normal University, initial student response would have been better. Again, the program itself was not an issue, but rather the scheduling and
technical problems which can be overcome.

In general the rhetoric department was favorably impressed with the program's potential. The head of the Rhetoric 102 sections, who had initially been skeptical about the replacement of the tours, agreed that points were made more
forcefully by TV than they could have been made by tour. Perhaps the most justifiable criticism was that too much material
was covered in too little time. Possibly a longer program or
a series of programs would do a more effective job. The rhetoric department still favors a program designed specifically

290

for the student doing a reference paper in which library orientation is only incidental. Such a program could easily be prepared by using the materials already gathered for the library's program, although it is the library view that such a program is a rhetoric department responsibility. No statistical data is available on the results of "Your Library," but there is general agreement that the program was well worth the effort and does as effective a job as the tours did. From the viewpoint of the library such an orientation program is definitely needed, and "Your Library" is a good first step.

What of the evaluation of the first program, "Education Library Tour?" Shortly before "Your Library" was completed, students in Education 101 again had an opportunity to evaluate "Education Library Tour." Again a ten-question test was given and again, although the results showed some slight improvement, the tape was demonstrated to be only as effective as the tours. The following table indicates the comparison of test results for tours and TV program for the education library.

	Tours (Spring, 1961)	Tape (Fall, 1961)	Tape (Spring, 1962)
No. Students	456	444*	304
Range	0–88	0–100	0–100
Right responses	62 per cent	65 per cent	66 per cent
Wrong responses	38 per cent	35 per cent	34 per cent

*Includes 56 students who took test but did not see program.

In using these results one should realize that they are at best a rough estimate. No control groups were set up and no thorough analysis of the different sections was made. Although the results fall short of expectations, they do provide some encouragement. The least that can be said is that the same amount of information is communicated with the expenditure of much less effort. With improvement in techniques and with a more careful analysis of student needs, the library should be able to prepare more effective programs and secure even better results.

One special comment can be made about test results from Education 101: the secondary education sections performed better than the elementary sections. Since the former group consists largely of sophomores and juniors who are expected to know their way around the library, while the latter group consists largely of freshmen, the question arises as to how well the program met the library needs of the incoming freshmen. However, a number of graduate assistants who led the discussion groups after viewing the film commented that the students appeared to learn more from the program than their test responses indicated. They also volunteered the opinion that the students might have been better prepared if they, as the instructors, had previewed the program first. Such comments reveal that much better coordination between class and library will be needed to achieve maximum results.

In an attempt to determine why one class was conspicuously successful in terms of test results, the education librarian met with students in that class to elicit their comments and criticisms. The students were candid and cooperative. Much of the discussion centered upon the technical details (blurred images, poor shots of books, pages, etc.) and poor scheduling; some questioned the necessity for including basic data such as an explanation of the card catalog in the video tape. Others, however, found this section very useful and wanted it retained. While there was no agreement on what could be left out, the class did agree on one point: there should be further library instruction in the use of specific reference works as had been done with Education Index, Buros' Fifth Mental Measurements Yearbook, and the Encyclopedia of Educational Research.

From the comments, test results, and general library evaluation it is apparent that the basic outline of the Education Library Committee stood up well. Many of the criticisms were concerned not with the substance of the program but with details which can be improved, either by revision of the programs in their entirety, or by splicing in better sections. Such problems as scheduling at the right time can be overcome during the coming year when the university will have more closed circuits available and more classrooms equipped to receive such broadcasts. Viewed in the total framework of library orientation, the year's efforts have been fruitful. With more refinement of the program there seems to be no reason why orientation by television cannot be made an effective and efficient part of the university's total instructional program.

After a year of rather intensive work with library orientation, the authors of this article submit the following comments for whatever help they may be to others who contemplate similar programs:

1. Television does hold good promise of orienting large groups to the library successfully.

2. There are no technical details which cannot be met by adequately planning the use of this medium. Indeed, in terms of explaining the catalog and certain reference books, this medium is superior to the ordinary personally conducted tour.

3. There are, however, difficulties involved in determining the best procedures and the best approaches for each university and each specific class.

4. Some of the questions which each librarian must answer for himself are:

A. What specific data do I want to communicate? Location data? How to use the card catalog? How to use specific reference works? How to write a term paper? No program can do everything.

B. Within the framework of what specific courses do I want this library program to fit? The basic English course? The basic education course? The advanced undergraduate course?

C. What techniques can most effectively communicate procedures by TV? Slides? Movies? Mockups? Narrator-lecturer?

D. In terms of cost is the closed circuit TV the most
economical method of library orientation?

If the answer to these questions is that TV orientation is
a particular library's solution, then one or two other major
points should be stressed here. Sufficient time should be allowed for adequate planning, writing, and production. Assuming that the entire production, other than the purely technical
aspects, is to be done by people who are untrained in script
writing, a year is not too long to prepare a finished script from
its committee and planning stage until it is filmed. It is also
wise to consult with the TV production staff several times before the final script is prepared. They may be able to offer
advice which can save time.

53. A MILITARY COLLEGE INITIATES
A LIBRARY INSTRUCTIONAL PROGRAM

Sidney E. Matthews

The Virginia Military Institute in 1959 radically changed
its concept as to the role of the library in a twofold educational
program—academic and military. This combination, in the
words of its originators, is designed to provide "practical util-
ity, through discipline and formative training," and to produce
men of "energy, efficiency and reliability."

The Virginia Military Institute is organized under the laws
of the Commonwealth of Virginia and is governed by a board of
visitors appointed by the governor and subject to confirmation
by the state senate. In accordance with provisions of the Code
of Virginia, the cadets constitute a military corps and officers
at the Institute are commissioned by the governor in the Virginia Militia, unorganized. Although V.M.I. requires rigorous
military training for its entire student body, the Institute al-

294

A LIBRARY INSTRUCTIONAL PROGRAM

ways has placed its first emphasis on its academic program. Colonel J. T. L. Preston, a prime mover in the founding of V.M.I., proposed that "the object is to prepare young men for the varied work of civil life . . . the military feature, though essential to its discipline, is not primary in the Institute's scheme of education." The Institute has followed this concept since 1839 when it was founded as the first state military college in the nation. V.M.I. offers nine degree-granting curricula—one each in civil engineering, electrical engineering, chemistry, physics, biology, history, and English, and two in mathematics.

When it was decided to alter the library's role, three major changes were made: (1) the library was made an academic department with the librarian reporting directly to the dean of the faculty, (2) the librarian was given academic rank and made a member of the Institute's Academic Board, and (3) formal and informal courses in library science were officially entered in the curriculum. The formal library science courses as described in the catalog issue of the Institute's bulletin embrace two areas: (1) "Library Science 101—Literature of the Natural Sciences. Reference materials, bibliographical methods, and use of the library in study of the natural sciences. This course is given in the fall semester and required of all biology majors." (2) "Library Science 301—Reference Materials and Bibliographical Methods. Basic bibliographical methods and reference materials used in the various fields of the liberal arts, science, and technology, with problems and practice. Problems will be adapted to needs of individual students and may be developed in conjunction with work on a senior thesis. This course is offered both semesters."

The informal freshman program of the Institute's library program consists of two parts: (1) a tour and (2) three one-hour lectures with problems on use of the library. The former is under the supervision of the commandant of cadets and professor of military science and takes place either during the cadre period or during R.O.T.C. class periods the first week of classes. All academic departments cooperate fully with the

R.O.T.C. instructors in conducting these tours so as to give
the freshmen a thorough examination of the academic facilities of the various departments. Any more than a cursory
tour at this point would be unnecessary as the cadets are confused by various tests and by the adjustment to a rigid military way of life. The informal program of lectures with problems is part of freshman English 101. These lectures are
usually given the first week in November, immediately preceding the cadet's term papers, and coincide with that part of
the freshman English course in how to prepare a term (research) paper. It is usually at this time that the cadet is
searching for book reviews for his history course and begins
to realize how necessary it is to know how to locate materials
in the library.

Instruction in the formal courses is given entirely by the
librarian, and the informal course is given by the librarian
with the assistance from the two other professional librarians
on the Preston library staff. All library instruction is given
in the library's auditorium or in its classroom.

The three one-hour lectures and problems on each in the
informal program are designed to: 1) acquaint the cadet with
the physical arrangement of the seven-story library building
(the building is on a slope and the front entrance is located on
the fifth floor which is also the first stack level) and location
of collections, 2) develop the cadet's ability in locating information and to make him as self-sufficient as possible in
the use of the card catalog and other reference tools, and 3) to
introduce the cadet to various types of sources available to
him and not to overwhelm him with too many titles.

The three lectures emphasize the dictionary catalog, reference books, and indexes. The lectures are illustrated with
two filmstrips series. It is planned to produce local slides of
Preston library's floor plan and reference items not included
in the films. As supplementary material the cadets use their
English textbook and appropriate titles from the library.

Problems are passed out at the end of each lecture and
the cadets have a two-week period to complete them. The

problems are designed to direct the cadet along subject lines which are of interest to him and to use his own family name or, if his is not found, to select another beginning with the first three letters. By using this procedure, some of the usual difficulties of freshman library problems, i.e. each cadet using the same part of a book, set, or the card catalog and passing answers, are avoided. These problems are graded by the librarian and the professional staff and the grades are recorded by the English department as three units of the cadet's grade in English 101 for that grading period. As a follow-up, most of the instructors in the English department include library questions of a general nature covered in these lectures as part of one of their regular English tests.

The cadet reaction to these lectures and problems has been largely favorable. The few unfavorable comments usually center on the amount of time required. Statistics were not recorded the first year, but this past year out of a total of 250 questions, seventy-four cadets missed twenty-five or less, 163 cadets missed thirty-seven or less, and 242 cadets missed fifty or less. No cadet has ever been proficient enough to obtain a perfect score on all three sets of problems. A check of the ten cadets achieving the highest grades on these problems with their grades in other subjects showed that they were proficient in their other freshman courses. Conversely the cadets receiving an extremely low grade on the library problems were failing one or more freshman courses. No valid inference should be drawn from this, but next year a large number of library grades will be compared with the cadets' grades in other courses.

English faculty comments have been extremely favorable and in agreement with the type of problems presented. Requests for one or two hours of library lectures with problems have also come from other instructors in the liberal arts program and in engineering. A condensed version of the lectures, with emphasis on the particular subject area involved, has been given in electrical engineering, civil engineering, economics, American government, and geopolitics classes.

297

The inherent difficulties of the program include: (1) scheduling nineteen sections of freshman English, usually 350 freshmen, for three different one-hour lectures in one week, (2) lack of any type of local library handbook, (3) large number of papers to grade in which there can be no "key" for the answers since each cadet has worked with subjects of interest to him, (4) having to schedule too many cadets at one period, (5) no opportunity to discuss and go over the papers with the cadets after they have been graded, (6) no opportunity for the librarians to give each cadet individual help and attention, and (7) extremely heavy use of the library's reference room and card catalog at this period of the academic year.

In spite of these difficulties there is general approval of the program, and for V.M.I.'s program it is highly desirable to integrate this instruction with freshman English classes. The cadet is introduced to the tools and research methods at the time he is ready to begin serious library use. This introduction is more thorough than the usual library orientation program that is often used in "freshman week" and is much more helpful. Several items indicate a degree of partial success. The cadets do not ask as many elementary questions, seem more at ease in the library, and have a clearer understanding of how to go about their work; and perhaps the 30 per cent increase in circulation over the last two years received some impetus from this program.

This joint instructional program has proved of value not only to English 101 but in subsequent courses requiring the use of the library. It has done much to make the library meaningful to the cadets of V.M.I.

54. THE HAPPY MEDIUM IN LIBRARY INSTRUCTION
AT THE COLLEGE LEVEL

Annie May Alston

In an effort to avoid the extremes of no library instruction for college students and the required library course for all students, library instruction has fallen in our institution—a liberal arts, church-related college with student enrollment of 1,000—at a midway point between these two extremes.

In an earlier self-examination of our library instructional program for students, we had reached the following conclusions about our offerings:

1. A freshman does not need to know in one hour what librarians have learned in one or more years of library school.

2. A freshman does not need to know specialized reference tools of which his own instructor may be unaware.

3. The guided library tour is the lowest form of instruction.

4. The copying by twenty-five students of problems solved by four students has no real educational value.

5. Our sophomores, juniors, and seniors are the forgotten students in systematic library instruction.

Our current program has been built around the concept that the library does have something for every student and there is a time in the academic life of the student when he will accept this fact.

FOR THE FRESHMEN

All freshmen, through their English classes (thirteen sections with an average of thirty students to the section this year), come to the library for one hour of library instruction near the beginning of the fall semester. During this hour a series of

slides is shown and a real effort is made to avoid crowding
in detailed information for which the student has no immediate use. In this first series slides are shown which illustrate (1) every aspect of the physical plant (a brief explanation is made of the various activities carried on in each
area); (2) arrangement of library materials; (3) library
policies and regulations (although the library handbook contains this information, the slides do a better job at this point);
(4) sets of catalog cards; (5) citations from Readers' Guide to
Periodical Literature.
During the second semester the freshmen come back
through their English classes for another hour of library instruction before beginning their term paper. A second series
of slides is shown including (1) detailed instruction on the card
catalog; (2) Library of Congress subject headings; (3) additional information on Readers' Guide to Periodical Literature; (4)
information on International Index; (5) periodical files; (6) Essay and General Literature Index.

FOR THE SOPHOMORES

In the second year, through the humanities classes, a one-
hour lecture on general reference books, with accompanying
bibliography, is given to all sophomores. Specialized reference tools are omitted from this instruction. Appearing on
this bibliography are unabridged dictionaries, adult encyclopedias, biographical tools, atlases, Statistical Abstract, World
Almanac, Brewer's Dictionary of Phrase and Fable, Bartlett's
Familiar Quotations, Granger's Index to Poetry and Recitations,
and the "Oxford Companions." An additional sheet of citations
from Essay and General Literature Index, Readers' Guide to
Periodical Literature, International Index, Education Index, and
Public Affairs Information Service is distributed to students.

FOR THE JUNIORS AND SENIORS

During the fall semester a one-hour meeting is held with
majors on the junior and senior level by departments of instruc-

tion. Faculty members in the department attend these meetings and make valuable comments on library resources. Meetings are held with the following departments: art, Bible and religion, biology, business and economics, education and psychology, English, home economics, music, social science, and speech. The chemistry department has its own course in chemical literature but follows the bibliographical guide prepared by the library. These meetings with the majors in different departments have the following objectives: (1) to teach students the approach to the specialized reference books in their major field; (2) to acquaint students with types of reference books in their area of specialization; and (3) to insure the fact that students know authorities and some of their contributions to their major field of study.

In this discussion on specialized reference tools the college library comes near fulfilling its mission of bringing teachers, librarians, and students together in a true spirit of learning from books.

All of the above sessions are initiated by the library but do meet with the full cooperation of the teaching staff. In addition to these classes, the library continues to welcome special invitations from faculty members for library instruction to groups throughout the year.

55. LIBRARY INSTRUCTION AT THE UNIVERSITY OF ILLINOIS IN CHICAGO

LeMoyne W. Anderson

Several years ago the need for library instruction at the University of Illinois, Chicago Undergraduate Division was demonstrated by the large number of elementary reference questions asked at the Library's public service desks, the patron's ignorance of basic reference tools, and the utter helplessness of students at the card catalog.[1] A method had to be found to reach all students and to give them necessary instruction. The College of Liberal Arts and Sciences and the Library administration subsequently recognized that the students required instruction in the use of libraries to save time and also to prevent an excessive burden on the library staff.

METHOD

The next logical question was, what type of program shall we offer? Orientation programs are ineffective generally, due to the detachment from a definite need and the lack of adequate follow-up. It was recognized, however, that a tour during Freshman Orientation Week is useful for acquainting students with the location, arrangement, and services of the Library. A separate library instruction course was, and still is, impractical because it lacked connection with definite student demands, required a large professional staff, and competed with an overcrowded university curriculum. Individual instruction as students come to the Library for help was most desirable because of the definite realization of need and also due to the possibilities of adaptation to individual differences in ability and experience. It is time-consuming, however, and the reference library staff could not give adequate assistance during peak hours of activity.

Instruction which could be integrated with subject classes was most effective, it was decided, if a cooperative relationship between librarians and instructors could be attained. This method has the advantage of illustrating definite needs (e.g. term papers) and it also provides an opportunity for adequate follow-up by the classroom instructor. In this type of program, the Library could serve as a laboratory for practical application of all principles taught in the library instruction class sessions. It was recognized that audio-visual aids were desirable in this program, and several methods were attempted. Unfortunately the physical arrangement of the classrooms and their distances from the Library have always militated against full exploitation of this medium.

THE TYPE OF STUDENT

An effective program of instruction can be formulated only with the knowledge of the student to whom it will be offered, especially their geographical origins, library experiential backgrounds, and the amounts of time available to spend in the Library. As would be expected, geographical distribution of U.I.C. students is mainly for Chicago and Cook County (approx. 88 per cent). Since the majority of students are Chicago residents, the need for library instruction in college based on the library instruction programs in the high schools of the city is a desirable step. A questionnaire for gathering the data has been devised. It is hoped that some time in the near future this information can be obtained and subsequently analyzed. Another factor in library instruction at U.I.C. is the amount of time a student has available to spend in the Library. Even though a student with ample time may choose to spend his leisure in ways other than visiting the Library, a knowledge of the extent of outside employment of students does appear pertinent to the planning of the program. Studies which have been made indicate that over one-half of the U.I.C. student body is employed part-time and full-time.[2]

LIBRARY ORIENTATION

Library instruction at the University of Illinois, Chicago Undergraduate Division begins with a librarian-conducted tour of the Main Reading Room and Fine Arts Reading Room during Freshmen Orientation Week at the beginning of each regular semester. The greatest advantage of the tour is that the students learn where the Library is located and they also lose some of the timidity which one naturally has when entering unfamiliar places. It is doubtful whether there are any additional benefits. During Orientation Week, students ordinarily do not feel the need of the Library services. They are having many new experiences and as a result often retain only confused impressions of their first week in college.

THE BACKGROUND OF LIBRARY INSTRUCTION AT U.I.C.

Despite the library instruction U.I.C. freshmen may have received in high school, they appear to be in need of help, chiefly in the development of techniques of bibliographical searching and obtaining the knowledge of basic library tools, such as the card catalog and the Readers' Guide to Periodical Literature. A need for a diagnostic test for determining the nature and extent of library instruction needed was recognized several years ago. Through the combined efforts of university librarians and psychometrists, a test was developed and used during past semesters. A true evaluation of this tool cannot be determined, however, as the testing program was discontinued in the fall of 1955.

THE PRESENT PROGRAM

The Rhetoric Department and the Library have attempted several forms of library instruction during the past few years. Since the Spring Semester, 1956, one lecture plus a ten-point laboratory exercise has been arranged for Rhetoric 101 students; for Rhetoric 102 students, two lectures and a 25-point

304

laboratory exercise. Especially important in 102 is the conference follow-up at the reference desk which has been very effective in maintaining a personal approach.

Library instruction classes are met during the first twelve weeks of the term. Rhetoric instructors are requested to express their preferences for specific dates and insofar as possible these are honored in making up the schedules. Library instruction in Rhetoric 101 covers: 1) parts of books; 2) the card catalog; and, 3) Readers' Guide to Periodical Literature. Instruction is intended to acquaint each student with the minimum skills and routines of library use. Instruction in 102 covers: 1) periodicals and periodical indexes; 2) reference books; and 3) bibliographical searching. Reading assignments in the Library Handbook and Library Instruction Text are made prior to the lectures.[3] Follow-up laboratory exercises are completed in the main reading room by the students after classes. Opportunities for librarian-student conferences are abundant during the time when the completed exercises are returned to the reference desks. This also gives the student a chance to discuss other library problems such as term paper topics, bibliographical documentation, etc.

THE OBJECTIVES AND AIMS OF THE PROGRAM

The objectives of the library instruction program are: 1) inculcation of such knowledge of general library tools, including the card catalog, that will enable the student to realize quickly the most likely sources of information needed in specific situations; 2) development of skills and techniques necessary for efficient use of all library facilities; 3) close cooperation with the English department and other faculties in the provision of experiences, the prevention of duplication of instruction, and the meeting of student needs.

The aim of the reference staff is to strive toward integrating library instruction with individual term paper assignments, especially in 102, although we do not limit the instruction to

this one paper.[4] We attempt to illustrate general principles
and procedures on the fundamental, functional level at which
most undergraduates operate. Recent experimentation with
audio-visual aids proved to be a valuable method of presentation; however, as previously stated it is not feasible to em-
bark on a full-scale program of this type at this time.

THE MATERIALS OF INSTRUCTION

The materials needed for the Rhetoric 101 library instruction unit are: the Library Handbook and Library Instruction Textbook; mimeographed instructions on how to locate
materials in the Library; five versions of ten-point 101 exercises; four versions of 25-point 102 exercises; mimeographed
instructions in letterform for rhetoric instructors regarding
choice of dates and purposes of program; instructions to the
101 and 102 students in form of mimeographed memoranda;
sample catalog cards for 101; copy of Webster's New World
Dictionary of the American Language;[5] superseded issues of
the Wilson indexes, New York Times Index, Public Affairs Information Service Bulletin, etc.; mimeographed copies of the
sample steps in the compilation of a bibliography for distribution to 102 students; and lecture notes as needed by the individual librarian-instructor.

THE PRESENTATION

The most effective and feasible form of instruction with
a mass student body seems to be the laboratory-discussions,
with guide and question sheets, accompanied by the Library
Handbook. The goal of the reference staff is to organize and
present library resources and services to students in such a
way that they may be used efficiently.

Each librarian-instructor is at liberty, in fact encouraged,
to present his lectures and conduct his discussions in any way
with which he is most comfortable and which he feels is most
effective with the students. The class could begin with an announcement of the problems and the purposes. This would be

followed by the presentation of the material by the instructor which could be interspersed, or followed by, discussion among the students. Each lecture could be illustrated by means of posters, catalog cards, blackboard notes, or filmstrips. Examples of the types of material being discussed should be available in the classroom, as discussing titles in the abstract is much less stimulating and often confusing to the student.

SUMMARY AND EVALUATION

A review and evaluation of the library instruction program can be done in several ways. A test could be given to the students after completing the program on the lectures, information in the Library Handbook, and as the result of experience in working the laboratory problems. Another method of testing could be to give pre-instruction tests and post-instruction tests and subsequently compare the results. Evaluation of a program can always be obtained by observation of the understanding of students in discussions and the scores on their problems. Perhaps the best evaluation will come through observation by the reference staff of the library competence of those who have taken the library instruction.

Frequently it is valuable to get the opinions of the students regarding the program. The completing of a questionnaire for purposes of improving instruction and requiring no signatures from the students often produces valuable information for the staff responsible for the presentation of a library instruction program.

56. TEACHING THE USE OF ENGINEERING LIBRARIES

William S. Budington

Among the many problems faced by librarians today is
the business of salesmanship. Most of us are familiar with
the usual devices some of which we employ, others of which
we enviously watch in use elsewhere—such as displays, lists,
advertisements and radio broadcasts. At colleges and universities we have a head start in that education depends
heavily on library resources. There is still a definite selling job to do—selling the faculty and especially the students
the concept of the library as a working tool rather than a
stockroom.

Salesmanship is largely a matter of personal contact,
no less in libraries than in business. Our most effective
work lies in direct dealing with the public through formal or
informal guidance or instruction. Teaching the use of libraries formally is carried out in several ways: the freshman orientation tour, a short talk by the librarian in a program meeting, the inclusion of one or more library periods
in a subject course and the separate library course. The latter is becoming more and more common, and interest in it is
increasing. In engineering schools, however, little at this
level has yet appeared. Since the course given at Columbia
University appears to be one of the first, it may be appropriate to describe it briefly before passing on to general discussion.

At present, Engineering 3 is a one-point, one-hour-a-
week course required of all undergraduate engineering students. Titled "Engineering Library Technique" it is taught
by the engineering librarian and is given during both winter
and spring semesters. Each of the seven engineering curricula (mechanical, electrical, industrial, etc.) has a section

308

to itself and, as far as possible, students are registered for the appropriate section. These usually have from 15 to 40 students, depending on the subject, and sometimes two sections are necessary for heavily enrolled curricula. Such instruction was initiated in 1933 in the form of library periods in one of the regular subject courses. This was expanded to a series of three lectures required of all students, then to a full semester, noncredit, required course. Since 1945 one point of credit has been given.

The present content of the course largely follows traditional lines. The approach is by form of material. The beginning is made with principles of classification, the card catalog and the making of proper references. Guides to the literature, encyclopedias and handbooks, national bibliographies, review sources and other bibliographies of various types then follow. The importance and use of serial literature brings in general and special technical indexing and abstracting. Standards and government documents, trade literature and directories have their part, and we conclude with something on documentary production and reproduction, microfilm and the like. In all, 15 lecture periods are planned. The examples are chosen to fit the major subject of each section. Many items are given to all sections, but wherever possible the class periods are tailored to fit.

Each student, as his project for the course, completes a bibliography on a topic of his choosing subject to the instructor's approval. The number of references and the number of sources from which they are obtained are specified. This precludes comprehensive bibliographies, but our intent is to obtain a fairly comprehensive coverage of sources rather than intensive searching. Although exceptions are made for thesis projects, we hope that students will thus come to recognize the value of source material in related fields as well as in their own. As a rule there have been no tests, daily assignments or final examinations. With two or three hundred students there is a limit to our capacity for including them. Attendance is regulated by general university procedure.

BUDINGTON

This course is taken during the junior year by all except
chemical engineers who take it as seniors. It comes during
their first year in the School of Engineering since the lower
two years are spent in Columbia College or the School of
General Studies. Thus our students have had college experience, and one-half to two-thirds of them have received some
library orientation in high school or college.

There is no need to elaborate greatly on the reason for
some such instruction. Occupied with the technics of laboratory and classroom, the student engineer often does not realize that the library offers as much in value as the rest of his
curricula. In the humanities, one's contact with library resources is more extended and more enforced. It must be
brought home to students of science and engineering that familiarity with current progress is an absolute necessity.
There is a need for recognition of what has gone before, and
a realization that knowledge has been recorded for many cen-
turies before the student became a novitiate engineer. He
should become familiar with the major library tools of research, and with the extent of the literature in his own field.
It is well that he learn that English is by no means the sole
language of communication. If he is to be aware of the world's
work, he must acquire a working knowledge of foreign tongues.

Basically, the library must be dissected and the machinery
of its use made clear. The student should come to understand
bibliographic practice as it affects his library research and
the preparation of reports and articles. When Columbia's
course originated, the dean's announcement said, "The engineering libraries are for the use and convenience of the students. The school is anxious that every student should learn
the possibilities of an engineering library." This has been extended to include the meaning and significance of engineering
literature and its organization.

In a number of schools, such instruction is given on a
graduate level, for credit in many instances and even required
in a few. The advantage to the graduate student is unquestioned.
That undergraduates as well may benefit is not as often recog-

nized. There is no reason why they, too, should not have the
ability to dig out information for themselves. A noticeable
improvement in report work for other courses was one of
the reasons the Columbia lectures were expanded. Such an
undergraduate course deals with more elementary materials
than a graduate offering and may be less intensive since immediate original research is not contemplated. There is a
very definite problem in getting across to undergraduates the
need for such information, whereas a graduate student facing
a thesis is acutely aware, or shortly will be, of the complexities of technical literature and his own shortcomings.

Choice of the instructor is up to the school, of course.
From the professional point of view, this duty is rightfully
the librarian's and so it is usually found. Teaching ability is
an important factor which is likely to be minimized in the
decision, "Let the librarian do it." It is particularly important in the undergraduate course, as mentioned before. Knowledge of the literature is another obvious prerequisite; faculty
members and specialists know better than the librarian the
literature of their own subjects, but for coverage of all fields
a bevy of such men would be required. A competent librarian
will have general acquaintance and familiarity with the materials of all branches of engineering. In addition, a more
uniform scheme is assured if instruction is centralized, and
related fields may be tied in more easily.

Another point gained by the librarian's instructorship
relates to the library's position in the educational pattern.
As a fellow teacher, the librarian is more likely to be considered a colleague by the faculty, as eloquently argued by B.
Lamar Johnson in his book The Librarian and the Teacher in
General Education. Furthermore, he is brought in contact
with most, if not all students, early in their engineering studies.
There is established an acquaintanceship which makes easier
the students' later use of the library and engenders a working
basis for further guidance.

As in nonscience curricula, library instruction may be
correlated with subject courses. Frequently, students are

311

required to present a senior thesis. Through consultation
with the department, it is possible to adjust requirements
and emphases toward that specific end. Where departmental research is under way, students in the library course are
able to do some of the bibliographical groundwork, thus aiding the department as well as themselves.

The question of the proper time for giving such a course
may be open to comment. The junior year appears to have
several advantages to recommend it. At this point the student
is entering his major field of work and may be assumed to
have a definite subject interest, giving point and direction to
any library work done. An added maturity over first-year
students also makes the task of teaching easier. This is not
to say that a first-year introduction to the library is undesir-
able; the freshman orientation tour or practice work in the
English course familiarizes the student with the library's
principal features—notably its location and arrangement. Extensive instruction, however, should wait until the teaching
can be done in terms of the subject field rather than in terms
of pure bibliography.

Credit for such a course should be arranged if at all possible. Its length, the time spent on it and its required status
are all deserving of recognition, not to speak of its real contribution to the training of engineers. A noncredit course
stands much less chance of attention from the students and
consideration from the faculty.

The content of the course will be largely a matter of individual organization, much as with any other subject course.
The various elements described in the Columbia course are
fairly standard items for inclusion, and others can be developed depending on circumstances. The number of students,
the types of curricula, size of library and staff, and physical
facilities will affect the content and teaching methods. Library tours or instruction periods in the library may be handled if conditions permit. Guest lecturers from the faculty
help to vary the program and lend a certain meaning and
authority. With large classes a lecture schedule is usually

called for, with less in the way of tests, homework and the like. Small classes permit the use of problems and more individual attention. Teaching aids may include pictures, enlargements, charts and samples. Slides have been used in some similar courses, although we have not yet attempted them in our large classes. Copies of books and materials are brought to class for use with the lecture and are there after class for examination. During the semester these materials are kept on a separate shelf in the reading room for the students' use.

Whatever teaching methods are used, great emphasis must be placed on practical uses. Examples should contain the technical vocabulary, and all explanations be made in those terms. The instructor must have a fair understanding of engineering subjects in order to explore the nuances of subject headings. In brief, the work must be strictly from the engineering point of view, and made, as far as possible, an engineering course in the literature rather than a library course for engineers.

The results from the course are rather difficult to pin down. The work turned in indicates how well students have grasped the principles of library research, but the application elsewhere of what has been learned is often not known. Our best indications come when we occasionally see their reports, and especially when we note the activity at the catalog, the indexes, use of bibliographies and the like. Student reaction to a one-point course is not likely to be rapturous, especially when there is not the obvious practicality of some of their other work. In a curricular survey conducted by our students, the library course received an over-all average rating slightly above the humanities and slightly below many of the engineering subjects. Our present school administration has been highly in favor of it, and it would be difficult to maintain the course without that support. As a whole, the faculty think it a good idea, though many of them are unclear as to just what it is all about. As might be expected, those faculty members who make considerable use of the library are more sympathetic than those who rarely pass through our portals.

Perhaps our most pleasant recommendations come from graduates who drop back for a visit. Frequently they tell of research work or assignments in which knowledge of information sources was an advantage. Sometimes undergraduates or graduates will call in knowing that there is a volume which will answer their questions, though perhaps not remembering its name. Even this is certainly better than floundering about in aimless search or prematurely assuming the unavailability of the desired material.

Similar coverage appears in science-technology literature courses found in library schools. More emphasis is being given to such instruction, and engineering librarians are naturally interested in it, both for their personal benefit and in the hope of trained assistants. Illinois has offered "Bibliography of Science and Technology" since 1948, aimed at large public library service and including four periods out of 48 on engineering. At Columbia, the classes in "Science Literature" cover only the basic sciences; medicine has been covered in "Literature of Special Fields," but as yet there has not been sufficient demand in the applied sciences. It would certainly be to our advantage to stimulate such a demand through our own studies and recruiting activities. However, I believe there are obvious differences between such library school courses and those given to undergraduate subject students. Their purposes are essentially the same—imparting knowledge of and familiarity with common materials. For the librarian these are the tools of his trade and the instruction must be more complete, more detailed, more comprehensive; for the engineer this knowledge is an adjunct only, and while it would doubtless be nice to include more, the essentials are all he should be expected to acquire. Principles of book selection and trade information are two items which the librarian needs but the engineer does not.

In almost all categories, whether it be bibliographical variations or knowledge of sources, the approach to the subject stems from a different viewpoint. The librarian tends to have greater interest in the book or periodical, per se, as a physical container; its many manifestations, its selection, care and preservation, and accessibility are his concern. The engineer, on the other hand, is interested only in the container's contents; what happens in the long chain of events bringing it to his use is of little or no real interest to him. His background and training have been entirely different. As a rule, he is not overly interested in books but in the accomplishment of factual results and the means for doing so.

Our basic problem is to convince him that the "means for doing so" include the library. Though it differs from what the engineer is accustomed to think of as instrument or apparatus, the written record of scientific knowledge can be fully as important in providing foundations for work and pointing the way. A library course may thus be compared to those in basic mathematics, instrumentation, drafting and other contributory instruction. The more salesmanship we can exercise the better. By familiarizing the engineer with the printed tools of his—and our—trade, we do him and ourselves a service.

57. LIBRARY EXERCISE FOR FRESHMEN

Hugh Pritchard, Edmund G. Miller, Alice H. Savidge,
   and Ezra C. Fitch

Freshman library exercises have suffered from two weaknesses: the questions were of very little interest to the students; and the answers could be much more easily obtained from another student than from the reference book in which they were buried. The reference librarians and the freshman English instructors at the University of New Hampshire have developed an exercise which does much to overcome these weaknesses. The University exercise attempts to direct each student's attention to a part of the card catalog and to those parts of selected reference books which will have immediate interest for him. In finding and identifying the facts then demanded, the student teaches himself the function and limitation of each reference aid.

For example, the student is asked to look up his own family name in the card catalog. If he finds it on a printed card, he is asked to copy certain information from the card. If the student's name does not appear, he is told to select another name beginning with the same three letters as his own. In either case he supplies the following information: Call number, Author, Birth date, Title, Place of publication, Publisher, Date of publication, Pages.

In doing this he teaches himself to recognize the essential information on a catalog card more effectively, it is thought, than he would by merely looking at a card with the components circled and identified.

The student's experience with the card catalog is reinforced as he uses it to find the reference books he must examine in the rest of the exercise. One of these is Who's Who in America. He is asked to look up his family name and fill in another set of blanks. If his name does not appear, he is told to select one on the page where it would be. He then supplies the following information: Full name; Occupation; Where and when born; Married? If yes, to whom?; A significant accomplishment; Home address; The main difference between Who's Who and Who's Who in America.

For some reference books, the student's interest in his own name cannot be exploited and other means must be employed to catch his attention. For example: Consult the Readers' Guide to Periodical Literature for articles on what you think will be your major at the University. After finding an article, write the subject heading under which it appears and copy the entire reference, placing each item of information in the proper place. If uncapitalized abbreviations, such as "il" or "por" appear before the name of the periodical, copy them opposite "Abbreviations" and write out their meanings in full. (For help see the "Key to Abbreviations" and "Explanation," found toward the front of the volume.)

Subject heading	Volume
Title of article	Page
Author (if given)	Date
Magazine (title in full)	Abbreviations (if any)

Now consult the Periodicals List and report whether the Library has this particular issue of the periodical and, if so, where it is found. It will not be necessary to see the periodical.

In UNH Library?   Location.

Other parts of the exercise deal with The World Almanac, Information Please Almanac, Statistical Abstract of the United States, The New York Times Index, The Dictionary of American Biography, The Dictionary of National Biography, and Bartlett's Familiar Quotations.

In dealing with each title, the student is asked to look up his name, his actual or tentative major, or some subject that appeals to him. Supplying the information shows what each reference book can do and what its limitations are. Wherever possible the questions are worded so that one student cannot give his answers to another.

The exercise was first suggested by the librarians in 1957 and was used that spring by six sections of English 1. The Chairman of Freshman English introduced it to the teachers of the course and has supplied copies to those who wanted to use it. The instructors have never been required to use the exercise, but an increasing number have elected to do so. They usually assign it after the library lecture and tour, which are fixed items in the curriculum. In the Fall of 1957 it was used by 24 sections and in the Fall of 1958 by 29 out of 35 sections. Including the sections which used it in the Spring of 1958, 65 sections, or approximately 1600 students, have performed the exercise.

The Chairman of Freshman English has reported the instructors' criticisms and suggestions regarding the exercise, and these have helped the librarians improve and clarify it. It has now passed the experimental stage and will not require fundamental changes.

What has been the student reaction to the exercise? As nearly as can be ascertained it has been largely favorable. Students usually work two hours or more on it and most have followed the directions carefully enough to earn good marks. As a means of seeing how the students performed the exercise, the librarians volunteered to correct as many papers as the instructors wished them to. They have now corrected 673 exercises. In this group 56 per cent of the students had three errors or less and 10 per cent wrote perfect papers. Such high scores might indicate an exercise that is too easy, but this conclusion does not seem justified. The students appear to work hard, and the instructors are satisfied that the exercise teaches the use of reference books better than anything else they have tried.

When the exercise was first used it was hoped that correcting it could be entrusted to clerical personnel, but this hope has not been realized. Rather it appears that the more the corrector knows about libraries, the more accurate the grading will be. For example, if a student on the card catalog question gives the author as John Jones, the title as Principles of Electrical Engineering, and the call number as $\frac{317.3;}{U58s}$ an alert grader would notice that the title did not fit the Dewey Decimal number and the author's name did not fit the Cutter number. Less obvious clues are also to be found in the other questions. To be aware of these, instructors should perform the exercise themselves before trying to correct students' papers. If a student is able to fabricate completely plausible answers which would fool a careful grader, he undoubtedly already knows all the exercise could teach him.

One aspect of the exercise which librarians like is the fact that each student's attention is directed to a different part of a book or set. In the past when students in a class or several classes were told to look up the same item in a reference book, the page on which the information appeared would soon be marred by underlining and dirt and the binding would often be weakened by excessive use at one place. The reference books used in the exercise are now more heavily used than before, but the wear is more evenly distributed.

The technique of teaching reference books by asking questions can also be applied to special subject fields. Hardly had the freshman exercise been started than a physics professor asked if a similar exercise could be designed for his upperclassmen and graduate students. The librarians undertook the task and produced an exercise which asks a student to answer instructive questions about Science Abstracts, Mathematical Reviews, Chemical Abstracts, Engineering Index, Handbuch Der Physik, and Applied Science and Technology Index.

Exercises have also been prepared for music and government. In the exercises for upperclassmen the instructor gives each student a topic which he looks for in the special sources for the subject. In other respects these exercises use the same basic technique as the freshman exercise. Librarians will make exercises for other subject fields as the need and opportunity arise.

58. LIBRARY INSTRUCTION ON THE GENERAL EDUCATION LEVEL

Annie May Alston

The objectives of the college library should harmonize completely with those of the institution of which it is a part, and the college library should seek to establish no objectives apart from those to which the whole institution is dedicated. Harding is a Christian college of arts and sciences, and the first two years of the student's academic life are committed to pursuance of the objectives of general education. A concerted effort has been made to integrate our library instructional program with this general education program for students during these first two years. The following discussion, therefore, does not include instruction which we give in non-general education courses nor the continuous instruction to individual students as the need arises.

I. Time of Instruction

    A. On the freshman level: all students are given one week of library instruction. Instruction begins in the third week of the fall semester, after students have had time to become somewhat adjusted to the strange, new life on the college campus, and when competition with other activities is not quite so keen.

    B. On the sophomore level: immediately after library instruction to freshman students is completed, instruction is begun for students on the sophomore level, and completed by the end of the first six weeks of the second semester.

Instruction on these two levels is staggered, because the librarian who handles the teaching program must simultaneously fulfill administrative responsibilities.

II. Prescribed General Education Courses Through Which Students Receive Library Instruction

    A. On the freshman level: all sections of Communications.

    B. On the sophomore level: all sections of World Affairs and Institutions, Humanities, Biology, Religion, Health and Safety.

III. Number of Class Periods of Instruction

    A. On the freshman level: three class periods, Tuesday, Thursday and Saturday of the same week.

    B. On the sophomore level: two class periods with a week's interval between classes (this interval is allowed in order that students may have sufficient time in which to prepare their assignment).

IV. Clear Statement of Objectives to Students

    A. On the freshman level:
       1. The position the library with its facilities holds in the student's program.
       2. The location of materials in our library.
       3. Library policies and regulations.
       4. Thorough understanding of the card catalog, Readers' Guide, general encyclopedias and yearbooks, dictionaries and biographical reference books.

It may be noted that instruction on the freshman level is confined to the learning of a minimum number of reference books which it is believed the student actually needs during his first year. An effort has been made to avoid the common mistake of crowding into this first library instruction reference titles for which the student has little or no use.

    B. On the sophomore level:
       1. Knowledge of basic reference tools in the subject area under consideration.
       2. Acquaintance with authorities in the field of study; e.g. Sarton in the history of science, Comstock in nature study, Ditmars in the study of reptiles.

   3. Knowledge of techniques involved in searching for material. A recognition of the type of library problem involved, and of the procedure to be followed in solving the problem.

V. Content of Instruction
   A. On the freshman level:
      1. Syllabus containing the floor plan of the library, policies and regulations, the second summary of the Dewey Decimal classification, and a bibliography of general reference tools.
      2. Lesson plans covering the card catalog, Readers' Guide and general reference books, and the location of various library materials.
   B. On the sophomore level:
      1. Bibliography of reference titles in the specific subject area.
      2. An assignment covering the periodical indexes to which our library subscribes: Readers' Guide, International Index, and Education Index; and Essay and General Literature Index, and the New York Times Index.
      3. A series of twenty questions to be answered by titles listed in the subject bibliography.

The following questions asked in Humanities are representative of the other subject areas. Where may I find:

A list of novels on the Civil War?
The author of the poem which begins, "Under the wide and starry sky"?
A discussion of twentieth century literature?
The most complete bibliography of John Ruskin?
Critical statements regarding Shakespeare's Merchant of Venice?
A discussion of patriotic songs and hymns in American literature?
An explanation of the term, poetic justice?

322

An illustration of the Globe Theatre?
The author of the quotation, "Life is not so short but that there is always time for courtesy"?
A full discussion of the life and work of John Milton?
An illustration of a flying buttress?
A reproduction of Da Vinci's Mona Lisa?
Illustrations of Italian dress in the fifteenth century?
A discussion of Latin American art?
Information on the various Madonna paintings?
Treatment of the musical career of Richard Strauss?
Material on German folk music?
The date of the first performance of Roy Harris' Third Symphony?
Information on the Anglican chant?

VI. Advantage of Library Instruction Offered through Regularly Scheduled Classes

1. Students are assured of obtaining basic library instruction in an organized manner.
2. Instruction in these library fundamentals through classes rather than through individual cases greatly conserves the time of the library staff. If a tool or a library procedure can be taught to a class of thirty in a matter of minutes, it is sheer extravagance to teach that tool or procedure on thirty different occasions.
3. When library information is disseminated through regular class channels, students are able to see the relationship of such instruction to specific courses offered. When library instruction is separated from specific courses, it may assume the role of an extra-curricular activity.
4. In classroom situations, faculty members have the opportunity of cooperating with the library staff in planning instruction and of participating actively in the discussion periods. Manifestation of the faculty member's interest in such a program of instruction has a very wholesome influence on students.·

5. Through such normal classroom procedures, the faculty member is in a position to make follow-up assignments in terms of the library instruction which the students have so recently received.

The library staff of Harding College would be the first to admit that the above outlined program of library instruction is not without its weaknesses; but we believe that in principle such instruction is sound. We have the testimony of many students who enthusiastically declare that it works.

NOTES

10. TEACHING LIBRARY SKILLS TO JUNIOR HIGH HONOR STUDENTS

1. F. R. Cyphert. "Junior High School Library Develops Investigative Skills." Clearing House. October 1958. pp. 107-108.
2. R. Will Burnett. Teaching Science in the Secondary School. Holt, Rinehart, and Winston. New York. 1957. pp. 206-294.
3. Exam marks showed that the fears many teachers have about student reports not covering sufficient and/or appropriate material or not holding class interest appear to be ill founded. These academically talented students tended to over-research rather than under-research their reports (which made checking all rough drafts advisable), and they paid keen attention to oral reports given by fellow students. They asked intelligent questions, took good notes, and got excellent test marks, which compared favorably with marks received on tests that covered material learned by more conventional methods.

12. "SLIDING" TOWARD PROGRESS

1. Chicago Board of Education. Supplement: Teaching Guide for the Language Arts: a Tentative Program. Chicago Public Schools, Chicago, 1958.
2. Richard K. Corbin and Porter G. Perrin. Guide to Modern English. Chicago, Scott, Foresman and Company, 1955. See also Lorraine F. Dangle and Alice M. Haussman. Preparing the Research Paper. New York, College Entrance Publications Corporation, 1957.

NOTES

16. TRAINING THE LIBRARY USER

1. ASLIB. Report of proceedings of the Seventh Conference. London, 1930, p. 98.
2. ASLIB. Report of proceedings of the Seventeenth Conference. London, 1942, pp. 27–30.
3. The Royal Society. Scientific Information Conference Report. London, 1948, p. 203.
4. Library Association Record, vol. 51, no. 5, May 1949, p. 149.
5. Ref. No. 3. Document No. 61, p. 694.
6. J. P. Lamb. Teaching the use of books and libraries: a Sheffield experiment. Library Association Record, vol. 51, no. 4, April 1949, pp. 102–8.
7. E. Scripture and M. R. Greer. Find it yourself. New York, 1928 (H. W. Wilson Co.).
8. W. W. Bishop. The backs of books. Baltimore, 1926 (Williams and Wilkins); London (Baillere, Tindall and Cox).
9. London School of Hygiene and Tropical Medicine. History of the Library. London, 1947, p. 17.
10. C. C. Barnard. Bibliographical citation. Librarian, vol. 39, July and August, 1950, pp. 105–10; 125–9; 171–5.
11. E. J. Crane and A. M. Patterson. Guide to the literature of chemistry. New York and London, 1927 (Chapman and Hall).
12. B. A. Soule. Library guide for the chemist. New York and London, 1938 (McGraw Hill).

27. HOW TO MAKE THE LIBRARY FUNCTION: TEACHING THE USE OF THE LIBRARY

1. Urdang, George. The American Institute of the History of Pharmacy. Bull. Hist. Med. 10: 690–700, Dec. 1941.

29. ORIENTATION OF THE USE OF THE COLLEGE
LIBRARY

1. Patricia Knapp, "The Montieth Library Project an
Experiment in Library-College Relationship", College and
Research Libraries, July 1961, p. 256.

30. FRESHMAN LIBRARY ORIENTATION PROGRAM

1. The following had most relevance for us: Brown,
Helen M., "The librarian as teacher in the college library,"
College and Research Libraries, X (1949), 119–23.
Chaney, Mary Lou, "Discovering the library," College En-
glish, XIV (1953), 407–8.
Erickson, Walfred, "Library orientation programs in American teachers colleges," Wilson Library Bulletin, XXII (1948),
62–63, 65.
Hamlen, Dorothy, "Initiating the freshman," Library Journal,
LXXIX (1954), 422–24.
Heathcote, Lesley, "Initiating the freshman," Library Journal, LXXVII (1952), 1959–60.
"Library orientation for college freshmen" [four short arti-
cles], Library Journal, LXXXI (1956), 1224–31.
2. Knapp, Patricia B., "A suggested program of college
instruction in use of the library," Library Quarterly, XXVI
(1956), 224–31.

41. THE SCHOOL LIBRARY: EACH TEACHER'S
RESPONSIBILITY

1. Desser, Maxwell, Producer. 18 East 41 Street, New
York 17. Library Tools Series, Young America Films, Inc.
New York.
2. Hook, Lucyle and Gaver, Mary Virginia. The Research Paper. Prentice-Hall, 1956. 85 p.

NOTES

3. Morris, Emmet. Exploring Libraries. School Necessities, 1954. 64 p.
4. Practical English Supplement. "How to Study and Use the Library." Scholastic Magazine, Vol. 21, No. 3, Part 11, September 27, 1956.
5. Gray, Albert, and others. English in Practice. McCormack-Mathers. Book 1, 1953, 224 p. Book 2, 1953, 224 p. Book 3, 1954, 232 p.

46. THE ROLE OF THE RESOURCE UNIT IN LIBRARY INSTRUCTION

1. Harold Alberty, Reorganizing the High School Curriculum (New York: Macmillan, 1947), p. 272-276.

49. TEACHING STUDENTS TO USE THE LIBRARY: WHOSE RESPONSIBILITY?

1. U.S. Bureau of Education. Public Libraries in the United States (Washington: G.P.O., 1876).
2. "Statistics of Libraries in Institutions of Higher Education, 1951-52," Chapter 6 of Biennial Survey of Education in the United States (Washington: Government Printing Office, 1952).

Institutions Reporting	107 Universities		552 Liberal Arts Colleges	
	(no.)	(%)	(no.)	(%)
1. Separate course	8	7.5	33	6.0
2. Part of subject course	30	28.0	104	19.0
3. Part of freshman orientation	24	22.5	112	20.0
4. Combination of 1 and 2	5	4.7	17	3.1
5. Combination of 1 and 3	6	5.6	29	5.3
6. Combination of 2 and 3	23	21.5	203	37.0
7. Combination of 1, 2, and 3	11	10.0	54	9.8

NOTES

3. L. W. Griffin and J. A. Clarke. "Orientation and Instruction of a Graduate Student by University Libraries," CRL, XIX (1958), 451–54; "Library Orientation for College Freshmen: Symposium," Library Journal, LXXXI (1956), 1224–31; M. C. Marquis. "A Study of the Teaching of Library Facilities to College Students." (M.A. thesis, George Peabody College for Teachers, 1952); Joseph N. Whitten. "Relationship of College Instruction to Libraries in 72 Liberal Arts Colleges." (Ed.D. dissertation, New York University, 1958).

4. E. M. Clark. "How to Motivate Student Use of the Library?" American Association of University Professors Bulletin," XXXIX (1953), 413–20; E. E. Emme. "Library Needs of College Students and Ways of Discovering Them," ALA Bulletin, XXX (1930), 134; Peyton Hurt. "The Need of College and University Instruction in the Use of the Library," Library Quarterly, IV (1934), 436–48; R. O. McKenna. "Introduction in the Use of Libraries; a University Library Problem," Journal of Documentation, XI (1955), 67–72; A. S. Powell. "Survey Pinpoints Library Attitudes," Library Journal, LXXIX (1954), 1463; L. R. Reed. "Do Colleges Need Reference Service?" Library Quarterly, XIII (1943), 232–40; J. S. Sharma. "Need for Library Education," Indian Librarian, XI (1957), 154–56; J. A. Wedemeyer. "Student Attitudes Toward Library Methods Courses in a University," CRL, XV (1954), 285–89.

5. B. Lamar Johnson, The Librarian and the Teacher in General Education (Chicago: ALA, 1948); Johnson, Vitalizing a College Library (Chicago: ALA, 1939); David K. Maxfield, "Counselor Librarianship at UIC," CRL, XV (1954), 161–66. (Or see any of the annual reports of the librarian, Chicago Undergraduate Division of the University of Illinois, 1951 through 1954.)

6. Teaching with Books (Chicago: ALA, 1940).

7. Griffin, op. cit.; S. E. Gwynn, "The Liberal Arts Function of the University Library," In Chicago. University. Graduate Library School. Function of the Library in the Modern College (Chicago: University of Chicago, 1954); Patricia

329

B. Knapp. "The Role of the Library of a Given College in
Implementing the Course and Non-Course Objectives of that
College" (Ph.D. dissertation, University of Chicago, 1957).
Knapp, "Suggested Program of College Instruction in the Use
of the Library," Library Quarterly, XXVI (1956), 224–31.
    8. Branscomb, op. cit., p. 52.
    9. Hurt, op. cit., p. 440.

50. THE ROLE OF THE COLLEGE LIBRARY STAFF IN
    INSTRUCTION IN THE USE OF THE LIBRARY

    1. Madeline G. Harrison, "Status of Card Catalog Use
at Savannah State College Library," Savannah State College
Faculty Research Bulletin, XIV (December 1960), 5–9.
    2. Letter from the chairman, Department of English,
Savannah State College, January 15, 1960.
    3. George S. Bonn, Training Laymen In the Use of the
Library. (New Brunswick, N.J.: Graduate School of Library Service, Rutgers — The State University, 1960), pp.
27–54.
    4. Letter from Richard A. Farley, associate director
of libraries, University of Nebraska, April 14, 1961.
    5. Letter from Donald J. Pearce, head librarian, Uni-
versity of North Dakota, April 4, 1961.
    6. Letter from Lucille Higgs, assistant, general edu-
cation division, Florida State University library, April 7,
1961.
    7. Letter from Katherine M. Stokes, librarian, West-
ern Michigan University, June 20, 1961.
    8. Letter from J. Isaac Copeland, librarian, George
Peabody College for Teachers, April 17, 1961.
    9. Letter from Victor Schaefer, director of libraries,
University of Notre Dame, March 31, 1961.
    10. Letter from Juliette A. Trainor, librarian, Pater-
son State College, April 5, 1961.
    11. Letter from Lillian M. Seaberg, assistant librarian,
University of Florida, April 6, 1961.
    12. Haskell M. Block and Sidney Mattis, "The Research
Paper: A Co-operative Approach," College English, XIII
(January 1952), 212.

NOTES

13. Letter from Josephine M. Tharpe, reference librarian, Cornell University library, April 7, 1961.
14. Patricia B. Knapp, "The Montieth Library Project: An Experiment in Library-College Relationship," College and Research Libraries, XXII (July 1961), 257-258.
15. Ralph E. McCoy, "Automation in Freshman Library Instruction," Wilson Library Bulletin, XXXVI (February 1962), 468-472.

52. UNIVERSITY LIBRARY ORIENTATION BY TELEVISION

1. U.S. Office of Education. Educational Statistics Branch. Opening (Fall) Enrollment in Higher Education, 1961: Institutional Data (Washington: Govt. Print. Off., 1961).
2. This program is described in "TV Library Instruction," Library Journal, LXXXVI (January 1, 1961), 42-46.
3. "Insulted the intelligence" was a common statement; this statement was also made about the education library tape, but less frequently.

55. LIBRARY INSTRUCTION AT THE UNIVERSITY OF ILLINOIS IN CHICAGO

1. Several words and ideas in this discussion are attributed to: Lewis, Katherine W. "A plan for instruction in the use of library materials to be given at the University of Louisville." Unpublished Master's Paper. Cleveland, Western Reserve University Library School, 1955.
2. University. Illinois. Chicago Undergraduate Division. Survey Committee on Student Employment. Location of employment of University of Illinois Chicago Undergraduate Division students. Chicago, 1956.
3. Illinois. University. Library. Chicago Undergraduate Division. Library Handbook and Library Instruction Textbook. 4th edition. Chicago, 1956.
4. In 1955/56, the reference staff met 107 sections of 101, or 2182 students. In Rhetoric 102, 82 sections, or 1548 students were given library instructions. In addition, 1296 students visited the library during the orientation period.
5. Webster's New World Dictionary of the American Language. College edition. Cleveland, World Publishing Company, 1956.

THE CONTRIBUTORS

ANNIE MAY ALSTON, Librarian at Harding College, Searcy, Arkansas.

LeMOYNE W. ANDERSON, Director of the Colorado State University Libraries, Fort Collins, Colorado.

LEONA B. AYRES, Librarian, Jefferson Elementary School of Richland, Washington.

MURIEL BENNETT, Librarian, Hillsboro Community High School, Hillsboro, Illinois.

MARY ANN BLATT, Librarian, Montgomery Hills Junior High School, Silver Spring, Maryland.

HELEN M. BROWN, Librarian, Wellesley College, Wellesley, Massachusetts.

WILLIAM S. BUDINGTON, Librarian, John Crerar Library, Chicago, Illinois.

HELEN M. CARPENTER, Professor of History at Trenton State College, Trenton, New Jersey.

VIRGINIA CLARK, Reference Librarian, Wright Junior College, Chicago, Illinois.

D. I. COLLEY, Chief Assistant of the Hull Public Libraries, England.

MARYLINE CONREY, Librarian, Verdugo Hills High School, Tujunga, California.

THE CONTRIBUTORS

MARTHA DALLMANN, Professor of Education, Ohio Wesleyan University, Delaware, Ohio.

CHASE DANE, Assistant Professor of the School of Library Science, University of Southern California, Los Angeles, California.

KERMIT DEHL, Reading Counselor, Oak Park and River Forest High School, Oak Park, Illinois.

ELEANOR DEVLIN, Assistant Librarian in Charge of Reference, Ohio University Library, Athens, Ohio.

BERNICE K. DONEHUE, Librarian, Lindblom Technical High School, Chicago, Illinois.

BERNICE L. DUNTEN, Librarian, School of Pharmacy, Purdue University, Lafayette, Indiana.

B. AGARD EVANS, Chief Librarian, Ministry of Public Building and Works, England.

MILDRED EYRES, Librarian, Dakota Wesleyan University, Mitchell, South Dakota.

IRENE FARNBACH, Librarian, Grandview School, Phoenix, Arizona.

EZRA C. FITCH, Assistant Reference Librarian, University of New Hampshire, Durham, New Hampshire.

ROBERT L. FOOSE, Principal, Westfield Senior High School, Westfield, New Jersey.

VERNON S. GERLACH, Assistant Professor of Education, Arizona State University, Tempe, Arizona.

THE CONTRIBUTORS

MARY YOUNG HALE, Assistant Librarian, University of Chattanooga Library, Chattanooga, Tennessee.

FREDERIC R. HARTZ, Assistant Professor of Library Science, Trenton State College, Trenton, New Jersey.

BEATRICE HERRMANN, Librarian, Lyons Avenue School, Lansing, Michigan.

EDWARD G. HOLLEY, Director of Libraries, University of Houston, Houston, Texas.

ELISABETH HURD was, at the time of writing "Now I Use the Library Even More," a sixth-grader at Casis School, Austin, Texas.

ROBERT U. JAMESON, Chairman of the English Department, Haverford School, Haverford, Pennsylvania.

ALICE E. JOHNSON, Librarian, Evanston Township High School, Evanston, Illinois.

GRIFF L. JONES, Librarian, Kensington High School for Girls, Philadelphia, Pennsylvania.

VALENTINE JONES, Librarian, Velasco Elementary School, Brazosport, Texas.

E. J. JOSEY, was Librarian at Savannah State College, Savannah, Georgia, at the time of writing "The Role of the College Library Staff in Instruction in the Use of the Library."

LORAINE J. KELLEHER, Librarian, South Junior High School Library, Newburgh, New York.

ELAINE LAPIDUS was, at the time of writing "Library Lesson Period in the Elementary School," a Librarian of the Marion Street School, Lynbrook, New York.

THE CONTRIBUTORS

CAROLYN LEOPOLD, Librarian, Curriculum Laboratory, Montgomery County Public Schools, Rockville, Maryland.

DOROTHY LIGDA, Librarian, Pleasant Hill Intermediate School, Concord, California.

RALPH McCOMB, University Librarian, Pennsylvania State University, University Park, Pennsylvania.

EDNA S. MACON was, at the time of writing "School Librarians and Teachers," a Librarian at the Ballard Memorial High School, Barlow, Kentucky.

SIDNEY E. MATTHEWS, Assistant Librarian, Southern Illinois University, Carbondale, Illinois.

EDMUND G. MILLER, Assistant Professor of English, University of New Hampshire, Durham, New Hampshire.

BARBARA A. MONROE, Children's Librarian, Laboratory School, State University Teachers College, Plattsburgh, New York.

ALBERT NISSMAN, English Teacher, Benjamin Franklin Junior High School, Bristol Township, Pennsylvania.

ROBERT W. ORAM, Circulation Librarian, University of Illinois, Urbana, Illinois.

WILLIAM H. OSTERLE, Librarian, Georgetown University, Washington, D.C.

ESTHER PINCH, Remedial Reading Instructor, Lincoln School, Wauwatosa Elementary Schools, Wauwatosa, Wisconsin.

HUGH PRITCHARD, Reference Librarian, University of New Hampshire, Durham, New Hampshire.

THE CONTRIBUTORS

BESSIE L. PUGH, Supervisor of the Institute of Logopedics, Wichita, Kansas.

DONALD D. RANSTEAD, Reference Librarian, College of the Pacific, Stockton, California.

HELEN REED, English Teacher, Verdugo Hills High School, Tujunga, California.

MARILYN ROBBINS, Chairman of the Junior High School Science Department, W. Tresper Clarke High School, East Meadow, New York.

DOROTHY ROCHE, Librarian, Belleville New Jersey High School, Belleville, New Jersey.

MARTIN ROSSOFF, Librarian, James Madison High School, Brooklyn, New York.

ALICE H. SAVIDGE, Assistant Reference Librarian, University of New Hampshire, Durham, New Hampshire.

BYRD FANITA SAWYER, Librarian, Churchill County High School, Fallon, Nevada.

LEAH M. SERCK is connected with the Redeemer Lutheran Church, Denver, Colorado.

ANN SHAFFNER, Librarian, High Street School, Lansing, Michigan.

GRACE M. SHAKIN, Librarian, Lakeville School, Great Neck, New York.

LILLIAN SHAPIRO, Librarian, Woodrow Wilson Vocational High School, Jamaica, New York.

THE CONTRIBUTORS

HILDA P. SHUFRO, Head Librarian, Paramus Public Schools, Paramus, New Jersey.

GLADYS BARRETO SPENCER, Librarian, Petersburg High School, Petersburg, Virginia.

SHERMAN H. SPENCER, Circulation Librarian, College of the Pacific, Stockton, California.

GERTRUDE STACY, Librarian, McKinley Elementary School, Sunnyvale, California.

ALENE TAYLOR, Elementary Librarian, Newton-Conover City Schools, North Carolina.

A. H. WATKINS, Borough Librarian, London Borough of Bromley, Kent, England.

AUTHOR-TITLE INDEX

AUTHOR-TITLE INDEX

AUTHOR-TITLE INDEX

AUTHOR-TITLE INDEX

AUTHOR-TITLE INDEX